The
West
Indian
Americans

Other Titles in
The New Americans Series
Ronald H. Bayor, Series Editor

The South Asian Americans
Karen Isaksen Leonard

The Cuban Americans
Miguel Gonzalez-Pando

The Dominican Americans
Silvio Torres-Saillant and Ramona Hernández

The Taiwanese Americans
Franklin Ng

The Korean Americans
Won Moo Hurh

The Soviet Jewish Americans
Annelise Orleck

The Vietnamese Americans
Hien Duc Do

The Filipino Americans
Barbara M. Posadas

The Chinese Americans
Benson Tong

Puerto Ricans in the United States
Maria E. Perez y Gonzalez

The West Indian Indian Americans

Holger Henke

THE NEW AMERICANS
Ronald H. Bayor, Series Editor

GREENWOOD PRESS
Westport, Connecticut • London

Library of Congress Cataloging-in-Publication Data

Henke, Holger.
  The West Indian Americans / Holger Henke.
    p.   cm.—(The new Americans, ISSN 1092–6364)
  Includes bibliographical references and index.
  ISBN 0–313–31009–2 (alk. paper)
  1. West Indian Americans.   I. Title.   II. New Americans (Westport, Conn.)
  E184.W54H46   2001
  973.04'96972—dc21   00–033130

British Library Cataloguing in Publication Data is available.

Library of Congress Catalog Card Number: 00–033130
ISBN: 0–313–31009–2
ISSN: 1092–6364

First published in 2001

Greenwood Press, 88 Post Road West, Westport, CT 06881
An imprint of Greenwood Publishing Group, Inc.
www.greenwood.com

Printed in the United States of America

The paper used in this book complies with the
Permanent Paper Standard issued by the National
Information Standards Organization (Z39.48–1984).

10 9 8 7 6 5 4 3 2 1

Copyright Acknowledgments

The author and publisher are grateful to the following for granting permission to reprint excerpts from their sources:

Christine Ho, *Salt-Water Trinnies: Afro-Trinidadian Immigrant Networks and Non-Assimilation in Los Angeles* (New York: AMS Press, 1991), by permission of AMS Press.

Catherine Sunshine and Keith Warner, eds., *Caribbean Connections: Moving North* (Washington, D.C.: Network of Educators on the Americas, 1998), courtesy of NECA.

Merle Collins, "Nabel String," courtesy of Merle Collins.

Fay Clarke Johnson, interview with George Hudson, 1995, courtesy of Fay Clarke Johnson.

Contents

Illustrations

FIGURE

Photo essay follows page 114

Series Foreword

Oscar Handlin, a prominent historian, once wrote, "I thought to write a history of the immigrants in America. Then I discovered that the immigrants were American history." The United States has always been a nation of nations where people from every region of the world have come to begin a new life. Other countries such as Canada, Argentina, and Australia also have had substantial immigration, but the United States is still unique in the diversity of nationalities and the great numbers of migrating people who have come to its shores.

Who are these immigrants? Why did they decide to come? How well have they adjusted to this new land? What has been the reaction to them? These are some of the questions the books in this "New Americans" series seek to answer. There have been many studies about earlier waves of immigrants—among them the English, Irish, Germans, Jews, Italians, and Poles—but relatively little has been written about the newer groups—those arriving in the last thirty-five years, since the passage of a new immigration law in 1965. This series is designed to correct that situation and to introduce these groups to the rest of America.

Each book in the series discusses one of these groups, and each is written by an expert on those immigrants. The volumes cover the new migration from primarily Asia, Latin America, and the Caribbean, including the Koreans, Cambodians, Filipinos, Vietnamese, South Asians such as Indians and Pakistanis, Chinese from both the People's Republic of China and Taiwan, Haitians, Jamaicans, Cubans, Dominicans, Mexicans, Puerto Ricans (even though they are already U.S. citizens), and Jews from the former Soviet

Union. Although some of these people, such as Jews, have been in America since colonial times, this series concentrates on their recent migrations, and thereby offers its unique contribution.

These volumes are designed for high school and general readers who want to learn more about their new neighbors. Each author has provided information about the land of origin, its history and culture, the reasons for migrating, and the ethnic culture as it began to adjust to life in the United States. Readers will find fascinating details on religion, politics, foods, festivals, gender roles, employment trends, and general community life. They will learn how Vietnamese immigrants differ from Cuban immigrants and yet how they are also alike in many ways. Each book is arranged to offer an in-depth look at the particular immigrant group and to enable readers to compare one group with the other. The volumes also contain brief biographical profiles of notable individuals and a short bibliography of readily available books and articles for further reading. Many contain a glossary of foreign words and phrases.

Students and others who read these volumes will secure a better understanding of the age-old questions of "who is an American" and "how does the assimilation process work?" Similar to their nineteenth- and early twentieth-century forebears, many Americans today doubt the value of immigration and fear the influx of individuals who look and sound different from those who had come earlier. If comparable books had been written 100 years ago they would have done much to help dispel readers' unwarranted fears of the newcomers. Nobody today would question, for example, the role of those Irish or Italian ancestry as Americans; yet this was a serious issue in our history and a source of great conflict. It is time to look at our recent arrivals, to understand their history and culture, their skills, their place in the United States, and their hopes and dreams as Americans.

The United States is a vastly different country than it was at the beginning of the twentieth century. The economy has shifted away from industrial jobs; the civil rights movement has changed minority-majority relations and, along with the women's movement, brought more people into the economic mainstream. Yet one aspect of American life remains strikingly similar: we are still the world's main immigrant-receiving nation and, as in every other period of American history, we are still a nation of immigrants. It is essential that we attempt to learn about and understand this long-term process of migration and assimilation.

Ronald H. Bayor
Georgia Institute of Technology

Acknowledgments

Although most books bear only the name of one, two, perhaps three, but rarely more than four authors on their front cover, in reality a greater number of people are involved in the process of researching and writing. The situation is no different with this book. I gratefully acknowledge my indebtedness to a number of people who helped with advice, who gave direction or materials, and pointed out inaccuracies. In particular, I would like to mention J. A. George Irish, director of the Caribbean Research Center at Medgar Evers College, who was there all along the way when I sought contacts with researchers and community leaders. I thank the many who freely offered their advice and assistance: Ronald H. Bayor, Coleen Clay, Nancy Foner, Nancie González, Charles Green, Herman Hall, Calvin Holder, Ramesh D. Kalicharran, Philip Kasinitz, Ransford Palmer, Frankie Ramadar, and Milton Vickerman, to mention the most important ones. Many others, whose names cannot be mentioned for lack of space, engaged in informal discussions that proved extremely beneficial in giving more depth and substance to this book. The able guidance of Wendi Schnaufer, the acquisitions editor, lifted me over many formal hurdles of preparing the manuscript. Betty Pessagno, the production editor, and Beverly Miller, the copyeditor, were extremely helpful in the final phase of the manuscript preparation. However, without the patience and loving encouragement of my wife and the disappointments of my son about forgone opportunities to play computer games, I could not have written this book. I want to thank all of you for contributing to this book.

Introduction

A look at the map of the Caribbean region instantly reveals that it consists of rather diverse societies and cultures. No consensus has emerged yet in the scientific community about which countries and territories should constitute the Caribbean and on the basis of which criteria they would be chosen. Considering the fact that, for example, during the time of the construction of the Panama Canal a sizable number of Jamaicans migrated to Panama as well as other Central American countries and that the Garifuna people of St. Vincent were forced to settle in Belize and Honduras, it would appear to make a great deal of sense to include at least the Central American coastline in the definition. However, even if we apply a relatively narrow definition of the Caribbean, this diversity is immediately visible. Perhaps somewhat surprisingly, we are still faced with a great variety of histories, dialects, and cultural traits when we apply the yet more restrictive definition used for the purposes of this book. This book focuses on the English-speaking Caribbean, which comprises Antigua and Barbuda, the Bahamas, Barbados, Belize, the Cayman Islands, Dominica, Grenada, Guyana, Jamaica, Montserrat, St. Lucia, St. Vincent and the Grenadines, Suriname, and Trinidad and Tobago. Although this definition appears to be straightforward, it camouflages the fact that some of the Dutch territories in the region use the English language in practically all aspects of their daily life except for the procedures of their parliaments. At the same time it has to be acknowledged that there are also significant parallels between these countries and the Spanish- and French-speaking Caribbean. This relatedness is testimony to the complexity and ongoing process of cultural mixing within the Caribbean.

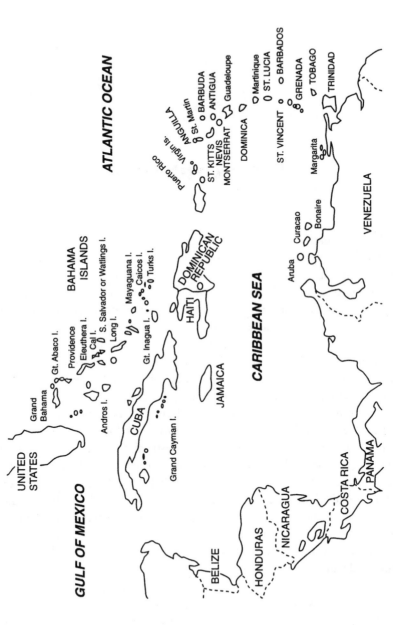

The Caribbean Area

Often this region is called the West Indies, and people within the English-speaking countries of the region regularly refer to themselves as West Indian. However, the term reflects the mistake Christopher Columbus made when in 1492 he landed in Hispaniola (the island that Haiti and the Dominican Republic share) and assumed that he had found the western route to India. Calling the region West Indies therefore mirrors a good deal of the colonial arrogance and ignorance that European settlers brought to this region. The term *Caribbean* also bears a negative connotation in that it evokes the native Carib Indians whom Columbus described as one-eyed men with dog snouts "who eat human flesh and who decapitate anybody they can catch to drink their blood and to castrate them." Nevertheless, the Caribs were indigenous to this region and gave fierce resistance to the Spanish conquerors, and for these reasons I consider the term *Caribbean* as the more appropriate one. Since this book focuses on immigrants from the English-speaking Caribbean, it was decided, however, to use the term *West Indian* in the title in order to keep it brief and plain.

Because the concept of "race" is unscientific and socially constructed, it will be put in quotation marks consistently throughout the text. While I acknowledge that belonging to certain ethnic groups is a very real day-to-day experience for people discriminated against on the basis of their skin color and/or other phenotypical features, I also believe that it is necessary to break away from such classifications. As a small step in this direction, the concept and term have to be regarded as pre-scientific and will be marked as such through my use of the quotation marks.

The term *Caribbean Americans* may at first sight surprise many readers who have grown up with the American taxonomies of "race" and ethnicity. However, if one recalls that most Americans lump all dark-skinned people together as African Americans and/or "black" regardless of an individual's "racial" background, the initial astonishment over the term becomes more understandable. Without doubt, most immigrants from the English-speaking Caribbean are of African origin and "conspicuously tanned." However, for Caribbean people, who for the most part have been used to a much subtler classification of color and "race," being thrown into a (often discriminatory) category that does not reflect their cultural background is an injustice. It is one of the most formidable contradictions with which they have to contend as newcomers to the United States.

As we shall see in this book, the Caribbean has historically been a crucible where ethnicities and "races" from all over the world met. It continues this function today. It should be no surprise, then, that the notion of networks and the practice of networking has become second nature for most Caribbean people. Thus, this second nature of networking means that most Caribbean people have very good interpersonal skills. Once the initial ice is broken and it has been established that there is no apparent reason to be distrustful, the overwhelming majority of Caribbean people are really easy to talk with. Networks of Caribbean families and friends have therefore spread all over the globe. In fact, in the late 1980s I left Europe to live and work in the Caribbean. Upon meeting and eventually marrying a young woman from the United States visiting her mother and grandparents in the Caribbean, I subsequently moved to the United States to join my wife. The network of this family now spreads from my home country in Europe to the Caribbean and along the eastern seaboard of the United States, where both my wife and I have relatives.

It should be apparent that the region is an eminently colonial creation and that its colonial past plays a paramount role in the identity of all Caribbean countries and both the festivities and everyday life of the various peoples living there. It is a product of an intense historical process of cross-fertilization that has conferred a unique character and culture on this fascinating region at the intersection of several world regions—Europe, Africa, Asia, and the Americas. Their history, a story of oppression and resistance, appears to have a much more vivid presence in the memories of Caribbean people than is true for most other peoples and regions of the world. As the following chapters demonstrate, English-speaking Caribbean Americans have used their history and cultures to carve out their own niche within the United States. In this process they have also left their mark on U.S. history and culture.

1

History of Jamaica and the English-Speaking Caribbean

FROM PLANTATION SOCIETY TO THE THIRD WORLD

When Christopher Columbus landed in Jamaica in 1494, he noted that he had never seen a "fairer isle." This can easily be said for most, if not all, other Caribbean islands, whose natural beauty has become in the twentieth century one of the greatest assets of their tourism industries. However, enjoying nature and its gifts had only indirectly been a motive of the Spanish conquerors and the various other European nations that followed them to what they called the New World. The aspect of nature they were pursuing, and the single most important motive for their exploration, was their thirst for gold. However, there were no significant amounts of gold to be found in the Caribbean. Although the expectation of finding the precious metal was dispelled soon after Europe's discovery of the new continent, the profit motive remained the main engine for the eventual subjugation of the native Amerindians as well as the establishment of colonial economies in the territories they inhabited. While the Carib Indians and others like them resisted the Spanish invasion, the Arawak Indians and similar peoples were enslaved. Within a few decades, many had succumbed due to the brutal conditions of the forced labor, as well as diseases that the Europeans brought to their lands. Eventually the Caribs had the same fate. With some justification, the killing of Caribbean indigenous peoples can be regarded as the first genocide in human history. Only small numbers survived. Many textbooks will say that today there are no more indigenous Caribbean people, but this is not entirely accurate. In fact, many Caribbean people can trace their heritage back to Arawak, Taino, or Carib Indians.

The predominance of the Spanish in the Caribbean did not last long. By the second half of the sixteenth century, other European powers followed, and a phase of intense competition for colonies with Spain began. Only with great difficulty did the British succeed establishing themselves between 1624 and 1635 in Barbados, St. Kitts, Nevis, Antigua, and Montserrat, and soon the Dutch and French installed themselves as neighboring powers (Craton 1982: 22). In 1655 the Spanish were ejected from Jamaica. After the British started to colonize the islands under their control, the slave trade (involving an ongoing series of slave wars in Africa) between Africa and the Caribbean, which had begun under Spanish rule, started to gather momentum. According to figures that are generally considered reliable, of the approximately 10 million Africans who were forcefully abducted from Africa during the 300 years of the transatlantic slave trade about 50 percent came to the Caribbean colonies and about 2 million died during the passage (Curtin 1969). The American director Steven Spielberg captured the inhumane conditions of this journey from Africa to the Caribbean, the so-called Middle Passage, in the impressive film *Amistad* (1998). Between 1670 and 1807 alone, an estimated 750,000 Africans were carried off to Jamaica, where they became slaves in the plantation system.

Throughout the region a belt of economies based on plantations was established to reap maximum benefits from agriculture. The plantation was more than an economic institution combining land and labor; it was a total organization giving structure and form to the political life and social relations in the islands as well. Basically, plantation society was a two-class system in which the white planters, due to their exclusive access to the colonial assemblies, became what is often referred to as a *plantocracy*—a class whose political and economic power was based on the plantation. The plantation owners, the (often absent) landlords, and a group of colonial administrators formed a small ruling class, which stood in opposition to the large majority of slaves working on plantations and was controlled by a comprehensive system of sanctions and incentives. The sanctions included a variety of often extremely cruel and violent punishments, while the incentives could reach from becoming a house servant to actually being set free (which, however, happened much less often). In 1770 about 23,000 whites and 200,000 black slaves lived in Jamaica. Given the continuing resistance by the slaves, this uneven relationship could be maintained only with an iron hand and the brutal rule of the whip.

After a few generations, an intermediate class started to develop, consisting of a few free blacks, some artisans, midwives, and a steadily growing number of descendants of mixed "race" (often derogatorily called mulattos) who often held privileged positions in or around the planter's Great House—the power center of the plantation. This mostly lighter-complexioned group was psychologically torn between its relative distance from the generally darker-skinned slaves and their attraction to the allegedly superior culture of their white masters. Because of their skin color, however, they were never able to ascend into the ranks of the white ruling class. As we shall see, this cultural dilemma eventually became what might be the most significant defining moment for the identity of the Caribbean countries subjugated to the plantation system (Beckford 1983; Henke 1997). The emergence of a tiny group of poor whites did not conceal the fact that color was the primary determinant for social status in the colonies; even the poorest white could generally count on greater legal protection than a free black or so-called mulatto.

In many of these rigidly stratified plantation societies, another important element emerged: runaway slaves (called *maroons*). These groups often managed to establish elaborate settlements deeply hidden within the jungles covering many of the Caribbean colonies. They often engaged the colonizers in lengthy guerrilla-type wars and were often able to secure favorable peace treaties from them, which guaranteed their independence. Thus, in Jamaica maroon settlements like Accompong, Moore Town (earlier Nanny Town), and Maroon Town even today possess a significant amount of self-government and maintain many of their African traditions. The legendary maroon priestess and leader Nanny, who supposedly died in 1733, is the only female national hero of Jamaica.

In the English-speaking Caribbean, slavery was abolished in 1834 by the British Parliament. In fact, only in Haiti was there a general uprising of slaves, in 1796, which led to their freedom and independence. The deeper reasons for the decision to abolish slavery were less of a moral nature than economic and political. With the beginning of the Industrial Revolution and the rise of industrial capital, the traditional influence of merchant capital in Britain started to wane. The need for new markets for the industrial products of the motherland increased, and it was reasoned that only "free" labor would create the necessary critical mass of consumers. It is therefore not surprising that one of the most influential and vocal "abolitionists" in Britain, William Wilberforce, was a factory owner who employed child labor. For the plantocracy in the colonies, the prospect of an end to slavery meant financial ruin. Consequently they fiercely resisted this initiative taken by the motherland. In Jamaica, for example, the governor dissolved the local parliament, but the newly elected parliament resisted abolition just as much. As a result Britain chose a more conciliatory approach and allowed local planters to decide the nature and speed of the abolition process.

Following the official abolition of slavery in Jamaica, about 60 percent of the former slaves left the plantations between 1838 and 1865 to settle in the hilly interior of the island and plant small plots of land. This was by no means a straightforward process, as the government imposed a number of restrictions on them, which in effect forced many to return to the plantations as seasonal low-wage workers. In addition, a sizable group of former slaves continued to work on plantations under slavery-like conditions as contracted labor. The reason was that they had to work to pay for the lease of a small plot of land and a hut, sometimes because they could not find any alternative means of income in the restrictive and racially stratified economy. In addition, the planter class searched for new, cheap labor, which it found in other parts of the British Empire, particularly in India and—to a lesser extent—in China. Clearly, abolition did not translate into an increase in political influence or power for the ex-slaves. Thus, in the 1863 elections in Jamaica, only 1,789 out of over 440,000 persons were allowed to vote.

The plantation-based economies determined how the English-speaking Caribbean countries would be part of the emerging global economy, dominated by the European powers, in particular Britain. Thus, the products (e.g., sugar, and later, bauxite) produced in these colonies were basically raw materials that were shipped to Britain for refining. Three structural elements were thereby established early in the colonization process. First, the economy generally was based on exports, which almost exclusively were shipped to Britain. Second, these products were shipped in a state that allowed further processing (i.e., adding of value) in Britain, a pattern that persists to this very day and also lives on in some of the preferential trading arrangements between the European Community and the Caribbean. For the Caribbean countries, this has meant that their productive potential has been stifled throughout their history. For example, Jamaica has produced mainly sugar for over 200 years, and consequently the fate of its economy depends to a large extent on the price of sugar in the world market. Third, agriculture in the Caribbean has been based primarily on a single product, so the economies were prevented from integrating. This means that the different industrial sectors in the Caribbean economies frequently operate independently of each other and without the linkages required for the attainment of sustainable development. Although these sugar economies subsequently started to diversify to other products like bananas, cocoa, coffee, and later bauxite, tourism, exotic fruits, telemarketing, offshore financial services and more, they basically remain an economic hinterland within the global economy.

After achieving their political independence in the 1960s, 1970s, and 1980s, many English-speaking Caribbean states intended to attain a more comprehensive economic independence and integrated themselves into the ranks of the Third World, particularly the Nonaligned Movement (NAM). Politically, the NAM sought to define a neutral position to the two big cold war rivals, the United States and the Soviet Union, and on the economic front it pursued closer integration with and cooperation between all Third World countries in Asia, Latin America, and Africa (Singham and Hune 1986). For the Caribbean, however, another factor was of additional relevance: the establishment of relations with regions and countries to which they had ethnic connections, particularly Africa, India, and China. This establishment of relations also had a cultural and historical dimension. The NAM can be understood as a kind of international lobby group seeking to coordinate and give coherence to the politics and economics of Third World countries, particularly in their interface with the West. As such it was—or at least seemed to be—particularly relevant to the development of small Caribbean nations in the 1960s and 1970s.

More than any other English-speaking Caribbean nations, Jamaica and Grenada in the 1970s became disproportionately important players. When during the 1970s left-leaning governments in Jamaica (1972), Grenada (1979), and Nicaragua (1979) came to power, several influential quarters in the United States, including the Carter administration, perceived an undue influence of communist rule within what they traditionally had considered as their sphere of interest. In order to strengthen their position against the growing storm of international resistance, these three states sought and managed to engage the support of the NAM. During the Sixth Summit in Cuba (1979), the Grenadian and Nicaraguan governments spoke about the experiences of their revolutionary removal of dictators in their countries. The Jamaican prime minister, Michael Manley, emphasized the need for stronger relations between developing countries. In this move deep into the Third World, "Manley spoke not isolation, but of collective self-reliance. Countries with similar difficulties but different resources could join together in meaningful and practical economic programs to develop their societies. This particular economic strategy was becoming more essential, as spiraling inflation and unemployment in Western economies left the North unwilling to negotiate with the South in ways which would contribute to resolving the economic problems of the majority of the world's population" (Singham and Hune 1986: 220).

THE CREOLIZATION OF CULTURES INTO CONTEMPORARY CARIBBEAN SOCIETY

The societies of the English-speaking Caribbean countries are composed of a diverse body of ethnicities, cultural traditions, colors, and languages. All

Table 1.1
Distribution of Ethnicities in Selected English-Speaking
Caribbean Countries, 1977 (in percentage)

	Blacks	Creole	East Indian	Chinese	Indian	White
Belize	51	22	-	-	19	-
Bermuda	63	-	-	-	-	37
Grenada[a]	84	11	-	-	-	-
Guyana[b]	30	11.3	52	-	4.4	-
Jamaica	76	29	-	1.5[c]	-	1.5[c]
Trinidad & Tobago	43	14	40	2[d]	-	1

[a] 1978 data.
[b] 1980 data.
[c] Original value was 3 percent for both groups; the split represents my estimate.
[d] Including "others."

Source: Compiled from Nohlen and Nuscheler (1982).

have contributed to the unique mixture of people and blend of cultures inhabiting this region of the world today. Perhaps with the exception of major cities such as New York City, Los Angeles, and London, the depth of this ethnic diversity is unparalleled anywhere else in the world. The composition of modern Caribbean societies is a direct consequence of the influence of European colonialism. Equally important, however, is the recognition that all Caribbean societies are more than simply the sum of their ethnic elements. In the process of several hundred years of immigration, regional migration, and emigration to foreign countries, these societies have undergone an extensive process of amalgamation that has led to a new culture. Despite the persistence of and, in some cases, increase in political conflict between the ethnicities of the region, it is fair to say that all of the cultural elements in the region contribute to a pan-Caribbean cultural heritage. In many cases different cultural traditions have merged and become integral parts of a widely shared local or regional way of life. The process that has led to this amalgamation and mixing of different cultural traditions, religions, and languages is referred to as *creolization*.

There are several dimensions to the process of creolization. The most basic aspect is the one that involves the merger of the different ethnicities that settled the Caribbean. It is necessary to keep in mind that much of this mixing of skin colors and ethnicities in the Caribbean involved significant force and violence. In the majority in cases in which slaves had one white and one black parent, this was the result of rape or forced relationships. The offspring of such relationships were mostly required to work in or around the "Great House," the private and administrative center of the plantation. This was considered a privileged position within the rigid social hierarchy on the plantation, but more often than not, this brown-skinned "middle class" was mistrusted by both the planter and the slaves, who rightly or wrongly felt that their proximity to the master corrupted them.

The black population of the region was not an ethnically homogeneous group when it arrived in the region but consisted of different African peoples. The local planters were well aware that the differences between these peoples played into their hands because they prevented the slaves, at least in the early days of colonialism, from uniting and organizing into a threatening opposition. Consequently they often made sure that slaves came from different regions along the coast of West Africa, from Senegal in the north to Angola in the south, and that they would be put together into heterogeneous groups. Thus, families and members from the same ethnic group were routinely split upon arrival in the Caribbean and family bonds brutally severed. Nevertheless, even in Africa itself the differences between various peoples was often blurred by strong traditions encouraging cultural cross-fertilization. Also, slaves who had survived the gruesome Middle Passage on the same ship regarded each other in a real sense as kin. Equally important is the recognition that African slaves were far from being docile workers who willingly submitted to slavery. Quite to the contrary, the list of local insurrections, rebellions, and other forms of resistance to oppression is long.

In light of this violent and involuntary transition, all ethnicities brought to the Caribbean by the British plantocracy were strongly inclined to maintain their traditions as a sort of spiritual connection with their homelands and their past. Language, dress, festivities, music, dance, theater, and religious rites may have changed over time, but in the case of the black population in the region, their African roots are not hidden from the surface and are increasingly displayed as integral parts of their culture. It is no exaggeration to claim that these cultural traditions were the most formidable aspect of the slaves' resistance and adaptation to the conditions in the colonies. As the Jamaican Rex Nettleford, a principal educator, artist, choreographer, intellectual, and now vice-chancellor of the University of the West Indies, rightly asserted, "dance was a primary instrument of survival" (1985: 20). Equally true is the awareness that these cultural traditions are today the greatest resource and most vibrant sectors of their societies, a realization that sadly is too often ignored in the region itself. In Jamaica, for example, dance-filled *jonkonnu* (often called John Canoe) masquerades, *dinkiminni, burru, bruckin party,* or pre-Lenten Carnival continue to be vehicles for stinging social commentary on society. Much the same applies to dances in other English-speaking Caribbean territories, such as the *jombee* in Montserrat (Dobbin 1983: 181). In addition, recreational and ceremonial dances of worship (for example, *pukumina* and *revivalism*) and, during the invocation of ancestral spirits (*kumina*), the medium of the drum serve to maintain this close link to the African motherland. Dance

> was the organic link with Africa, helping to alleviate the isolation that threatened the cultural heritage of the individuals who ended up in the Caribbean. Life itself continued to be viewed in cyclical terms, involving the dead, the living, and those unborn. . . . The dance is not only a performing art, it is also an art of community effort that proclaims the virtue of cooperation over unrestrained individualism. It is self-evident how this relates to self-government, nation-building, and social organization. (Nettleford 1985: 21)

Religions

As has been described in a seminal work on the African roots of Jamaican culture, *kumina*, the most African religion in Jamaica, has both Christian (e.g., David, Ezekiel, Moses, Cain, and Shadrach) and African (e.g., Oto, King Zombi, Shango, and Obei) gods in its pantheon of deities (Alleyne 1989: 92ff.). Similar to Brazilian *cambinda*, the Jamaican *kumina* religion worships ancestral spirits called *zombi*, which take possession of the living. *Pukumina* and *revivalism* are largely urban phenomena in Jamaica and build on a religious framework inherited from *myalism* (a religious movement similar to West African "secret spiritual societies"), and all three incorporate elements of possession by ancestral spirits, dance, and chant. Both *pukumina* and *revivalism* rank figures from the Old and New Testament in a loose hierarchy and endow them with particular characteristics. Thus, under the restrictive conditions of plantation societies, central figures of Christianity, from Jesus Christ to the Apostles, were often transformed into deities within a pantheon based on African religious traditions. They basically served as a legitimization for Africans to continue practicing their religions, which was officially forbidden.

A melding of European and African cultures occurred in the English-speaking Caribbean to a rather significant extent. A critical role in this process was played by Christianity and the influence of Christian missionaries. Borrowing elements of Christianity often gave some legitimacy to the African forms of worship. This influence is visible to this very day and readily acknowledged. Whether it is true or not, many people in Jamaica will tell you that their country boasts the greatest number of church buildings per square mile in the world. Baptists, Methodists, Anglicans, Roman Catholics, and dozens of other mainly Protestant Christian churches punctuate the urban and rural landscape in the English-speaking Caribbean with their church buildings, and many communal activities and initiatives, particularly in the ghetto, continue to have the churches as their organizational support and operational base. The graveyards of many churches in the countryside can tell silent stories of a time past. But here too influence was not a one-way street as the slaves had not come to their new homes without religious traditions of their own. Africans had indeed come to the Caribbean with a long history of *syncretization*, that is, the gradual blending of different strands of culture, and converting to Christianity promised real benefits to the increasingly creolized slaves of the English-speaking Caribbean. Apart from that, there were a variety of "common and transferable elements in European and African religions" (Craton 1982: 248). Not only did African religious practices such as *vodun, obeah*, or *shango* retain a number of Christian rituals, iconographies, and beliefs,

> [e]ven Protestants, who dismissed Catholic practices along with African as idolatrous or superstitious, retained easily transferable symbols and imagery: the cross, communion wine as blood and sacrifice, the "Rock of Ages, cleft for me," and the Holy Book, toward which they displayed an almost talismanic reverence. Even the solemn oath sanctioned and enforced by religion, so vital to both subversive organization and its uncovering, was a feature common to Europe and Africa. (Craton 1982: 248)

The importance of suffering (indeed, slavery itself) and redemption in Christian writing and history provided slaves with a powerful narrative through which they could express their plight and voice moral appeals for an improvement of their situation.

The Caribbean religion most visible outside the region and most universally appealing and influential on other cultures is without a doubt Jamaican Rastafarianism, a religion based on the Christian bible (both Old and New

Testaments) and a mixture of various Afrocentric philosophies. The name refers to the Ethiopian emperor Ras Tafari, whose name as emperor of Ethiopia was Haile Selassie I. When Ras Tafari was crowned in November 1930, an event widely reported in the Jamaican press, he instantly became a symbol for the European lies about Africa as a decrepit and downtrodden continent inhabited by an inferior race of peoples.

Earlier, during World War I and the 1920s, a Jamaican journalist and political activist, Marcus Mosiah Garvey, had attempted to awaken the awareness of his countrymen for their African roots. His Universal Negro Improvement Association (UNIA) was not particularly successful in Jamaica, but it eventually became the largest organization of black people in the United States (and the world). Although his message did not strike a common chord among Jamaican people, at the time of the crowning of Ras Tafari many of Garvey's followers recalled that he had predicted the coming of a black monarch in Africa. Garvey thus became the first prophet of the Rastafarian movement, and Haile Selassie soon assumed mythical stature. In fact, Rastafarians to this day regard Selassie as a divine Messiah figure, which is based on their reading of the Old Testament. In Revelations 5:5, the returning Messiah is identified as the Lion of the Tribe of Judah and a descendant of David, and in 19:16 as the King of Kings and Lord of Lords. Selassie himself traced his family lineage back to the Queen of Sheba and King David, and his official title was "King of Kings, Lord of Lords, Conquering Lion of Judah." Suddenly there was a black emperor in a country that had successfully rejected its submission to colonialism and represented a sense of African pride, selfhood, and glory. Even the British Crown, then and still the official head of state in many English-speaking Caribbean countries, showed its reverence to the African emperor by sending its son to the crowning ceremony in 1930. Particularly among the marginalized rural and urban Jamaicans, the conjunction of these facts and events served as a great boost to Rastafarianism, a nationalist response to colonialism.

The first Rastafarian communities developed soon after 1938 in the hills around Jamaica's capital Kingston (Campbell 1990: 93ff.). Among the symbols used by the Rastafari to identify themselves as members of the movement are the colors red, gold, and green; the symbol of the lion; the distinctive use of the Jamaican language and many words and phrases specific to the Rasta religion; and, true for many, but by no means all, of its members, the use or advocacy of the use of *ganja* (marijuana). The most characteristic outward mark of a Rastafarian are dreadlocks. Since the 1950s this style of wearing the hair in a natural fashion and curling it into long locks, which the Rastafarians adopted as a symbolic rejection of established society or, as others claim, from the Land and Freedom Army (Mau Mau) in Kenya, became a trademark of this religious movement (Chevannes 1998). (This does not mean that everybody wearing dreadlocks is automatically a Rastafarian.) True Rastafarians in the English-speaking Caribbean are among those who have the best work ethic and are usually dedicated to their work as artists, agriculturists, and artisans (to mention only their most common occupations).

Jamaican Language

African dialects have survived as part of religious rituals and in many ways have given shape to the Jamaican language, called *patois*, as well as other local dialects in the region. Many dialects in the English-speaking Caribbean developed from African vocabulary, grammar, and construction of sentences, plus the English language. In the case of Jamaican *patois*, the phrases or versions of the same sentence can look like the following sequence:

(i)	*î a nyam î dina*	"He/she/it is eating his/her/its dinner"
(ii)	*shi a nyam shi dina*	"She is eating her dinner"
(iii)	*im a nyam im dina*	"He is eating his dinner"
(iv)	*shi a nyam ar dina*	"She is eating her dinner"
(v)	*im a iit im dina*	"He/(she) is eating his/(her) dinner"
(vi)	*(h)im iitin (h)im dina*	"He/(she) is eating his/(her) dinner"
(vii)	*(h)im iz iitin (h)im dinner*	"He is eating his dinner"
(viii)	*hi iz iitin hiz dinner*	"He is eating his dinner" (Alleyne 1989: 138–139)

In describing this sequence, the "absence of gender and case distinctions in the pronominal system in (i) has West African antecedents" (Alleyne 1989: 139). The root of *nyam*, the phonetic *î*, and the abbreviated *a* (for English-*er*) are also West African in origin. Similar amalgamations of African and European languages can be found in the other territories of the so-called English-speaking Caribbean.

Emancipation and New Immigrants

The creolization process experienced another boost with the formal end to slavery, the so-called *Emancipation*, in 1834. After Emancipation, most slaves left the plantation to work their own land, which they mostly found in the less fertile or accessible regions of the colonies. This sudden loss of plantation workers gave rise to a massive importation of contracted workers, so-called *indentured laborers*, from the Far East, particularly India and China. In Trinidad, for example, after some experimentation with former slaves from Cuba, immigrants from the United States, Madeira, China, and African, East Indians came in large numbers.

By that time, most of India was under also British control. India had an immense population, and millions of its peoples lived in poverty and were therefore likely to emigrate in the hope of a better life. Consequently, a huge traffic of Indian laborers was established that brought them to a number of places along their way to the Caribbean—South East Asia, East Africa, South Africa, and Mauritius. Nearly 144,000 Indians arrived in Trinidad between 1845 and 1917, most of them from Calcutta and—to a lesser extent— Madras (Brereton 1985: 21). About 37,000 East Indians were imported to Jamaica between 1845 and 1916 (Shepherd 1993: 245). They came from all castes, and non-Hindi speakers in Trinidad became so outnumbered that they or their children learned to speak Hindi. The rigidities of the Indian caste system faded in the new environment and with a male-female ratio sharply unfavorable to maintaining caste purity. Marriage across castes, widely considered as a taboo in India, became much more common. In fact, in all receiving countries, the Indian custom of providing a *dowry* (a sum of money given to the husband by the family of the bride) was reversed because of the shortage of marriageable females (Reddock 1993: 234). Nevertheless, within the British colonial context of the Caribbean plantation societies, the East Indians were often treated as outsiders—as intruders, "heathens," or "barbarians"—and their language, dress, food, religion, and value systems were ridiculed. Little or no attempt was made to integrate them into the wider society, and their legal status was for a long time secondary to that of other Trinidadians.

As did the African slaves, the East Indians brought a number of traditions to the Caribbean, many of which eventually became part of the local culture. In this process, Trinidad Indians resurrected skills and crafts to lay the basis for their eventual escape from plantation life. They "also rediscovered the economic usefulness of traditional institutions, such as the *bhaiacharaya* or cooperative brotherhood, which proved especially helpful in the cultivation of rice, and the box money arrangement—a kind of pool to which all would contribute at stated times and from which each in turn would draw a lump sum" (Haraksingh 1985: 161). Such practices had almost identical counter-parts in several institutions among the black population.

Widely used in Trinidad and Tobago (as well as in Guyana and—to a lesser extent—in other English-speaking Caribbean countries like Jamaica) are food items of a distinctly Indian background. Thus, *roti, bhaht* (boiled rice), *dal* (lentils), *bhaji* (spinach), *chatni, jhingi, karaili,* and *sahijan* (a green stick of about eighteen inches), to mention only a few, are common foods. Spices (*mashalas*) used in Indian cuisine, such as *hardi* (turmeric), *jeera* (cumin seed), *dhania* (coriander), *sonf* (anis seed), *elayachi* (cardamom), *dalchini* (cinnamon), and many others can be found readily in local markets. The sacred basil plant (*tulsi*) often decorates Hindu homes. While the reverence for the cow is not as deep as in rural India, the eating of beef, pork, and even chicken is still taboo for many. Among Muslims, the taboo for alcohol and pork persists. Apart from these traditions, strong remnants of Indian folk traditions and a number of festivities, like *phagwah*, which celebrates rebirth and triumph over evil in Hindu mythology, survive to this day. These traditions represent a distinct contribution to English-speaking Caribbean countries, particularly Trinidad and Tobago and Guyana, where a renewed interest in them can be noted.

British Standard

An implication of the discussion is that the colonial British culture set the standard for what was regarded as respectable and civilized. In many instances this remains so. Not only do judges in the English-speaking Caribbean still wear wigs in court, but also the usual formal dress code of suit and tie (rather unsuitable for a tropical climate) for persons of social status signifies that Anglo-European traditions remain influential. Indeed, even rather casual affairs like jazz concerts with foreign guest artists may turn out to become an occasion for little speeches, official introductions by (state or municipal) dignitaries, and the playing of national anthems. Parishioners who attend church are often dressed in fancy and glamorous attire. In many countries, the British monarch has remained the titular head of state.

Given this picture of the official culture, it is interesting to take a brief look at white immigrants from Europe to the Caribbean and the influence they exerted on local culture. In what can perhaps be described as an early attempt at social engineering (that is, the conscious shaping of society), the white plantocracy in British Guiana (later Guyana) decided after Emancipation to import Portuguese immigrants into the colony. This was done in a conscious attempt to create a white middle-class to serve as a social buffer between the dominant white classes and the black and creole masses (Moore 1993). In order to facilitate the establishment of the Portuguese in such a socioeconomic position, they were granted—by a variety of economic incentives not given to creoles or blacks—the opportunity to become retail traders.

Because of this competitive advantage handed to them by the white plan-tocracy, they were able within a few years almost to monopolize this aspect of commercial activity at the expense of the creoles, who after Emancipation had also begun to venture into this business. Despite their economic fortune, the Portuguese remained cultural outsiders and they eventually attracted the anger of creoles, which at various occasions turned into open hostilities. Their middle role, determined by race, fulfilled two functions: "first, to erect a physical human barrier to protect the dominant whites from the mass of the black population—which emphasized the importance of their numerical po-sition; and secondly, to foreclose to the Creoles the most lucrative economic challenge by the latter to the social supremacy of the dominant white mi-nority, while effectively reducing the Creoles to chronic socio-economic deg-radation" (Moore 1993: 159). It can therefore easily be seen how the mix of racial prejudice and economics continued to determine life in the aftermath of slavery, particularly for blacks and creoles.

The Indigenous People

In all of this, one should not overlook the continuing presence of the indigenous Indians in some of the English-speaking Caribbean territories. In Dominica, for example, about 3,000 Carib Indians survive, largely ignored by their government and mostly living with little or no infrastructure (for example, running water, sewage systems, or roads) on a small piece of land given to them by the British monarch early in the twentieth century. There are contingents of about 400 Carib Indians living in St. Vincent and a com-munity in Trinidad. Although their language has more or less died, they have preserved a few of their skills like the craft of building canoes. Incidentally, *canoe* is a word that goes back to the Caribbean Indians. Similar words that have become fixed terms in many languages are *barbacoa* (barbecue), *batate* (potato), *cacao* (cocoa), *chili, huracan* (hurricane), *mahiz* (maize), *papaya, tobago* (tobacco), and *tomatl* (tomato).

Of particular interest are the Garinagu, sometimes called Black Caribs or Garifuna people, descendants of the Caribs and maroons who originally set-tled and lived together in St. Vincent. Because of their resistance to slavery, they were later deported to Central America, particularly Honduras and Be-lize. The Garinagu still have a number of cultural traditions in common with the Indians of the Amazon (the origin of the Carib Indians), such as language, the use of yucca, circle dances, and several religious practices and beliefs. Their African ancestors have also left a deep mark, bringing with them dances, oral traditions, and drumming. The Garinagu are an ethnically distinct people and continue to preserve their traditions such as a common language, called Garífuna, which derives from native Carib culture.

Garinagu have also migrated to the United States, where they have a sizable community, particularly in and around New York City. The estimates vary, but there are likely between 30,000 and 50,000 Garinagu living in the New York City area and at least another 10,000 to 20,000 in the rest of the country (e.g., Washington, Chicago, Saint Louis, and Los Angeles) (González 1992). Garínagu have their own language, Garífuna, but usually speak English or Spanish, depending on which country they grew up in. Consequently, in a strict sense, only those who are from Belize are relevant for this discussion.

Garinagu children born in the United States seldom learn to speak Garífuna well; many do not speak it at all. They know little of their heritage and often are embarrassed or ashamed by the elders' beliefs in the spirit of the dead and the powers of the priest, called a *buwiye*. There are traditional curers working in the United States, but major rituals to placate the ancestors are believed to be best held in Central America. Many Garinagu, however, have found comfort and help in the rituals of other African Americans living in New York. Some of the elements of these have been taken back to villages and have found a place in curing practices here. The New York Garinagu are pushing a new way of thinking that the Garinagu at home do not appreciate. They are actively (and without scholarly evidence) promoting the idea that Garinagu have derived primarily from Africa, thereby demoting the Amerindian basis of their culture. Their language, religion, diet, and technology are basically those of the Arawak Indians, with an African overlay that is fairly recent. Some Africanisms were adopted in St. Vincent, but others in Honduras and Belize, and still more from other African-Caribbean peoples with whom they have come into contact in New York. The people at home resent this and point out that there are millions of African Americans but relatively few with Amerindian roots as well, and only the Garinagu are Arawak-African.

MODERN POLITICAL SYSTEMS IN THE ENGLISH-SPEAKING CARIBBEAN

Much of the marginalization of the English-speaking Caribbean is also a consequence of their inherited political systems. In most of these countries, the traditional British-type political system has perpetuated and in many instances even reinforced rifts within these societies. In Guyana and Trinidad, for example, the two dominant political parties are closely identified with the strongly represented African or Indian descendants living there. This division has become a serious stumbling block to any attempts to establish national unity on the basis of racial and ethnic equality. In Jamaica, the same system has led to two rival political camps (closely aligned to the two major parties) vying for political power and until very recently to a large extent dependent on clientelist politics (that is, politics based on handouts to the electorate). In some instances this has led to virtual garrison constituencies (that is, electoral districts in which a party candidate, due to intimidation and political violence, has no fear of competition from another party), fiercely defended by political delegates elected there and their thugs who are controlling power within these constituencies.

In Guyana the People's Progressive party (PPP) developed at the beginning of the 1950s out of the trade union movement. The PPP, which consisted of both the Afro-Guyanese and Indo-Guyanese membership, was a broad coalition of all national forces interested in ending British rule and was led by the Indo-Guyanese Cheddi Jagan and the Afro-Guyanese L.F.S. Burnham. When in 1953 the party formed the first government elected in Guyana by general elections, the British governor quickly suspended the constitution out of fear that Marxist Prime Minister Jagan would establish a communist state. The subsequent intervention by the British contributed to a deepening of tensions between Indians and Afro-Guyanese within the PPP, which in 1955 led to a party split. The new faction, led by Forbes Burnham, constituted itself as the People's National Congress (PNC), and ethnicity eventually became the most significant marker for membership. Thus, the PPP became the party of the Indo-Guyanese, and the PNC identified with Afro-Guyanese interests. With the financial and organizational support of the CIA, British and U.S. trade unions, and the U.S.-based Institute for Free Labor Development, an eighty-day general strike in Guyana in 1963 led to almost civil war–like conditions and a loss of the PPP at the December 1964 polls (Henfrey 1972). Shortly thereafter, on May 26, 1966, Guyana achieved its independence from Britain.

In Trinidad and Tobago the situation was until recently less tense, but nevertheless similar in terms of the ethnic-political divide. From the time of Trinidad and Tobago's independence in 1962 until about the early 1980s, the political process in the twin republic was clearly dominated by Afro-Trinidadians despite the black power protests that shook the country in 1970 (Premdas 1993). Under Eric Williams, the premier party in Trinidad and Tobago, the People's National Movement (PNM), ruled without interruption from the 1960s into the 1980s. In 1976, Trinidad and Tobago changed its constitution and became a republic with a president as the head of state (as opposed to the British queen, as it was before). This did not fundamentally change the distribution of power. While politics was in the hands of the black Trinidadian population, East Indians developed their stronghold in the economy, which in many sectors they came to dominate. Even when a long-lingering economic crisis broke into the open during the 1980s, ethnic identification and interests continued to determine partisan choices among the mainly middle-class electorate.

In 1986 the PNM was ousted by an ethnically diverse coalition grouped together in the National Alliance for Reconstruction (NAR) under the leadership of former PNM stalwart A. N. R. Robinson. When Robinson's government was introduced, it shocked the Indian population who had voted in large numbers for the NAR and who had expected greater representation in the new government. Despite apparent unity, ethnic polarization entered politics again. In 1987 Robinson, apparently annoyed at the constant criticism from the Indian faction in his coalition, reduced the influence and governmental responsibilities of his Indian ministers. This step led to further dissatisfaction and in the following year several Indian ministers were relieved from their responsibilities; "national unity had been sacrificed to preserve cabinet solidarity" (Premdas 1993: 110). After a failed coup attempt in 1990, which symbolized the fragility of the Robinson government, the PNM returned to power in the 1991 elections and ruled until 1995, when the Indian-based United National Congress (UNC) narrowly won the elections and gave Trinbagonians their first Indian prime minister. Politics and daily living in Trinidad and Tobago have become much more racialized; in particular, African Trinbagonians perceive a systematic attempt by the Indian population to put them at a disadvantage (Allahar 1998). In fact, at the time of writing this book, charges are being laid against the UNC that it intends to "steal" the next elections and to absorb the PNM into its party. Whether the accusations against the government, in particular, and the Indian segment of the society, in general, are based on fact (and it is questionable that they are) is not important. It is important, however, to realize that the perceptions of African Trinbagonians are real and that, in such a polarized climate, social order and development are becoming goals harder to achieve.

Other English-speaking Caribbean countries have experienced various forms of party and political strife. For example in Antigua and Barbuda, under various prime ministers from the influential Bird family, corruption has deep roots both in the political and economic system, and credible charges of government involvement in drug trafficking and money laundering schemes have done serious damage to the reputation of this island and— by implication—that of other small islands in the region (Griffith 1997). In Grenada, a popular social revolution (1979–1983) that turned on itself

brought the world's attention to the region. The revolution was unceremo-
niously terminated in October 1983 when a multinational force under the
leadership of the United States invaded the country and restored order.

In the largest of the English-speaking Caribbean islands, Jamaica, the heritage of the colonial past also continued to be a considerable handicap for
economic and political development after independence. In this country the
two major parties, the PNP and the JLP, developed out of the labor unrest
of the late 1930s. Although this development seemed to copy the British
system and—by implication—therefore to guarantee stable and continuous
progress, the result was that the working class was split between the two
parties. This is important to keep in mind because only a united labor force
would possibly have been in the historical position to rectify the rigid, unjust,
and ethnically reinforced patterns of property that prevailed in the island
since colonial days. The process of developing a constitution and political
processes in the years preceding independence were biased because they operated in the interest of the elite and small middle classes in both Jamaica
and Britain and did not sufficiently encompass the interests of the majority
of poor people. Thus, of the members of the parliamentary committee that
in 1961/1962 was authorized to prepare proposals for Jamaica's new constitution,

> all . . . with one certain exception only, had gone beyond the elemen-
> tary school level. No less than six were lawyers. In contrast active trade
> unionists for example were conspicuously by their absence from the
> Committee. Its middle-class character showed itself even in the com-
> plexion of the members less than one-quarter of whom could have been
> described as predominantly of African stock in a population which was
> almost 80 per cent black. (Munroe 1984: 139)

The new constitution can therefore be described as an "opportunity lost to
try to compensate for traditional mass apathy by creating popular awareness
around, at least, some symbolic break with the past" (Munroe 1984: 151).

More significant, the consensus that ran across both parties that this system
would constitute the best constitutional arrangement became the basis for a
democratic process that to a large extent was nothing more than a political
spectacle. The government had little incentive to make a national effort for
genuine development that would benefit the mass of Jamaican poor in both
the countryside and the cities. Eventually, government policies became characterized by political clientelism. This subsequently led to the formation of
so-called garrison constituencies in the ghettos of Kingston—a development

that was promoted by politicians who in essence paid for their votes (Stone 1986). When in the 1970s the PNP under Michael Manley attempted to institute a political process aimed at the development of the lower classes, it was quickly overtaken by its middle-class leadership and opposition from the economic elites in the country who in tandem successfully managed to derail this process. This experiment was one of the reasons for the huge debt that Jamaica acquired during this time and through the 1980s, which is probably the main cause of its stagnating economy. Development in this political and economic climate was, despite the rhetoric of the political classes, never much more than an afterthought. Through the 1980s and into the 1990s large numbers of Jamaicans felt compelled to migrate in order to improve themselves.

REFERENCES

Allahar, Anton. 1998. "Popular Culture and Racialization of Political Consciousness in Trinidad & Tobago." *Wadabagei: A Journal of the Caribbean and Its Diaspora* 1, 2 (Summer–Fall), 1–41.

Alleyne, Mervyn. 1989. *Roots of Jamaican Culture*. London: Pluto Press.

Beckford, G. L. 1983. *Persistent Poverty: Underdevelopment in Plantation Economies of the Third World*. Morant Bay: Maroon Publishing House.

Brereton, Bridget. 1985. "The Experience of Indentureship." In *Calcutta to Caroni: The East Indians of Trinidad*, ed. John La Guerre, 21–31. St. Augustine: University of the West Indies, Extra Mural Studies Unit.

Campbell, Horace. 1990. *Rasta and Resistance: From Marcus Garvey to Walter Rodney*. 3rd ed. Trenton, NJ: Africa World Press.

Chevannes, Barry. 1998. "The Origin of the Dreadlocks." In *Rastafari and Other African-Caribbean Worldviews*, ed. Barry Chevannes, 77–96. New Brunswick, NJ: Rutgers University Press.

Craton, Michael. 1982. *Testing the Chains: Resistance to Slavery in the British West Indies*. Ithaca, NY: Cornell University Press.

Curtin, Philip D. 1969. *The Atlantic Slave Trade: A Census*. Madison: University of Wisconsin.

Dobbin, Jay D. 1983. " 'Do'en Dee Dance': Description and Analysis of the Jombee Dance of Montserrat." Ph.D. dissertation, Ohio State University.

González, Nancie L. 1992. "Garifuna Settlement in New York: A New Frontier." In *Caribbean Life in New York City: Sociocultural Dimensions*, ed. Constance R. Sutton and Elsa M. Chaney, 138–146. Staten Island, NY: Center of Migration Studies.

Griffith, Ivelaw Lloyd. 1997. *Drugs and Security in the Caribbean: Sovereignty under Siege*. University Park: Pennsylvania State University Press.

Haraksingh, Kusha R. 1985. "Aspects of the Indian Experience in the Caribbean." In *Calcutta to Caroni: The East Indians in Trinidad*, ed. John La G. Guerre, 155–169. St. Augustine, Trinidad: University of West Indies.

Henfrey, Colin V. F. 1972. "Foreign Influence in Guyana: The Struggle for Independence." In *Patterns of Foreign Influence in the Caribbean*, ed. Emmanuel de Kadt, 49–81. London: Oxford University Press for the Royal Institute of International Affairs.

Henke, Holger. 1997. "Towards an Ontology of Caribbean Existence." *Social Epistemology* 11, 1: 39–58.

Munroe, Trevor. 1984. *The Politics of Constitutional Decolonization: Jamaica 1944–62*. Mona: University of the West Indies, Institute of Social and Economic Research.

Nettleford, Rex. 1985. *Dance Jamaica: Cultural Definition and Artistic Discovery. The National Dance Theatre Company of Jamaica, 1962–1983*. New York: Grove Press.

Nohlen, Dieter, and Franz Nuscheler, eds. 1982. *Handbuch der Dritten Welt: Mittelamerika and Karibik*. Hamburg: Hoffmann und Campe.

Premdas, Ralph R. 1993. "Race, Politics, and Succession in Trinidad and Guyana." In *Modern Caribbean Politics*, ed. Anthony Payne and Paul Sutton, 98–124. Kingston: Ian Randle Publishers.

Reddock, Rhoda. 1993. "Indian Women and Indentureship in Trinidad and Tobago 1845–1917: Freedom Denied." In *Caribbean Freedom: Economy and Society from Emancipation to the Present*, ed. Hilary Beckles and Verene Shepherd, 225–237. Kingston and London: Ian Randle and James Currey.

Shepherd, Verene. 1993. "Emancipation through Servitude: Aspects of the Conditions of Indian Women in Jamaica." In *Caribbean Freedom: Economy and Society from Emancipation to the Present*, ed. Hilary Beckles and Verene Shepherd, 245–250. Kingston and London: Ian Randle and James Currey.

Singham, A. W., and Shirley Hune. 1986. *Non-alignment in an Age of Alignments*. Westport, CT: Zed Books and Lawrence Hill.

Stone, Carl. 1986. *Class, State and Democracy in Jamaica*. New York: Praeger.

2

Patterns of Migration to the United States in the Twentieth Century

The movement of peoples in and through the Caribbean has been a feature since prehistoric times, although in this it did not differ much from any other region in the world. What is distinct in the Caribbean of modern times are the extraordinarily high numbers and diversity of the peoples that came to the region or left it in search of a better life. The result of this long history of (largely involuntary) migration is a psychological mind-set characterized by a remarkable "strategic flexibility" by which the people of the region make decisions about the choices in their everyday life (Carnegie 1987). This flexible attitude has evolved over generations as a survival strategy in response to the difficult social, political, and economic conditions that have hampered the development of Caribbean peoples since the times of slavery, indentureship, and national independence. Prejudice, classism, racism, and various forms of dependence have historically formed a tight system in which the disenfranchised majority of Caribbean peoples have little choice than trying to rise above these obstacles by working in several jobs. In modern times an important part of this multi-occupational strategy has been their migration to metropolitan countries in order to attain professional skills and/or employment. Thus, travel, (temporary) migration, (temporary) return, and (temporary) migration again have been regular features of life in the English-speaking Caribbean from the very beginning.

Even in the seventeenth and eighteenth centuries, relatively close contacts between the British West Indies and the American colonies existed. At the end of the American Revolution, about 14,000 blacks went with the departing English forces, and many of them settled in the Bahamas, St. Lucia, or Jamaica (Kaplan and Kaplan 1989). At the end of the eighteenth century, influential religious leaders from the United States, such as the Reverend George Liele, preached and baptized in Kingston, Jamaica. Regiments from Haiti that fought in the American Revolution returned to Haiti to fight for their country's independence.

There was also movement in the opposite direction, although on a much smaller scale. In particular, many wealthy planters sent their children to study in British North America. In 1720, Judah Morris, a Jamaican Jew, was lecturer in Hebrew at Harvard College. Other students went to schools like the College of William and Mary and the College of Philadelphia. One of these students was Alexander Hamilton, who was born in Nevis in 1755 and attended King's College (later Columbia University). His activities attracted the attention of George Washington and Hamilton served Washington and his new country with distinction, eventually becoming the first secretary of the treasury of the United States (Knight 1990: 284).

With the end of slavery, most Caribbean migrants at first did not move out of the region but stayed relatively close to their points of origin. By the middle of the nineteenth century some governments sought to relieve population pressures by encouraging people to leave. In 1861, for example, a comparatively large number of Barbadians moved to (then) British Guiana (later Guyana) and Trinidad. Since these early days, however, people from the English-speaking Caribbean have never ceased to migrate to even the most distant places.

The first large wave of migration occurred probably during the time when the Panama Canal was built (1904–1914), when thousands of workers from Barbados, Jamaica, and other territories flocked to Panama to secure work. In fact, of the more than 50,000 (and perhaps as many as 100,000) workers who were recruited, most came from neighboring Caribbean islands. Thousands of them died in the process of building the canal. After its completion many returned to their home country, many stayed, and others continued to migrate. They have significantly contributed to the ethnic and cultural diversity of this Central American country, and English, French, Indian, Dutch, and Portuguese names, which can be found throughout Panama, bear witness to this. More than any other single event, the construction of the Panama Canal signaled to Caribbean peoples that in order to find work with meaningful—if unequal—pay, they would have to be willing to leave their home country. From their point of view, moving always was more a necessity than a matter of choice or even a preference.

GLOBAL FACTORS IN CARIBBEAN MIGRATION

Both structural factors (such as economic links) and public policy have shaped the flow of immigrants from the Caribbean. While the first phase in the development of migration in the English-speaking Caribbean was determined to a large degree by the relationship with Britain and by internal economic and social dynamics, from the late nineteenth century on, the United States increasingly came to play a role in the region. Although it would be inaccurate to say that U.S. policies actually determined the flows of migration, there is no doubt that the United States' budding assertion of regional and global power and aspiration to shape affairs in what was widely regarded as an American "backwater" had a strong impact on the region. America's growing role in the international and regional economies provides "bridges" for potential migrants. Thus, as the example of economically vibrant countries (e.g., Taiwan, South Korea) with high migration to the United States shows, this contact factor is not to be underestimated when attempting to explain flows of migration.

Following the Civil War, a consolidation of domestic and external power allowed the United States to look beyond its borders. In the Caribbean this coincided with the weakening of Spanish rule, which in 1898 allowed the United States to occupy Cuba and Puerto Rico. Building on the Monroe Doctrine of 1823, U.S. military strategists had argued that the country needed military bases from which it could venture forth. However, probably more important was that American business interests were looking for new business opportunities and markets.

Since the 1930s the population in the Caribbean has increased steadily. In fact, between 1940 and 1980 it tripled, from 55 million to 166 million (Maingot 1991). Due to this rapid population growth, by the 1950s large numbers of young people in the region were seeking employment, which the economies were not able to supply. The growth and contraction of new arrivals from the region also responded to policy shifts in U.S. immigration laws. For example, in 1952, the McCarran-Walter Act imposed a limit of 100 immigrants per Caribbean colony per year, which was aimed at significantly reducing the number of immigrants from this region. It particularly affected the English-speaking countries of the region, still under colonial rule. Thus, although the total number of arrivals from the Caribbean increased over the next twelve years, immigration from the major islands in the British West Indies fell. The main impact of the McCarran-Walter Act was that migration shifted to the United Kingdom until the immigration laws there were tightened in 1962. Between 1962 and 1965, when the discriminatory provisions in the United States were repealed, West Indians again shifted their direction back to this country, "first coming through the side door (as spouses, relatives, and so on), then the back door, and finally, with independence and subsequently the 1965 immigration act, through the front door as well" (Pastor 1987: 251).

It can be argued that from the beginning, labor markets and agricultural and industrial production in the Caribbean have been subject to the development priorities of the industrialized countries. Foreign economic priorities contribute to the crisis conditions that eventually developed, and in this they are aided by individuals and organizations within each Caribbean territory. In the context of the world economy, Caribbean exports have been produced with incentives given by the state. In addition, some of these commodities (e.g., sugar) have received preferential treatment in world markets. Bauxite and crude oil have been produced and marketed by transnational companies that employ pricing and other practices that are designed to increase their profit margins while weakening the economic position of the producer countries. Forms of state intervention produce direct and indirect consequences for production, employment, and the creation of profits and investment capital. Labor migration continues to be a basic response to the resulting crisis. In the case of the English-speaking Caribbean, this has created a socioeconomic system that puts their economies at a disadvantage.

Migration is also a direct consequence of the requirements of freely growing economies, in general, and the recently accelerated process commonly referred to as globalization. Most national policies do not pay sufficient attention to this link and consequently fail to achieve their desired intentions: the regulation of legal immigration and the suppression of illegal immigration. Nevertheless, the desire to migrate is influenced by the readiness of employers in the industrial world (including the United States) to employ workers for low wages even if the workers are known or suspected to be illegal. This point has been forcefully argued:

> It is pure folly to attempt to curb the flow of immigrant labor into the U.S. labor market, without understanding the economic forces that propel multitudes from the Third World to the United States. Attempting to limit the inflow without simultaneously prohibiting the flight of U.S. capital overseas to places where labor is less expensive is even more futile. The two phenomena are simply two sides of the same coin. To deal with one and ignore the other is plainly absurd. (Ho 1991: 28)

Globalization has created the situation that when businesses see wage levels or environmental standards as limiting their profits, they are now freer than ever to shift their operations to other countries. This gives them increased influence over political decisions and an immensely increased power over decisions concerning wages and employment. It is therefore not surprising that employer sanctions have failed in twenty other nations and ten states in the United States to prevent employers from hiring illegal workers. The intensification of international trade and the new opportunities for businesses to threaten the move their operations abroad have allowed certain industries to keep wages down and employ people willing to work for less. On the other hand, the growth in employment has created demand for new services, which are often filled by immigrants (e.g., maids, private nurses, nannies, and private chefs). Without doubt, globalization has given a new lease on life to both legal and illegal immigration.

Particularly relevant for the Caribbean remains the impact of the U.S. economy, the largest market in the world. Most recently U.S. insistence on the abolition of certain European Union trade preferences for Caribbean bananas has threatened to disrupt seriously several Eastern Caribbean economies in which this is the major export product. The unemployment resulting from this initiative will not alleviate any population pressures and provide a new push for migration.

Some observers object to establishing a direct relationship between the levels of development in one country and the numbers of its migrants. Although there might not be a relationship, this objection appears to underestimate the importance of opportunity (or the lack thereof). Certainly, the Reagan administration's Caribbean Basin Economic Recovery Act (CBERA) cannot be cited as evidence against any relationship between the importance of economic development and levels of migration. Too little was intended and achieved by this law, better known as the Caribbean Basin Initiative, than that it could possibly be held responsible for any significant, positive economic impact on Caribbean economies scholars (Pastor 1982/83; Payne 1984; Ramsaran 1982). Moreover, economic growth can not simply be equated with genuine development. In fact, there are numerous examples which demonstrate that an economy can grow without actually improving the situation of most of its people.

The United States absorbs about 70 percent of all migrants from the Caribbean region. Most come from Jamaica and the Dominican Republic. The large majority comes to this country legally. As in the past, they are driven by a combination of factors. With the persistent lack of development and opportunities for employment, many people in the English-speaking Caribbean continue a decades-old culture that regards migration as just another option to eke out a living for themselves and their families. They do not migrate because they want to, but because they see few other chances to earn a living, send their children to school, and comfortably retire. In fact, quite a few of them return to their home country to retire or to build a business there from their savings.

PATTERNS OF MIGRATION BEFORE 1965

Before 1965, four periods or phases of migration within and away from the Caribbean are often distinguished (Blackman 1985; Marshall 1987): (1) the 1830s to the 1880s, (2) ca. 1890 to the 1920s, (3) the 1920s to 1940, and (4) from 1940 to 1965. To a large extent, the first phase was characterized by in-migration from East Asian contract workers, particularly from India and China. Following the abolition of the British slave trade and then slavery itself in 1834, the Caribbean islands in British possession experienced a severe labor shortage since many former slaves were no longer willing to work on plantations. Together with declining profits for sugar in the international markets, this caused a crisis in these economies, which had centered on sugar production. In response, the planters decided to import contract workers, mainly from India and China. Until the end of this arrangement in 1917, Indian immigrants to British Guiana numbered about 240,000, to Trinidad 145,000, and to Jamaica 37,000. Their presence contributed to another brief period of sugar prosperity. Toward the end, however, the importation of indentured laborers from India and China became "a means of cheapening labor rather than a necessity for the maintenance of the sugar industry" (Hope 1985: 239). Smaller contingents of workers from China, Lebanon, and Syria also contributed to the inflow of foreigners to the English-speaking Caribbean during this phase, and they established a tight (often commercial) network of close family relationships throughout the region. Indeed, in many cases, families from Lebanon or Syria or of Palestinian background (all three groups sometimes referred to as Levantines) can trace their origin to the same village. Most of these immigrants came for economic reasons or because they had been discriminated against in their home countries. While many of the Chinese became involved in the retail trade, the Levantines operate many Caribbean hotel chains, cinemas, travel or real estate agencies, and soft drink operations, and some members of both groups have become quite wealthy. In many instances they (in particular the Levantines) have become influential in chambers of commerce, tourist boards, political parties, and state organizations.

A secondary wave of migration, one that already foreshadowed the second phase, occurred within the region during this period. Dominated by Barbadians, significant numbers of mostly seasonal laborers in search of better wages and land moved around in the English-speaking countries of the Eastern Caribbean. Because the plantations occupied most of the cultivable land, in many of the smaller Eastern islands moving from the plantation automatically meant moving away from the island. The labor shortage was particularly acute in Trinidad and British Guiana, and wage rates there were twice as high as in the other islands. Consequently they became attractive targets for migrants from the other islands. Between 1850 and 1921 Barbados alone sent 50,000 persons to these two countries. Between 1835 and 1846, 19,000 Eastern Caribbean migrants entered British Guiana and Trinidad and Tobago. Smaller contingents of several thousand moved during this period from Dominica to the gold fields of Venezuela and from Barbados to Surinam. In many instances these movements continue.

These early streams, or rather spurts, of intraregional migration were largely determined by global conditions affecting the sugar market, and the sudden emigration became a concern for planters in the islands affected by it. By 1839 Barbados had enacted two laws to discourage emigration, and in 1973 it made amendments to assist certain poor classes of emigrants. However, presumably because of the high population growth rate in Barbados following the end of slavery, emigration was soon regarded "as the only alternative to starvation and pestilence" (Marshall 1987: 18). The situation was similar in many of the other islands and marked the beginning of a continuing policy of active encouragement.

Following the collapse of sugar prices in the 1880s, Caribbean workers left their countries in search for job opportunities. During this second phase, thousands migrated from the British West Indies to the United Kingdom, Cuba, and several countries in Central and South America. Just like the subsequent labor exodus into the Panama Canal Zone, in the mid-1880s substantial numbers of workers went to Costa Rica, where they participated in railroad construction and agricultural labor. A secondary wave during this period went to Brazil, Colombia, the Dominican Republic, Haiti, and Honduras. With the beginning of World War I, the search for military forces and labor power attracted contingents of Caribbean migrants to the United Kingdom.

The second phase set the pattern for Caribbean migration for much of the rest of the century: the majority of the migrants moved around either within the region or (at least temporarily) out of it. Caribbean migration during this phase was dominated by the construction of the Panama Canal, although banana cultivation in Central American countries and Colombia caused many Caribbean workers to move among these countries, depending on where labor was needed. Their tendency to work for a specified time and then move back to their home countries, either to invest or spend the earned money, allowed a relatively large number of Caribbean laborers during this time to participate in the economic opportunities offered to them in Central America.

Due to the increasing involvement of U.S. economic and political interests in the region, it is hardly surprising that during this phase, the United States also became a target for Caribbean migrants, and this inflow constituted the first wave of West Indian immigration to this country. Although in 1914 a bill had been placed before Congress (subsequently blocked by President Wilson) to exclude West Indians because of their race and although many of them came only as seasonal workers, an increasing number of Caribbean migrants stayed permanently in the United States. According to U.S. population census data, the number of foreign-born blacks in the United States grew from about 20,000 in 1900 to almost 74,000 in 1920 (Kasinitz 1995). There was a clear acceleration of West Indian immigration during this time as annual inflow rates increased from 832 in 1902 to a relatively stable rate of between 5,000 and 8,000 per year afterward and reached a high of over 12,000 in 1924, shortly before new immigration restrictions went into effect. The vast majority of these were West Indians (including Haitians). Between 1900 and 1920 alone, for example, 10,000 to 12,000 Bahamians went to Miami in order to work in the booming construction industry there, and between 1904 and 1914 an estimated 44,000 Jamaicans alone migrated to the United States.

This second phase of migration in the Caribbean also ushered in new relationships between the islands that had been impossible under colonialism, when most foreign relations of the colonies were directed to their "mother country." Between 1902 and 1932, over 120,000 Jamaicans traveled to Cuba to work in the cane fields. Many of them stayed permanently and thereby contributed to a deepening sense of relationship between these neighboring islands.

The third phase, roughly the time between the two world wars, was marked by a steady reduction of opportunities for migrants, which prompted the first significant wave of returning migrants. The new U.S. immigration law of 1924 established national quotas, which restricted immigration from the Caribbean. At the same time, those who in search of work had earlier migrated to other Caribbean territories increasingly were forced to return to their home countries as economic opportunities contracted in their hosts' economies. For example, Venezuela, whose oil fields had attracted thousands of West Indians in 1929, restricted the entry of foreign-born black people. In addition, a number of migrants returned from the United States and Cuba. The swelling numbers of the unemployed contributed to the acceleration of the thrust for independence in several of the English-speaking Caribbean countries.

In the fourth phase, war and the postwar period provided an opportunity for Caribbean workers to alleviate sometimes severe labor shortages (e.g., farm labor, domestic helpers, and seasonal workers) in the United Kingdom, Canada, and the United States. This was the smallest of the waves of Caribbean immigrants coming to the United States; it "probably never exceeded 3,000 per year until the close of this period and was generally far below that" (Kasinitz 1995: 26). Many of this group were people joining family members who had come to the United States previously and young professionals who came as students and stayed after completing their degrees.

THE POST–1965 GENERATION OF IMMIGRANTS

The year 1965 marks the probably most significant turning point in the history of Caribbean-Americans' migration to the United States. In this year the Hart-Cellar Immigration Reform Act became law and abandoned the national quota system established in 1924. In its stead, a ceiling of 120,000 immigrants for the entire Western Hemisphere (however, there was no ceiling from 1965 to 1968) with no preference system and without country quotas was imposed. After 1976 a limit of 20,000 immigrants per country was imposed. This arrangement proved to be of particular advantage to the microstates of the English-speaking Caribbean that had become independent after 1962. Whereas during colonial times they had been allowed to send only 600, they were now allowed to send 20,000 per year (immediate family members not included in this number), which for many of them was a huge proportion of their total population (Miller 1985). On the one hand, this was a great economic relief for their beleaguered economies. From another point of view, however, the large outflow of often highly qualified citizens meant a serious loss of people in the smaller countries. Countries like Dominica, Belize, Grenada, St. Lucia, and St. Vincent lost between 16 and 23 percent of their base population during the 1970s (Simmons and Guengant 1992).

Between 1965 and 1975, the total immigration from the West Indies to

Table 2.1
Immigration to the United States from the Caribbean,
1961–1984

Year	English-Speaking Caribbean	Total Caribbean	English-Speaking as % of Total Caribbean
1961-1970	142,345[a]	470,213	30.3
1971-1980	331,365	741,126	44.7
1981-1984	134,638	213,986[b]	62.9

[a] Figure for the period 1960–1970.
[b] Figure for the period 1981–1983.

Sources: Kasinitz (1995; Table 2); Pastor (1985; Table 1.2); author's calculations.

the United States surpassed that of the previous seventy years: approximately 50,000 mostly middle-class immigrants from the English-speaking Caribbean were legally entering the country annually by the early 1980s. Immigration from Jamaica alone reached approximately 20,000 during that time. It is hardly a surprise, therefore, that the number of total immigrants from the Caribbean increased from 123,000 in the 1950s, to 470,000 in the 1960s, and nearly 750,000 in the 1970s, creating serious backlogs of persons with approved visas but unable to enter the United States because their country's limit had been exhausted.

With the 1965 act, the United States also changed the racial and ethnic composition of its immigrant population. Between 1900 and 1965, 75 percent of all immigrants had been Europeans. After 1968, 62 percent came from Asia and Latin America, and by 1978 this percentage had grown to 82 percent (Pastor 1987). As Table 2.1 indicates, the number of immigrants from the English-speaking Caribbean as a percentage of immigrants from the entire region has also steadily increased since the 1960s.

Immigrants from the English-speaking Caribbean consisted increasingly of single women or female-headed households. In the past, immigration from the region was often depicted in terms of male migration, and certainly before the late 1950s, women as a group did not figure prominently as immigrants. This, however, changed during the 1970s. Between 1972 and 1979 at least 51 percent of the immigrants from Trinidad and Tobago, Barbados, Guyana, Jamaica, St.Kitts/Nevis, and Antigua were female (Bonnett 1990: 140). As Table 2.2 indicates, the ratio of female-to-male immigrants from the first four countries reached about 80 to 87 percent in 1980.

Table 2.2
Gender Ratio of Immigrants from Selected Caribbean
Countries, 1980

Country	Male	Female	Total	Gender Ratio*
Barbados	12,230	14,617	26,847	83.7
Guyana	22,562	26,046	48,608	86.6
Jamaica	87,264	109,547	196,811	79.7
Trinidad & Tobago	29,752	36,155	65,907	82.3

*Male/female.

Source: Gordon (1989: 91).

Several reasons are behind this change in the gender composition. Apart from the liberalization implied in the Hart-Cellar Act, which allowed women to take advantage of the family preference scheme, shifts in the U.S. labor market proved beneficial for a number of Caribbean women with or even without higher education. From the late 1960s, more and more American middle-class women moved into jobs previously considered a male domain, which created demand for the jobs they vacated. For example, many of them left hospital nursing to better-paying and more prestigious positions in the private sector (Toney 1989). The same mobility also created a demand for services, such as general domestic helpers or caregivers for children, the elderly, and even for pets. These jobs were typically closed to men who, in addition, suffered from the decline in the industries (e.g., manufacturing or trades) they had traditionally been able to join upon arrival in the United States. Another reason is that with the greater independence most female migrants experience in the United States, many husbands or male common law partners refuse to follow and stay with their female partner. From their perspective, the female employment situation implies a loss of their own power, particularly if they are not able to find comparable or better employment in the United States. The gender imbalance among English-speaking Caribbean immigrants to New York City evened out between 1985 and 1990 period (Conway and Walcott 1999). However, most recent data indicate that the trend has again reversed and that women once again seem to be in the majority of immigrants from the region. According to the Immigration and Naturalization Service (INS), of 19,089 entries from Jamaica to the United States in 1996, 10,280 were females and 8,809 were males; the figures for

Guyana were 5,120 and 4,369, respectively (U.S. Immigration and Natu-ralization Service 1997, Table 13, 55).

While both women and men immigrants have improved their labor force participation rates, the increase was much more marked for new female im-migrants. Between 1975 and 1980, 68 percent of male arrivals from the four most important English-speaking Caribbean countries (Jamaica, Guyana, Trinidad and Tobago, and Barbados) sending immigrants to New York City were able to enter the labor force; this percentage had risen to 79.3 percent in the 1985–1990 period. The corresponding figures for the female arrivals from these countries are 56.3 percent and 82 percent, respectively (Conway and Walcott 1999).

In 1990 the United States put another immigration act into effect, which intended to finetune the demands of the domestic labor market and the potential supply of international migrants to this country. While the new act remains neutral to ethnicity, race, and national origin, family immigration was strongly reaffirmed as the defining feature of policy. In fact, four-fifths of all visas will be allocated on this basis. However, employment-based im-migration doubled under this act to 120,000 visas. Whether this new system accounts for the increase in female immigrants from the English-speaking Caribbean is not clear, but the overall effect—if there is any—on the total number of admissions from the region was only marginal and temporary. As Table 2.3 indicates, this figure seems to have recovered from a drop in the post–1990 period and reached almost the level it stood at in the late 1980s.

Finally, it has to be pointed out that migrants from the Caribbean used to be recruited from the middle and upper classes rather than from the bottom of the social ladder. This is particularly true for the migrants of the first half of the century. Since the 1965 Immigration Act, this trend has dissipated. Indeed, as Table 2.4 indicates, by the end of the 1990s, the num-ber of Caribbean immigrants in the professional, executive, and managerial category was a mere 6 percent of the total admitted number of persons. At the same time, two-thirds of all Caribbean immigrants in this year did not report an occupation, and although this figure includes minors, this trend represents a clear deviation from previous immigration patterns from the region.

Immigration cannot only be regarded as a safety valve, as some commen-tators and regional governments have claimed. (This term refers to the real or assumed release of the beleaguered Caribbean economies of their surplus labor force, which is permanently unemployed.) However, the consequences of migration for the sending countries are more complex. Besides possible

Table 2.3
Immigrants Admitted from Selected English-Speaking Caribbean Countries, 1986–1996

	1986-89	1990	1991	1992	1993	1994	1995	1996
Anguilla	164	41	56	46	23	31	26	36
Antigua[a]	3,502	1,319	944	619	554	438	364	406
Bahamas	3,270	1,378	1,062	641	686	589	585	768
B.'dos	6,331	1,745	1,460	1,091	1,184	897	734	1,043
Dominica	2,663	963	982	809	683	507	591	797
Grenada	4,031	1,294	979	848	827	595	583	787
Jamaica	88,233	25,013	23,828	18,915	17,241	14,349	16,398	19,089
St. Kitts[b]	2,617	896	830	626	544	370	360	357
St. Lucia	2,313	833	766	654	634	449	403	583
St. Vincent	2,907	973	808	687	657	524	349	606
Trinidad[c]	15,775	6,740	8,407	7,008	6,577	6,292	5,424	7,344
Guyana	41,287	11,362	11,666	9,064	8,384	7,662	7,362	9,489
TOTAL	173,092	52,557	51,788	41,008	37994	32,703	33,189	41,304

[a] Including Barbuda.
[b] Including Nevis.
[c] Including Tobago.

Source: U.S. Immigration and Naturalization Service (1997:Table 3, 30).

relief, there is also a loss of skills and people power—often referred to as "brain drain"—involved in the exodus from the region (Duany 1994). Thus, in the early 1990s the active recruitment of nurses to the United States created a serious crisis in the Jamaican and Trinidadian health sectors, which suddenly found their hospitals understaffed. At the same time, the need to train new nurses and the investment in the training of those who left have to be factored as losses to the national economy. It is a matter of great concern when, as has been reported, between 1977 and 1980 50 percent of the output of Jamaica's training institutions migrated (Maingot 1991, 111).

Table 2.4
Caribbean Immigrants Admitted by Major Occupational Group, 1996

	Jamaica	Trinidad/Tobago	Guyana	Caribbean
Professional	921	478	460	5,015
Executive/ administrative/ managerial	218	200	213	1,464
Sales	232	124	181	2,107
Administrative Support	919	240	336	2,938
Precision Production/craft/ repair	306	292	606	4,493
Operator/ fabricator/laborer	744	376	582	13,075
Farming/forestry/ fishing	303	19	259	1,583
Service	4,376	1,114	622	11,069
No Occupation or Not Reported	11,070	4,501	6,230	75,057

Source: U.S. Immigration and Naturalization Service (1997:Table 21).

REFERENCES

Blackman, Courtney N. 1985. "Factors in the Development of a Migration Policy for the Caribbean." In *Migration and Development in the Caribbean: The Unexplored Connection*, ed. Robert A. Pastor, 262–272. Boulder, CO: Westview Press.

Bonnett, Aubrey W. 1990. "The *New* Female West Indian Immigrant: Dilemmas of Coping in the Host Society." In *In Search of a Better Life: Perspectives on Migration from the Caribbean*, ed. Ransford W. Palmer, 139–149. New York: Praeger.

Carnegie, Charles V. 1987. "A Social Psychology of Caribbean Migrations: Strategic Flexibility in the West Indies." In *The Caribbean Exodus*, ed. Barry B. Levine, 32–43. New York: Praeger.

Conway, Dennis, and Susan Walcott. 1999. "Gendered Caribbean and Latin American New Immigrant Employment Experiences in New York City." *Wada-*

bagei: A Journal of the Caribbean and Its Diaspora 2,1 (Winter–Spring): 53–112.

Duany, Jorge. 1994. "Beyond the Safety Valve: Recent Trends in Caribbean Migration." *Social and Economic Studies* 43,1 (March): 95–122.

Gordon, Monica. 1989. "Gender in Selection of Immigrants and the Impact on Caribbean Women in the United States." In *Establishing New Lives: Selected Readings on Caribbean Immigrants in New York City,* ed. Velta J. Clarke and Emmanuel Riviere, 84–109. New York: Caribbean Research Center, Medgar Evers College, CUNY.

Ho, Christine. 1991. *Salt-Water Trinnies: Afro-Trinidadian Immigrant Networks and Non-Assimilation in Los Angeles.* New York: AMS Press.

Hope, Trevor J. 1985. "The Impact of Immigration on Caribbean Development." In *Migration and Development in the Caribbean: The Unexplored Connection,* ed. Robert A. Pastor, 237–261. Boulder, CO: Westview Press.

Kaplan, Sidney, and Emma Nogrady Kaplan. 1989. *The Black Presence in the Era of the American Revolution.* Amherst: University of Massachusetts Press.

Kasinitz, Philip. 1995. *Caribbean New York: Black Immigrants and the Politics of Race.* 3rd ed. Ithaca, NY: Cornell University Press.

Knight, Franklin. 1990. *The Caribbean: The Genesis of a Fragmented Nationalism.* New York: Oxford University Press.

Maingot, Anthony P. 1991. "Emigration and Development." In *Determinants of Emigration from Mexico, Central America, and the Caribbean,* ed. Sergio Diaz-Briquets and Sidney Weintraub, 100–119. Boulder, Co: Westview Press.

Marshall, Dawn. 1987. "A History of West Indian Migrations: Overseas Opportunities and 'Safety-Valve' Policies." In *The Caribbean Exodus,* ed. Barry B. Levine, 15–31. New York: Praeger.

Miller, Harris N. 1985. "U.S. Immigration Policy and Caribbean Economic Development." In *Migration and Development in the Caribbean: The Unexplored Connection,* ed. Robert A. Pastor, 348–370. Boulder, CO: Westview Press.

Pastor, Robert A. 1982/83. "Sinking in the Caribbean Basin." *Foreign Affairs,* 1038–1058.

Pastor, Robert A. 1985. "Introduction: The Policy Challenge." In *Migration and Development in the Caribbean: The Unexplored Connection,* ed. Robert A. Pastor, 1–39. Boulder, CO: Westview Press.

Pastor, Robert A. 1987. "The Impact of U.S. Immigration Policy on Caribbean Emigration: Does It Matter?" In *The Caribbean Exodus,* ed. Barry B. Levine, 243–259. New York: Praeger.

Ramsaran, Ramesh. 1982. "The U.S. Caribbean Basin Initiative." *The World Today* 38,11 (November): 430–436.

Simmons, Alan B., and Jean Pierre Guengant. 1992. "Caribbean Exodus and the World System." In *International Migration Systems: A Global Approach,* ed. Mary M. Kritz, Lin Lean Lim, and Hania Zlotnik, 94–114. Oxford: Clarendon Press.

Toney, Joyce. 1989. "The Changing Relationship between Caribbean Men and Women in New York City." In *Establishing New Lives: Selected Readings on Caribbean Immigrants in New York City,* ed. Velta J. Clarke and Emmanuel Riviere, 65–83. New York: Caribbean Research Center, Medgar Evers College, CUNY.

U.S. Immigration and Naturalization Service. 1997. *Statistical Yearbook of the Immigration and Naturalization Service, 1996.* Washington, D.C.: U.S. Government Printing Office.

3

Patterns of Adjustment and Adaptation

There are a variety of aspects giving shape and substance to the complex process of adjustment and adaptation of Caribbean-Americans to their new home. Like all other immigrants, Caribbean peoples in the United States regularly compare their memories of home to the realities of their life in a new country. The clash of cultures has perhaps nowhere been better captured than in the following lines from the poem "Nabel String" by the Grenadian Merle Collins:

> The blank stare from the unknown
> next door neighbor kills something inside
> and the sound that pulls
> is of the heartbeat, of the drum
> voice. Is River Sallee, is a drummer
> soaring, is Victoria, is Belmont,
> those places that you, I, we left
> left to search, as always, for a better life.

This sense of inner conflict is known to most migrants who have left their home country after growing up there and becoming socialized to its customs, social norms, and traditions. For immigrants from the English-speaking Caribbean, there is an additional dimension of "race," which often acts as a barrier that white migrants are not exposed to or even aware of. Overcoming these sociopsychological odds takes tremendous inner strength and can distract energies that could be more usefully directed (Henke 1998).

At the most general level, adjustment and adaptation can be understood as a psychological and social process in the course of which English-speaking Caribbean immigrants learn to negotiate various economic, administrative, and social requirements, norms, and value systems imposed by U.S. society. They bring both cultural assets and liabilities to the table. Depending on what they identify as the more valuable and practical asset, Caribbean Americans will adopt the requirements of the host society, manipulate and modify them to their advantage, or let them coexist with attitudes they really consider superior but are detrimental to insist on in an environment that is inclined to discriminate against them.

COMMUNITY STRENGTH

Values and attitudes that can create trust, justice, and voluntarism (known as social capital) are not new concepts to Caribbean peoples, who make every effort to retain their strong African (or, for that matter, Indian) traditions of community even under adverse conditions. By establishing networks, social clubs, organizations, festivals, and so on, Caribbean peoples who have migrated to North America have made it abundantly clear that they are not a somewhat casual gathering of rather disjointed individuals. Drawing on their traditions and values brought from the Caribbean, they have established themselves as a veritable and clearly identifiable community of people living in urban America. In doing so, they have adapted themselves to the living conditions in this new environment and made their mark on their communities.

Undoubtedly bonds between core family and extended family grow stronger among most migrants under the often adverse conditions of becoming integrated (or not) in the United States. However, in the case of Caribbean migrants in general and English-speaking Caribbean immigrants in particular, this general predisposition assumes a broader scope than for practically all other immigrant groups. Indeed, in the tradition of their experience of the Middle Passage, Caribbean immigrants continue to integrate people whom they regard as "adopted family" (and to which anthropologists sometimes refer as *fictive kin*). Slaves who arrived in the Western Hemisphere on the same slave ship would, despite possible different ethnic backgrounds, genuinely regard each other as brothers and sisters and treat each other as such. Generally Caribbean Americans are extremely open to accepting outsiders who prove themselves as very loyal or as good (new) family members into their midst and to welcome them as equal kin. This willingness to create "fictive kin" may very well transcend the boundaries of "race" and ethnicity and include members of groups that are generally perceived as unfriendly or even hostile (e.g., whites).

The notion of social capital has both material and immaterial aspects to it. Among the immaterial aspects one can count strong community values. One of the most remarkable material components of social capital among English-speaking Caribbean immigrants are their savings clubs and rotating credit associations, often called *susu*. Although this institution is also known among certain Asian communities in the United States, one study ascertains that "by far the most extensive use of these associations in the United States is among black West Indian immigrants" (Bonnett 1981: 53).

The most important function of the *susu* is to create capital for individuals intending to set up a business or buy property (e.g., a house), or for funds used to bury the dead or form burial societies, save for remittances (that is, money sent back to the islands), and supplement family budgets. The precondition for membership in such a saving circle is that members are reliable and trustworthy "working people" and have a regular income (Bonnett 1981). These associations are open to outsiders too. The size of the *susu* may range from approximately ten to fifty members depending on the size of required contributions (called the "hand"). The *susu* is an informal community of people based on mutual trust. There is no formal constitution with rules, regulations, or other contractual terms. A *susu* comes together informally. The individual members are drawn together by word of mouth rather than formal advertisements. The saving circles serve as a pillar among West Indian immigrants in their efforts to establish businesses and acquire property. They consequently facilitate adaptation to the new environment, particularly for relatively new immigrants and illegal aliens who tend to avoid opening savings accounts at banks.

Usually the members of a *susu* "throw their hand" once a week (normally a Sunday), with a regular monetary contribution to the "bank." The contributions vary in size and are made in cash. Since the entire process is informal, no receipts are issued, although records are kept about each member's share. At a consensually determined time, each contributing member will receive the entire "bank" and this will constitute his or her share in the entire scheme. No interest is paid, because more often than not the organizers perceive themselves as helping their members in an altruistic way. As one of them points out: "My son, I think it is mean to take out interest. God! It's poor people using this 'box,' you know. I have seen members take that money—all of it—and go right to purchase something they really need" (Bonnett 1981: 62). Individually, members may decide to give the organizer of the *susu* a small share of the hand they receive. There are no limitations imposed on how each member can spend his or her share. The average size of a fund is about $500 to $600, but sometimes larger "banks" of up to $4,000 may be established. In this case, the weekly contribution would be $60 and the association would run for the entire year. Smaller funds run for only about 20 weeks. A *susu* is usually constituted for a limited time only, but it may develop into a revolving scheme.

Because a *susu* is an informal, trust-based association, conflicts among and default in paying of members' payment cannot be ruled out. To minimize the occurrence of such conflict situations, the organizers try to limit membership to people they personally know to be upstanding members of their community or who have been recommended to them as trustworthy. This procedure usually creates a strong sense of solidarity and cohesiveness, and default becomes a severe risk to a person's reputation and respectability within the wider community. In some cases, organizers convene their *susu* from among members of the same island, which increases this risk in the case of such a misconduct. Information about an individual's default may spread to relatives and the wider community in the homeland, or in the individual's community in Canada or England, thus maximizing the embarrassment. In other cases, the organizer may walk to the house of the defaulting member and "cuss them out" in front of relatives and neighbors. In one instance it was reported that a defaulting nurse's reputation was damaged by information spreading about her financial irresponsibility, and it was widely perceived that this led to her being passed over for promotion at her workplace (Bonnett 1981: 64). Clearly, participation in a *susu* involves a substantial commitment and tangible sanctions. Thus, the possible loss of reputation in the case of an inability or, worse, unwillingness to pay one's dues can have serious consequences.

Apart from its function as a short-term savings mechanism, the *susu* is both an expression of social cohesiveness among West Indian immigrants and a tool for the creation of community. It can lead to a deepening sense of mutuality and trust, which has positive implications for the welfare of the rest of the community. One member has vividly expressed these dimensions of the rotating credit associations among English-speaking Caribbean immigrants:

Well, Mrs. _____ has been "throwing" a "box" with me for years. Often she tells me why she needs it and we share our mutual problems. She is like part of my family. For instance, when my mother died, Mrs. _ felt so concerned that she got the girls together at work and they started a "box" just so I could get some extra money for the funeral expenses.

My son, there is so much more to this "box" thing than mere economics. A lot of us immigrants needed it when we came here first. If only to get to see each other on days off and talk about how we [are] doing. (Bonnett 1981: 67)

Where membership is diverse, the *susu* also tends to build bridges between immigrants from the different islands and in this way gives rise to the construction of a Caribbean American identity, rather than the persisting identification with the different countries of origin. Some participants therefore aptly describe it as a "West Indian thing." Finally, new bridges are also established between the community of Caribbean people and American society. The *susu* have been recognized by institutions of the official economy, such as banks, mortgage loan associations, and insurance schemes (for example, the Fannie Mae Foundation). By having such relatively loose and informal schemes recognized as social capital, Caribbean Americans achieve a higher level of integration into the United States.

Another source of community strength should be mentioned. Caribbean people, as members of a strongly oral culture, have an inclination to emphasize social life and active interpersonal relations among each other. Undoubtedly, this has to be regarded as a source of community. A study about Trinidadians in San Francisco found that some not only make conscious attempts to keep up home country traditions of visiting unannounced at the house of their friends ("dropping by"), spending time together ("liming"), and exchanging news and gossip ("ole-talk"), but also that contacting friends and relatives via telephone has caused others to incur such high phone bills as to prevent them from purchasing a house (Ho 1991). In this way news from "back home" can spread within a very short time from the east to the west coast of the United States, which helps to deepen their sense of belonging.

Finally, there is a strong emphasis among English-speaking Caribbean immigrants to have their children acquire a good education. Indeed, many of the early immigrants came to this country specifically with this goal (and perhaps a scholarship) in mind. The high regard for a good education in the West Indian community has also been a source of economic strength for the second generation. U.S.-born children of West Indian immigrants usually have more years of schooling and higher incomes than whites in the United States (Sunshine and Warner 1998). Clearly, West Indian Americans have become a significant component of the black middle class in this country. Nevertheless, this social capital cannot be taken for granted. However, "assimilation to American culture for these immigrant children often means giving up the dream of making it in America through individual achievement" (Portes and Sensenbrenner 1993, 1342). In particular, some children reject their parents' West Indian identity and generally positive attitudes toward their American experience.

EMPLOYMENT PATTERNS

Another aspect of community strength and social capital is that people in the English-speaking Caribbean have been socialized into a relatively less racially oppressive environment. Growing up in a country where most people are dark-skinned led to greater self-confidence and self-worth despite the fact that in the early decades of this century, the ruling elites were still largely composed of whites and light-complexioned creoles. When Caribbean people arrived in the United States, they approached the question of job search and willingness to work certain professions with slightly different attitudes than did native blacks. From the beginning they were prepared to accept jobs that African Americans often shunned because of their low wages, low status, or generally poor working conditions. Because of this disparity, informants from the English-speaking Caribbean often report negative impressions of native black Americans and look down on this group for not being enthusiastic enough about all the opportunities in the United States.

In New York City, their preferred place of settlement, the integration of West Indians into the economy during the first three or four decades of the twentieth century has to be seen in context and as a consequence of the overall growth in the city's black community. As a consequence of this growth, a consumer market developed in New York. Because they were often not welcome in white establishments, Caribbean people required their own stores, shops, beauty parlors and barber shops, real estate agents, bars, and restaurants. Although most of those who were able to profit from this growing market were white, a number of Caribbean immigrants in both Brooklyn and Harlem were able to establish themselves as small retailers and providers of personal services. These stores often became harbors for illicit gambling, such as a popular numbers lottery that apparently had been brought by West Indians who had formerly worked in Panama. Small as these "ghetto capitalist" opportunities might seem, they offered the first substantial inroads into the market for West Indians with entrepreneurial aspirations and employment possibilities for others. Many of them, having owned small businesses and shops in their home country, sought to continue this way of earning their living after they arrived in the United States.

The skilled, white-collar, and semiprofessional occupations others had hoped to secure because of their middle-class status and education did not materialize. Like other blacks, they only had the most unskilled jobs to choose from. This was certainly true in the beginning of the twentieth century, and more often than not they had to accept work not commensurate with their education and skills. If they had a choice, they opted with great regularity for service-sector occupations: 87.1 percent of the West Indian workforce in 1905, 89.9 percent in 1915, 76.1 percent in 1925, and 76.3 percent in 1940 had to work as unskilled workers (Holder 1998; Reid 1939). In the order of their importance for English-speaking Caribbean Americans, such jobs were categorized as menial service workers, operatives, and manual laborers. They held jobs like porter, waiter, or elevator operator in the economy. Indeed, so prominent was their number among elevator operators that some members of the wider black community would, sometimes scornfully, call them "pilots of the indoor airplane" (Holder 1998: 38). Despite the discrimination from various groups that working these jobs implied, West Indians' choice under the circumstances was a good one. Elevator operators did not have night shifts; they did have regular hours, free Sundays, and higher pay than other available jobs. A similar case could be made for another favorite choice for West Indian men: chauffeuring. Preferred jobs for women in the early days of immigration were in the garment industry and as domestics. Many of these women had been skilled dressmakers or seamstresses in their home country and found it relatively easy to establish themselves in this market.

Without doubt, Caribbean men and women suffered job discrimination from both white and black Americans. On the other hand, many whites regarded West Indians as better workers than African Americans, because they were seen as less demanding, more docile, and easier to satisfy. It has been reported that their "British" background and good command of the English language were sometimes regarded as assets over native blacks. To the extent that these stereotypes applied to them, they became doubly vulnerable to discrimination. On the one hand, white employers regarded them as rebellious when West Indian workers decided to protest workplace discrimination. On the other hand, native African Americans would regard them as defeatist and accuse them of lowering the standards for working conditions for blacks (Green and Wilson 1990; Kasinitz 1995). Consequently, finding and keeping employment involved a precarious tightrope walk by these immigrants between the different communities with which they had relations.

Caribbean immigrants clearly did not have a preference for manual work, presumably because of its implicit association with slave work. Although most of the women who arrived in the early immigration worked under worse conditions and for less pay in nonunionized enterprises, they quickly joined trade unions, which helped them to improve their wages and guarantee continued access to the few available jobs in the garment industry or as nurses. As one said, "West Indians did not need to be told by whites that they seek membership and influence in the unions. Nobody had to tell us to do so" (Holder 1998: 37). Similarly, West Indian men often angrily renounced racist and denigrating designations by their employers, which at times cost them their jobs. With that kind of progressive and no-nonsense attitude, however, they occupied a trailblazing position among the black community in the United States and set a perhaps not yet fully appreciated early precedent for what would be demanded as a matter of course and on a broader scale by the civil rights movement twenty or thirty years later. And yet, for immigrants from the English-speaking Caribbean, working in menial service jobs also implied a considerable psychological burden. Although for some of them it meant an improvement over their occupation back home, the majority of these early West Indian immigrants suffered downward mobility (that is, they found employment only in jobs socially below their former occupation and/or below their skill levels). The men, who had been skilled and white-collar workers in the Caribbean, had grown up regarding menial work as degrading and reminiscent of slavery days. For the women, doing household work for white people often did not appear appropriate. Many of them came from a middle-class background and in their homeland had other people doing this work for them.

A number of immigrants from the English-speaking Caribbean wanted to become economically independent. This was an option not only for relatively unskilled workers with ambition, but also professionals; West Indians with degrees, diplomas, or certain skills also pursued this route. In the first decades of the century, this was still extremely difficult to achieve, but nevertheless there were some remarkable successes. Particularly worth mentioning are the inroads they made in the real estate business; even today they still own a relatively large number of companies. The Manhattan-based Antillean Holding Company (AHC) was the major black realty company in New York City in the 1940s and had holdings in excess of $1 million in the 1930s and more than $3 million in the early 1940s (Holder 1998). Some of its owners made a fortune, but by and large they were more significant by virtue of their function as suppliers of housing and real estate property to West Indian immigrants. Out of this and other businesses, the first fully or partly West Indian–owned financial institutions grew—for instance, the Paragon Credit Association, which in the 1950s and 1960s became instrumental in supplying the mortgages to prospective West Indian home owners; the Carver Federal

Savings and Loan Association, now the largest black financial institution in the United States; and the United Mutual Life Insurance, which, with assets of $1.6 million in the late 1940s and 1950s, was the most impressive business West Indians had established. Interestingly, United Mutual Life Insurance arose out of a burial society founded in 1929 that paid sick and death benefits to its mainly West Indian membership. A number of Caribbean physicians ran successful practices catering to the black community, but sometimes also to a white clientele.

As any visitor to some sections in Brooklyn can attest, the growth in self-employment and business ownership has been particularly vibrant in the area of restaurants, bakeries, small groceries, travel agencies, hair salons, and similar services. Many owners had already had such stores prior to their migration, and thus there is a certain tradition. In the first years of the twentieth century, English-speaking Caribbean immigrants were disproportionately well represented among New York black business owners and by the 1930s they were "clearly the majority of black businesspersons in New York and . . . the only blacks with businesses connected to the skilled trades" (Holder 1998: 53–54).

Just as finding employment was a problem that required flexibility, unemployment also required adjustment. The evidence appears to be that during the early decades of the twentieth century, unemployment never was a major concern among English-speaking Caribbeans, although it certainly existed. According to the 1940 census, 19.3 percent of the West Indian workforce were seeking employment (Holder 1998). In fact, they enjoyed a high reputation for being a frugal and hard-working people.

The U.S. economy of the 1920s or 1940s was very different from that of the 1970s, 1980s, or 1990s, and in the face of these changes people had to find new ways of making ends meet. During the first half of the century, Caribbean immigrants and African Americans were involved in building up the ghetto communities where they were forced to live, and this had offered them opportunities, albeit limited, to find employment or build their own businesses. In the second half of the century and particularly after 1965, immigrants from the English-speaking Caribbean were faced with an entirely different economic scenario, with new challenges and opportunities. For example, the U.S. labor market was deregulated in the late 1970s, which allowed the economic integration of illegal immigrants. This was a direct consequence of international efforts to the general reduction of labor costs. A number of so-called sweatshop industries, known for their poor working conditions, and other forms of extremely low-wage service jobs were created, which led to a growing informal economy (that is, businesses which operate

without state approval and without paying taxes) and the increasing importance of a secondary market for labor (that is, illegal workers hired by legitimate businesses), which included jobs such as security personnel, nursing
aides, data entry personnel, (seasonal) farmworkers, babysitters, dogwalkers,
secretaries, messengers, machine operators, assemblers, and maids. In New
York, the garment industry would have collapsed without the supply of new
immigrants in the 1980s. Paradoxically, as growing U.S. overseas investments
led to an increased readiness of people living in the receiving countries to
migrate, the growth of an informal economy in the U.S. helped to accommodate and actually attract illegal immigrants. The consequence for Caribbean immigrants was that they faced a new, higher level of competition for
labor by immigrants from other ethnic groups. This development was accompanied by a fundamental reorganization of the U.S. economy, which can
be broadly characterized as a deindustrialization in the traditional manufacturing sectors and an expansion of the service sector. At the same time,
particularly in the wake of the civil rights movement, new opportunities in
education offered broader possibilities for career and employment diversification. This has been an advantage for the second generation of Caribbean
immigrants. By and large, however, this and any cultural advantages may
have been neutralized by the fact that the educational achievements of recent
immigrants have been lower than of those who arrived before 1965.

A consequence of these changes in the economy during the 1970s was
that while native and foreign-born whites lost jobs disproportionately,
foreign-born blacks (the vast majority of whom are from the Caribbean) were
increasingly able to find jobs. However, most of these jobs were at the lower
end of the emerging service economy. Compared to native-born blacks, Afro-
Caribbean gross and net earnings in 1980 did not justify the opinion that
they had fared better economically than that group (Model 1991). In fact,
in the case of West Indian males, their earnings in 1980 were just 88 percent
that of African Americans, 60.6 percent that of foreign-born whites, and 59
percent that of native-born males. By 1990 the comparison was somewhat
better: both West Indian and African American men earned approximately
the same mean income (Vickerman 1999). For females the comparison is
somewhat less complex. In 1980 they earned 95.4 percent that of African-
American women, 98.1 percent that of foreign-born white women and 94.5
percent that of native white women. If Caribbean immigrants ever enjoyed
any cultural advantages in the economy over native blacks, this seems to have
been true only in the early decades of the twentieth century.

Unemployment today is a greater problem than it was for early Caribbean
immigrants. Of the estimated 648,615 English-speaking Caribbean immi-

grants living in the United States in 1990, 320,809 lived in New York state (Irish and Murphy n.d.). Of these an average of 8.5 percent were unemployed nationwide, and 8.7 percent were unemployed in New York. Barbadians were below these average figures, and Trinidad and Tobagonians were above them. For Jamaicans, unemployment was lowest in Maryland and New Jersey and highest in Washington, D.C., where the rate among male Jamaicans was particularly high (20 percent). The fact that male Jamaicans had higher unemployment rates than their female counterparts, coupled with the fact that they differed little in their educational attainment, points to the relatively stressful economic environment for Jamaican males (Irish and Murphy n.d.).

The relative success of West Indians in this changing economic environment is a consequence of their skills and qualifications that are particularly useful at the lower rungs of a service economy. In particular, their mastery of the English language and high rates of literacy, as well as the high female labor force participation, are responsible for this. But most English-speaking Caribbeans working in these sectors usually are employed below their levels of skill and education (Afflick 1989).

There is, however, reason to be optimistic. Despite the changing economic fortunes in the 1970s and 1980s, it appears that West Indians remain actively involved in business enterprises. Thus, the last available data show that in the 1980s over 50 percent of New York City's black businesses remain in their hands (Foner 1992, 111). Following the earlier established patterns of business ownership, they are particularly prominent in publishing, taxi companies, real estate, advertising, banking, insurance, and retail clothing. Consequently they continue to build on their established economic bases, while showing also a clear sign of flexibility.

BUILDING NEW COMMUNITIES

Social capital and employment are but two preconditions for the establishment of communities in cities where most English-speaking Caribbean immigrants settled. The majority of them settled in the metropolitan Northeast of the United States (particularly in New York City), Florida, or California. In other parts of the country where they decided to settle or move to, it is not easy to discern actual communities or neighborhoods in a geographical and/or demographic sense.

Although the early immigrants did not tend to concentrate in particular areas in New York City, eventually they clustered in parts of Brooklyn, Queens, Harlem, and the Bronx, where vibrant and distinctive West Indian neighborhoods emerged. The gradual transition from mere presence to the establishment of distinct Caribbean neighborhoods marks a process paralleled by the institution of organizations and processes of ethnic identification. Like other ethnic communities, Caribbean Americans have added local color to the neighborhoods in which they settled. Their bakeries, grocery and barber shops, betting shops, shops selling patties and other take-out food, bars, and restaurants all demarcate a Caribbean territory "in exile." They are, at the same time, a wall behind which West Indian immigrants can withdraw.

The development of Caribbean neighborhoods was not entirely a matter of free choice. In New York City in 1920, race rather than ethnicity was the main factor determining where they lived. Due to racial discrimination in the New York housing market, most West Indians during the first decades of the twentieth century ended up living in Harlem, where they constituted an estimated 25 percent of the growing total black population in this area.

The Caribbean migrants did not readily blend into the communities into which they moved. In fact, there were conflicts between them and the native black Americans, who often ridiculed the speech, behavior, and dress of the newcomers. As had happened in the eighteenth century, many West Indians took psychological refuge in their status as "British subjects," celebrating the British monarch's birthday in public events and engaging in the ultimate West Indian activity—cricket. In 1937, a group of West Indians conducted a reenactment of King George VI's coronation, at the St. Ambrose Episcopal Church. Before the war it was often reported that West Indians who were confronted with racism or discrimination would exclaim: "I am a British subject. I will report this to my consulate!" (Kasinitz 1995; 48). By considering themselves as having an English background, they regarded themselves having a cultural background superior to that of African Americans. It should therefore be no surprise that the Jamaican novelist Claude McKay reprimanded his countrymen for being "incredibly addicted to the waving of the Union Jack in the face of their American cousins" (quoted in Kasinitz 1995: 47).

Over the years, however, African Americans and West Indians have gained a better mutual understanding. Since about the 1930s, an increasing realization that their position in the wider society and economy was in effect determined by the color of their skin led to a closer identification and also first steps toward a closer relationship with each other. While West Indians continued to establish their own ethnic organizations, they also joined the broader black community, more often in leadership and spokespersons' functions than as regular members. They became engaged in political representation of the black community as well as economic organizations such as the trade unions. This is particularly true for the second generation of West

Indian immigrants, who shared the ambitions of their parents with African Americans' sense of entitlement and rights.

Only from the mid-1960s onward can we speak of Caribbean communities in a stricter sense. After 1965, with their numbers increasing and their concentration in certain urban areas growing, distinct geographical and social communities emerged that made it clear to every outsider that Caribbean peoples were dwelling there. New York, the center of gravity for West Indians, shifted from Harlem to parts of central Brooklyn, Queens, and the Bronx. For example, in Brooklyn the number of non-Hispanic Caribbean residents increased from about 165,000 in 1980 to 205,000 in 1990. In 1960, the foreign black population in the entire city was estimated around 68,000.

Parts of central Brooklyn in particular are immediately identifiable as Caribbean neighborhoods and the geographic area in the United States most densely populated by its peoples. Crown Heights, Bedford-Stuyvesant, and East Flatbush are the preferred areas of settlement and business activity for English-speaking West Indians in Brooklyn (Conway and Bigby 1992). Crown Heights is the city's oldest and most diverse Caribbean neighborhood. In the 1950s the migrants started to move into what was then a predominantly Jewish neighborhood. This is a diverse community. There are well-maintained buildings and others in disrepair; large brownstone apartment buildings and one-family houses; and small buildings with apartments above stores.

About 80 percent of the population in Crown Heights is black, about 10 percent Hispanic, and another 10 percent non-Hispanic whites, a situation that has created strong competition over limited space and tensions between the ethnic groups living in the area (Vickerman 1999). In August 1991, the car accident caused by a Hasidic Jewish driver killing Gavin Cato, a Guyanese youth, led to the fatal stabbing of a rabbinical student named Yankel Rosenbaum by a group of about twenty black youths. Three nights of rioting followed during which groups of blacks and Hasidim engaged in street fights, stores belonging to all ethnicities represented in the community were looted, and Jewish families were attacked in their homes. The riots occurred shortly before the famous Labor Day carnival parade on Eastern Parkway, and although there is some evidence that the events were exploited by attempts from politicians not representing the community, the two main groups, Hasidim and Caribbeans, finally agreed that two weeks of tensions were enough; the parade was an opportunity to engage in a collective process of healing.

East Flatbush is probably the most West Indian neighborhood of contemporary New York, although it does not have as many cultural institutions as

Crown Heights. East Flatbush has a similar ethnic composition of its population, but almost half of its black population in 1980 was from the Caribbean region. There are currently around 60,000 West Indians living in this section of Brooklyn. Quite a few of them moved into the rows of so-called Trump bungalows, built in the 1930s by real estate mogul Donald Trump's father, Fred Trump. In the late 1980s seventy-two condominium units were constructed in East Flatbush and specifically marketed to Caribbean households. In the 1970s the demand for housing among English-speaking Caribbeans spread from East Flatbush to Flatbush proper. Parts of Flatbush have become thoroughly Caribbeanized, although with just 32 percent black population in 1980, the overall percentage is comparatively lower than in other sections of Brooklyn. The Caribbeanization of parts of Brooklyn was also reflected in a weekly radio drama entitled "Flatbush USA," which came on the air in 1990.

Although Crown Heights, East Flatbush, Flatbush, and parts of Queens all contain significant pockets of poverty, there are also numerous areas with middle-class households. According to the New York City Department of City Planning, the median household income in Crown Heights in 1990 was $21,295, in Flatbush $27,620, and in East Flatbush $30,367. This does not compare entirely unfavorably with the citywide median household income of $29,823 (1990); in fact, in the case of East Flatbush it exceeds this average. In sections of Queens with a comparatively high rate of Caribbean population (for example, Queens Village, Laurelton, Cambria), the median household income of $46,000 and the high number of one-family houses with about a 70 percent owner-occupancy rate indicate a thoroughly middle-class status achieved by an increasing number of immigrants from the Caribbean region. Indeed, since the late 1970s growing numbers of middle-class Caribbean home buyers have moved out of Brooklyn into southeastern Queens, New Jersey, and Connecticut suburbs. Because sociologists increasingly recognize the importance of wealth creation (that is, owning assets like houses or businesses) in determining who is economically successful and who is not, it is also important to mention that these families have laid a strong foundation for their children's accomplishments (Miller 1999).

It is important to realize that the symbolic and psychological values of the new ethnic neighborhoods are significant to West Indian immigrants because the existence of these neighborhoods is often "misread" by outsiders as a sign that these immigrants are not integrating themselves into the (mainstream) society. However, this view more often than not mistakes assimilation (that is, assuming society's value systems while rejecting own traditions in order to be accepted) for integration (that is, a mutual coming closer) and does not factor in the rejection that minorities experience daily whenever they get into close contact with the host society. Ridicule of their accent, dress, or mannerism are constant reminders to the immigrants that not everyone accepts them as equals. Given this situation, it ought to be understood that building and withdrawing into ethnic neighborhoods is simply a reaction aiming at avoiding assimilationist pressures. "In some cases, such as real estate agencies, an island-oriented name or a palm-tree on a sign may serve as an assurance that one's business is welcome. In the case of personal services the symbol may assure the customers that their accent will not be ridiculed, and that they will deal with people they feel at home with" (Kasinitz 1995: 70). Many English-speaking Caribbean immigrants proudly display national symbols, such as flags on the back of their cars. Some stores (for example, little take-out restaurants, mom-and-pop stores, bakeries, and bars) serve to create a sense of community by creating public spaces where people who live or work in the neighborhood can meet for conversation. The same is true for local social clubs and community organizations (for example, health services, immigration-related services, ethnic clubs, and fortune-tellers). Of course, in a multiethnic urban community like Brooklyn, a number of cross-overs occur and so it is of little surprise when the media report that, for example, the Jewish owner of a carwash opened a new branch with an island motif as decoration and a Caribbean steel band to attract the attention of potential customers. Nevertheless, such hybrid forms also enhance the distinct ethnic flavor of the neighborhood and reinforce the identification of the neighborhood with the presence of the ethnic group.

More than ever before, some sections of Brooklyn have assumed a distinct Caribbean American identity, which is proudly, and often loudly, displayed on the streets and storefronts of this vibrant borough of New York City. To the extent that this new identity exists, it affords English-speaking Caribbean immigrants a place that they can call their "home abroad."

ADJUSTMENT PROBLEMS: ETHNICITY, "RACE," CLASS, AND GENDER

For immigrants the process of adjusting to new and unfamiliar environments occurs at different levels of social life. The demands for adjustment are "channeled" by different concepts ordering the functions, rights, and duties each of its members has within society. For people from the English-speaking Caribbean, the most important concepts determining their socioeconomic experiences and chances in the United States are "race," class, and gender, all three closely related.

The fundamental contradiction that immigrants from the English-speaking Caribbean are faced with is this: they have been socialized in societies that do not attach as much significance to "race" as U.S. society does, but rather emphasize such values as hard work, delayed gratification, or personal austerity, but as dark-skinned people of either African or East Indian origin, they are placed into the category "black" (with all the prejudice and stigma whites attach to this category) the minute their foot touches American soil. This discrepancy has been described by E. Leopold Edwards, who came from Jamaica to the United States in 1948:

> My first experiences upon arriving here as a student were terribly unfortunate. Upon arriving at the airport in Miami, when I went to catch a cab, the ladies got in first, and then the men, and then the cabs stopped coming. And I was still standing there. After about ten minutes I said to someone, "This is very strange. Why have the cabs stopped?" He said, "Sir, you will need to take a colored cab." Well, in Jamaica the word "colored" means multicolored—like multicolored clothing. We don't use the word colored referring to people. So I said to him, "I don't care about the color of the cab! What difference does it make? I just want a cab." So he took me around the corner and there was a cab which, as it happened, was painted purple and white and something. This reinforced my idea that a colored cab was a cab that had many colors. And I got into the cab intending to go to the hotel where I had a reservation. When I told the cab driver the name and address of the hotel, he told me firmly that someone had made an error. That was a "white hotel" at which I would not be welcome. I had to go to a "colored hotel." He said it was obvious that this was my first visit to America and he was therefore trying to be helpful and to save me from embarrassment. I told him I was tired and that he should do whatever he thought was best. So I went to the black hotel; not black in those days—"Negro hotel." (quoted in Sunshine and Warner 1998: 46–47)

Edwards's experience is very typical for the kind of "learning curve" West Indians discover very soon after their arrival.

The Reverend George A. Lloyd, a prominent community leader who was born in Anguilla, describes the extreme pressure on black immigrants from the Caribbean like this: "When they come here, and they see discrimination on a color basis, it knocks some of them out. And they can't function" (Caribbean Research Center 1997). Because they are to such a great extent unacquainted with or unwilling to apply racial criteria in the process of creating a self-identity, they often find themselves reluctant to use these criteria as guideposts for their own actions and decisions. The average West Indian immigrant usually tends to seek explanations or justifications in terms of personal responsibility, merit (professional or personal), social adeptness, or business acumen (or the lack of such qualities), rather than attributing misfortunes or successful experiences to racism or racial solidarity. This, however, often brings them into conflict with native blacks, who are generally more prepared to use racism to explain political, social, or economic events that affect them. For African Americans, the attitudes of Caribbeans often smack of overaccommodation of rules, regulations, and values imposed by American whites. Allegations that they are "Uncle Toms" or intending to "pass" (i.e., leave the black "camp" to join whites) have not been uncommon. Even in the benevolent and compassionate environment of churches, conflicts between the two groups can be sensed. Thus, the pastor of a Brooklyn church felt a need to caution his parishioners not to prejudge their Caribbean brothers and sisters:

> It does not appear that Afro-Americans read correctly the game Caribbean people play, which is that some things are means to an end. It is, therefore, their hope that someday the faithful Afro-American believers at the Brooklyn Temple will free themselves of the idea that West Indians are always trying to make themselves be in good grace with whites at the expense of making native blacks look bad. West Indians are in search of money, not white friends per se. (Ashmeade 1990: 85)

Clearly there is mistrust between these groups about the real motives for their social and political actions.

However, this does not mean that West Indians have been insensitive or even oblivious to racial discrimination. Quite to the contrary, they have stood in the forefront of the struggle against racism and for civil rights from the very beginning. An early example of West Indian leadership can be seen in the example of Captain Hugh Mulzac. In 1942, he became the first black merchant marine naval officer to command an integrated crew. Born on Union Island, St. Vincent Island Group, in the British West Indies, the young Mulzac entered the Swansea Nautical College in South Wales to prepare for a seaman's career. In 1918 he became an American citizen and continued his training at the Shipping Board in New York. He earned his captain's rating in the merchant marine, but racial prejudice denied him the right to command a ship. Later Mulzac was offered the command of a ship with an all-black crew. He refused, declaring that "under no circumstances will I command a Jim Crow vessel" (U.S. Maritime Service Veterans 2000). Twenty-two years passed before Mulzac was again offered command of a naval ship. During World War II, his demand for an integrated crew was finally met, and he was put in command of the SS *Booker T. Washington*. With a crew consisting of eighteen nationalities, the *Booker T. Washington* made twenty-two round-trip voyages in five years and carried 18,000 troops to Europe and the Pacific. On the day his ship was launched, Mulzac recalled, "Everything I ever was, stood for, fought for, dreamed of, came into focus that day. . . . The concrete evidence of the achievement gives one's strivings legitimacy, proves that the ambitions were valid, the struggle worthwhile. Being prevented for those twenty-four years from doing the work for which I trained had robbed life of its most essential meaning. Now at last I could use my training and capabilities fully. It was like being born anew" (U.S. Maritime Service Veterans 2000).

Earlier in this chapter I noted the impact of women on trade unions. Early in this century Jamaicans and other West Indians had earned a reputation for not accepting racial discrimination at the workplace, to an extent that certain firms no longer would hire them. Being able to look back on a long tradition of civil disobedience and passive resistance, even the average Caribbean immigrant became a leader in the struggle against racism at work and in the wider society. One Jamaican immigrant had this recollection about the 1940s:

Prejudice was there, so we did not go out of our way to experience it. Most of the people [in the area] did not know anything about black people. There were a few American blacks before we came, but they did not mix in the suburbs too much. . . .

Many of the discrimination barriers were broken down by us. For example, there was a theater called the Strand. They did not want to admit us, but we showed up in force, sometimes 10 or 15 of us, and demanded they let us in. After a while there was no more problem in us going to any theater. . . . The people were also aware that we were here working for the government and our behavior was also commendable.

The restaurants were the same thing. I did not experience this, but I heard that in the bars, when you went in to have a drink, the bartenders would break the glass when you left. The men found out about this and they would go in a restaurant in a busload. They would all order drinks for the group. When the owners found out that they were breaking 40 to 50 glasses a night, they then stopped the practice. (quoted in Sunshine and Warner 1998: 81–82)

In this and other ways, West Indians stood up against maltreatment and discrimination. The Jamaican-born Harlem Renaissance figure W. A. Domingo stated in 1925: "The outstanding contribution of West Indians to American Negro life is the insistent assertion of their manhood in an environment that demands too much servility and unprotesting acquiescence for men of African blood" (quoted in Kasinitz 1995: 47).

If it is true that English-speaking Caribbean immigrants learn what it really means to be black only after they arrive in the United States, it is equally true to say that their island identity changes into a more comprehensive West Indian identity. In the Caribbean there are sometimes fierce rivalries between different islands (sometimes within the same country, as the examples of St. Kitts and Nevis, as well as Trinidad and Tobago demonstrate). In the United States, however, when they are exposed to the "racialized" climate, they realize that pressures to integrate into the United States force them to let go of their island. Also, the merging of the different island identities can be seen in the fact that in urban Caribbean centers such as New York City, most subgroups (the Spanish-speaking Caribbeans tend to be the exception) live close together. Sometimes people from the French-speaking Caribbean, for example, Haiti, live in the same apartment block as people from the English-speaking Caribbean, such as Jamaica or Trinidad, and attend the same community events (e.g., Labor Day parade, dances, parties, concerts). Consequently, they tend to shed their island identities and embrace a more inclusive pan-Caribbean identity. One woman from Montserrat, an acquaintance of the author, says that she has been asked so many times if she is from Jamaica that she now does not bother to explain anymore, but usually just answers, "Yes, from May Pen." West Indian identity in the United States has a different meaning from the one applied to it in the Caribbean itself; it is more inclusive, fluid, and open than in the region itself.

Racial Categories

Many English-speaking Caribbean immigrants have difficulty adjusting to the more rigid application of racial categories and their (mostly demeaning) connotations. For one, as Edwards's testimony showed, racial and color descriptions in the Caribbean itself are used in a much subtler way and are usually not intended to mean any particular character trait of a particular person. Also, the Caribbean has a much higher degree of creolization of its people than to allow a simple distinction between blacks and whites. The presence of African, Chinese, East Indians, Middle Eastern, and European peoples and their conscious and subconscious mixing have created a new society. Blacks, no longer a minority or the exception, supply role models for young people. Standards of beauty include African features to a larger extent than in the United States. In other words, black and mixed people are the standard, white folks are the exception. Moreover, they signify a history of oppression and exploitation.

For a Caribbean person to call or (nick-)name a fellow islander of Chinese background "Mr. Chin," a mixed person a "browning" or "red skin girl," a white person "whitey," or a black person "Blacka" is usually not a show of disrespect but rather a neutral observation turned into a form of address; it may even be meant as a show of respect for the ethnic background of the addressee. Whereas in the United States the category white generally means to exclude all those who have any "nonwhite blood," in Jamaica "white" has been an inclusive category that embraces not only Anglo-Saxons, but also Jews, Syrians, and even some people with multiracial or Chinese background. This is a clear contrast to the color schemes in the United States.

I do not mean to imply that Caribbean people are unaware of issues surrounding "race." Certainly the Caribbean islands are not a paradise of racial harmony. However, in societies where the majority of people are nonwhite and where—at least since independence—an increasing number of black people belong even to the (formerly exclusively white) upper classes, economics has come to play a much more important role than issues of color and "race." Thus, Reverend Lloyd from Anguilla points out that in the Caribbean islands "discrimination is more on a class basis than on a color basis" (Caribbean Research Center 1997). But most Caribbean people are acutely aware that no slaves were white. They are equally aware that skin shade was also a marker for different positions within the slavery system, because usually individuals with lighter skin were also higher up in the social hierarchy. The best-known example of this hierarchy were the "brown" house slaves, who had a more comfortable life than the black field slaves. During that time too a number of other positions of relative privilege (e.g., artisans, skilled workers, midwives, and freed slaves) were held by individuals with lighter skin.

Most English-speaking Caribbean immigrants arriving in the United States have a natural inclination to see themselves as part of an ethnic group in a nation composed of many ethnic groups. Although they often tend to downplay the relevance of "race" and emphasize the importance of personal initiative and entrepreneurial astuteness, it would nevertheless be completely inappropriate to assume that they are less concerned or even unaware of the relevance that "race" holds in American society and politics. Thus, the racial identity assigned to them by American society intrudes on their efforts to view themselves simply as another immigrant ethnic group. While it may take the newly arrived migrant from the islands a little while to realize the greater saliency of ethnic prejudices and outright racism in the United States, it is important to note that Caribbean immigrants have nevertheless played an important role in the fight against racism and for civil rights. Indeed the Universal Negro Improvement Association (UNIA), founded in 1914 by the Jamaican Marcus (Mosiah) Garvey, was probably the largest and one of the most successful early black mass organizations in this country. The UNIA had branches in thirty-eight states in the United States and fifty-two all over the rest of the world.

Garveyism

In its desire to provide for the spiritual and material liberation of black people all over the world, the Garvey movement probably went further than any other black organization of its time. It proudly proclaimed that black people—like all other people—ought to worship God in their own image and actually created an autonomous religious institution, the African Orthodox Church, led by a minister from Antigua, "Bishop" Alexander McGuire. Far from being concerned only with providing symbols and imagery, Garveyism also engaged in the creation of an ownership and business base for blacks. The movement's business arm, the Negro Factories Corporation, owned restaurants, removal trucks, publishing companies, and laundries all over the United States. Its most ambitious project was the Black Star Line Shipping Company, which sought to engage in trade with Africa and the repatriation of blacks to the African continent. This venture failed for a variety of reasons, among them a lack of rigid application of business principles and the influence of more selfish elements within the Garvey movement. The Black Star Line Shipping Company was organized on the basis of the indigenous Caribbean cooperative system, the *susu*.

Despite its laudable goals, the Garvey movement ran into trouble. The ruling elites (that is, government and economic stewarts) in the United States and the United Kingdom regarded the Garvey movement as a threat. Here they had not only a black nationalist, but even an internationalist, who was able to mobilize and organize millions of black people under the umbrella of a single organization and who was preaching practically everything from black self-sufficiency and black ownership to black resistance and repatriation. When Garvey returned to Jamaica for a visit in 1921, the British were so apprehensive that they positioned battleships in the harbor. The U.S. government, for its part, put diplomatic pressure on Liberia to abort a UNIA settlement planned there. In 1923 Marcus Garvey was indicted under a phony charge of mail fraud and subsequently deported to Jamaica.

To a significant extent, the importance of Garvey lies in the new symbols of black sovereignty and self-awareness he introduced in his quest for racial equality (Carnegie 1999). At public rallies and demonstrations he often appeared in a field marshal's uniform or the scarlet and blue robe worn by an English honorary doctor of civil laws which unmistakably signified a new, sovereign, and ennobled image of black people. His vision of creating a transatlantic shipping enterprise for the repatriation of black people, although it invoked painful memories of the Middle Passage, also cast black people into the role of successful global entrepreneurs and appeared as a symbolic reversal of the Middle Passage. At yet another level, his vision of a worldwide community of black peoples foreshadowed the transnational tendencies of our own times (for example, global corporations, and global family networks).

Garvey's significance can also be seen with regard to his prophetic influence in the Rastafarian movement. As a playwright, he had staged a play in Kingston showing the crowning of an African king. When in 1930 Haile Selassie was crowned emperor of Ethiopia, many remembered Garvey's play and his prophesy that a king would be crowned in Africa. Garvey (with his middle name Mosiah, meaning Moses) became, and still continues to be, the most important prophet of the Rastafarians.

"Race" Relations

Many Caribbean people have a slightly different attitude toward the problem of racism in the United States. In essence, they generally proclaim a rather conservative ideology, which, despite the prevalence of racism, sees sufficient opportunities in the United States for hardworking individuals to succeed. This belief is sustained by their implicit comparison with the real and potential life and career chances in their Caribbean home countries, where opportunities are much more limited by the beleaguered economies typical of many Third World countries. Even hard-working individuals may eventually lose the belief in their own capabilities and self-worth when they are unable to find work.

Relations between blacks and Jews in the United States deteriorated notably after the civil rights era, and West Indian/Jewish relations were not spared from these increasing tensions. This conflict has been focused on the main concentration of Caribbean immigrants in Brooklyn. Since the 1920s, sections of Brooklyn have been predominantly Jewish. However, with the constant inflow of Caribbeans into Brooklyn, conflicts over space, power, and influence developed. This conflict was heightened by the fact that both groups are highly visible and have distinctive cultures, which led to mutual stereotyping.

In the 1950s, Hasidic Jews still owned a disproportionate share of the local retail trade and faced the black immigrant population in their role as land-lords. Following an increasing number of incidents in which Jewish merchants had been beaten, robbed, or even stabbed or shot, the Jewish shopkeepers in Brooklyn began to close their stores and move out of the community. On the other hand, it is certainly true that some of them held stereotypes about black people and treated them unfairly from the beginning (Clifford 1978). Conflicts continue between both groups. Nevertheless, despite these racial and ethnic tensions, there is cooperation between the groups. A good example is the political support that the Caribbean American Chamber of Commerce and Industry enjoys from both Jewish and African American politicians.

Home Societies

The discourse about "race" and the experience of racism also has implications for the home societies of English-speaking Caribbean immigrants. Particularly during the late 1960s and into the 1970s, concepts like the black power movement were directly or indirectly imported to the Caribbean. Through the media and politically active returned migrants, "race" became a much more explicit topic during this period and a challenge to the ruling elites in their home countries. Afro hair styles and *dashikis* (colorful patterned African shirts) were beginning to make an appearance, soul music became a much stronger influence, and there was a much greater demand for information about black America. Along with these cultural influences came political ideas on black solidarity, community empowerment, and autonomy and rejection of deference to Western (i.e., British) social norms. There was a demand for books by U.S. black leaders such as Malcolm X and Eldridge Cleaver, whose ideas seemed to herald political change. In the words of a young Barbadian militant, "Ten years ago ninety percent of the Bajans [that is, Barbadians] thought that the White man was superior. Today, I would say that seventy percent think he just another man—or another crook—or 'tief', we call it. And with some help by the outsiders, I think we'll make it" (Sutton and Makiesky-Barrow 1992: 101). Migrants and returned migrants became an important conduit of the fundamental social and cultural change that swept through several Caribbean countries during the 1970s and actually caused a revolution in Grenada (1979) and an experiment with quasisocialist forms of economic and political organization in Jamaica (1974).

It should not be surprising that the economic and political leadership in the English-speaking Caribbean largely rejected the introduction of foreign political concepts and idioms into the political discourse of their countries. They had managed a relatively smooth transition to independence and understandably had little interest in dealing with potentially disruptive issues of race. Instead, they tended to assert that "black power" already existed in the form of their leadership and that there consequently was no need to put this issue on the political agenda. In reality, however, they were frightened by these ideas about "race" and racism, which threatened to mobilize people into demanding fundamental changes in political and economic power. There were book bans in Jamaica, serious alarm in Barbados about a visit by the black power activist Stokely Carmichael, denials of entry visas to known political activists from the United States, and, in Barbados, new laws forbidding public meetings without police permission. In Jamaica, suspicion of the radical teachings of the prominent Guyanese university teacher and Africa scholar Walter Rodney led in 1968 to his ban from the island and the subsequent "Rodney riots" (Payne 1988). All these actions were attempts by the ruling elites to control the spread of ideas that to a large extent were transmitted by returned migrants.

Gender and the Migration Experience

Apart from issues of "race," ethnicity, and class, questions of gender also shape the migration experience of English-speaking Caribbeans. Thus, while, as Ralph Ellison pointed out in his novel *The Invisible Man* (1952), black men in the United States have suffered from a certain invisibility and black foreigners have suffered a double invisibility, West Indian women can be said to have suffered from a triple invisibility: as a black, a foreigner, and a female (Marshall 1987). From their beginning as immigrants in this country, they had to fight for liberty and equality simultaneously.

In their Caribbean home societies women are assigned specific gender roles (as are, of course, the men). All social classes in the region tend to emphasize the woman's role as partner and mother. Nevertheless, there is a difference in the marriage patterns of Caribbean social groups. Men and women are involved in three basic types of relationships: (1) married, (2) living together in more or less stable and permanent common law relationships, or (3) visiting relationships (that is, the man does not share the same home as the woman, but is there as a regular visitor). The latter two types are more typical for members of the "lower classes"; members of the middle class are more likely to be married. For them, visiting and common law relationships often lead to marriage. In all three cases the woman is often almost completely dependent on the male partner's financial support.

West Indian women are on average very independent. Although the stereotype of the powerful black matriarch is hardly grounded in reality, it is true to say that, due to the insecure financial and economic conditions under which Caribbean people live, West Indian women increased their power in the household through outside work. Historically they were forced to accept many of the roles that Western society attributes to men, which strengthened their position within the family. Nevertheless, women remain at the bottom of the socioeconomic ladder. To a larger extent than in industrialized countries, West Indian women work outside the home and at the same time assume full responsibility for child care. While middle-class women often can afford domestic help, poorer women have greater problems coordinating both responsibilities. Often the extended family (e.g., sisters, grandparents, or substitute mothers) provides childcare while the mother works.

Although the history (which separated male and female slaves on a regular basis) and contemporary strain of Caribbean life often lead the male and female partners to view each other with suspicion, it is important to point out that "there remains an abiding respect, and appreciation for family life in any form. While it is true that some men give no physical or financial support to their children, others, from all social classes, have warm abiding relationships with their family" (Toney 1989: 70–71).

The traditional gender roles assigned to West Indian women are challenged when the women are exposed to different role models in the United States. Many women experience these challenges as a liberation from traditional constraints. As we have seen, in recent years increasing numbers of women from the region migrated and in this way divided up existing households at home. Most often this has resulted in a new independence for the women because their employment affords them financial emancipation and greater leverage in their relations with the male partner. In the words of one woman: "Here, you become independent, and don't look for a husband to provide things. You may eventually find that you don't need one" (quoted in Toney 1989: 77). On the other hand, women who migrate often have to leave their children behind in the Caribbean. This phenomenon has given rise to the term *barrel children*, meaning those who were left behind and receive regular parental assistance in the form of barrels of consumer goods sent to them from the United States (Pragg 1999). In cases where the male partner stays behind, perhaps with the idea that he will follow later, new forms of stress are introduced, in particular, estrangement between mother and child or children. Men tend to be skeptical about or even reject the new freedom of the women, fearing that the female partner may become unfaithful. In the words of one informant, "Women are changed by work here. They earn more, have more and become independent. She may have become possessive because she has an income. They become more demanding. They increase their bargaining power. Sometimes in professional fields when the wife makes more money, she acts like the head of the household. . . . There are no jobs for women at home. Here women wear the pants" (quoted in Toney 1989: 74). Traditionally, in the Caribbean female infidelity has been regarded as much more serious than male infidelity. In any case, this new sense of "inequality" experienced by the husband can easily become a reason for divorce, which is not uncommon in this type of scenario. However, most men adjust to the new patterns, accept the wife's more equal status, and assume household duties traditionally regarded as the sole domain of the woman.

While living in the United States, many Caribbean men attend dances and other events without their partners. There are growing numbers of social clubs in the West Indian American community, and some have an unwritten "men-only" policy. Most women feel uncomfortable attending these clubs, where men spend many hours playing billiards, cards, drinking, or discussing politics. Women feel uncomfortable and unwelcome in such clubs and, like the men themselves, fear that their presence may be seen as an attempt to control their husbands. In this, attitudes from home are still very much alive, and it demonstrates that despite the new status women may achieve in the host society, one cannot easily speak of the emergence of a female-centered family. Caribbean women are, due to gender and "race" discrimination, twice removed from the equal participation in society, while they are enduring the same disadvantages that migration tends to produce.

IMPACT OF CARIBBEAN AMERICANS ON U.S. SOCIETY

Economic Impact

As consumers and as producers of services and goods, West Indians have an increasing and growing presence in U.S. markets. First, it is important to mention that, particularly in the urban centers, there are two economies—a formal and an informal (that is, semilegal or illegal and untaxed employment) economy. Informal activities (e.g., private taxis, household workers, street vendors, nannies) have greatly increased as the traditional formal sectors of the economy have either shrunk or moved away from these urban areas. West Indian immigrants who in the past greatly relied on jobs offered in certain formal economic sectors either followed these jobs or shifted to other, often informal, economic activities.

For the formal economy, there are very few, if any, large Caribbean businesses with large numbers of employees or large amounts of investments. In part, this reflects the fact that going into business is most often a consequence of the lack of opportunities in the formal labor market and/or discrimination. Not surprisingly, the majority of Caribbean enterprises are small businesses with a sole owner and few, if any, employees. They are mostly labor-intensive ventures with low-risk activities: groceries, record or hardware stores, bakeries, real estate or insurance services, food services, or car repairs. Only about a third of these businesses are incorporated (Afflick 1990). Few of these are knowledge- or technology-driven businesses.

By and large, Caribbean businesses mainly cater to other Caribbean immigrants, African Americans, and Hispanics, and most of these customers are locals. Similarly, employees are recruited mainly through social networks or by direct application. These businesses attract customers through word of mouth, and any advertising is mainly in ethnic-based media. Because English-speaking Caribbean immigrants place a greater emphasis on finding employment than starting their own businesses, their business successes are far less important than their employment record. Consequently, their influence over economic community resources and activities is minuscule. Another problem in the formal sector is the relative lack of established businesses that keep thorough records of financial and business transactions.

The challenge remains—as Marcus Garvey had formulated at the beginning of the century—to establish ownership patterns that are distinctly ethnic Caribbean in nature. In other words, compared with other ethnic groups there are not enough Caribbean-owned businesses. Only if a critical mass of independent economic entrepreneurship is reached can Caribbean immigrants be expected to play a more influential economic role in their host society.

An important organization provides formal and structural support for English-speaking Caribbean (as well as other minority) entrepreneurs: the Caribbean American Chamber of Commerce and Industry (CACCI), established in 1985. With a membership of around 1,500, this umbrella organization provides a wide and growing variety of services, such as business development seminars, technical assistance, referrals, and training programs in how to start, operate, and manage a business. In addition, CACCI provides technical assistance, loan packaging, business planning, legal, accounting, bookkeeping services, and mortgage counseling. Through its Micro Enterprise Loan/Grant Trickle Up/CACCI program, the organization assists disadvantaged home-based businesspersons with small grants and training. Its international programs include trade missions and trade expositions to the Caribbean region and international forums.

In recent years the informal sector of the economy has rapidly expanded, but its importance and impact on the employment of West Indian immigrants are difficult to gauge. To a significant degree, the incomes earned in the informal economy supplement total household income and are sometimes its only source. Although a number of people working in the informal sector have incomes higher than entry-level salaries, many informally self-employed Caribbean Americans regard this only as a temporary solution. Individuals may be trying to earn money to start a business or to attain skills or documentation (legal immigration status) for work in the formal sector.

Few jobs in the informal sector are in manufacturing enterprises, such as garment factories, found among other ethnic enclaves, for example, the Chinese communities in the United States. A possible reason is that Caribbean immigrants for historical reasons refuse to work below the minimum wage; with a history of slavery embossed in one's consciousness it is quite hard to accept wages below what is legal. On the other hand, some like these jobs because of the independence and flexibility they offer.

The overriding reason for West Indians to enter the informal economy, however, is the small number of alternative or acceptable options in the formal sector. Other factors are increases in the cost of living, economic uncertainties, increased life-style expectations, and search of additional income to maintain the current or gain a desired standard of living. Finally, it has to be kept in mind that the informal sector offers opportunities for illegal aliens to earn money. Particularly in light of recent new legislation making employment in the formal sector much more difficult to obtain than in the past, this is an increasingly important option for such individuals.

More women than men work in the informal sector. Thus, household work is commonly performed by women, while men prefer jobs like home repair or transportation. Despite the long hours (on average about twelve hours per day), many workers in the transportation and home repair sectors intend to remain in this sector indefinitely. Most enterprises in the informal sector are started with personal savings or family money.

Political and Social Issues

Because of their history of slavery, Caribbean people have a deep-seated suspicion of leadership and people who lay a claim to such a position. This suspicion explains in part their relative reluctance to become involved in the political process in the United States. It continues even today to influence the politics of second-generation Caribbean immigrants, albeit to a lesser extent.

In the 1920s, organizations like the West Indian Committee on America and the West Indian Reform Association urged immigrants to become citizens and asked African Americans to scale back their antagonism toward English-speaking Caribbean immigrants (Clifford 1978). Frequently, however, this is where the immigrants' involvement stopped. More interested in improving themselves economically than in politics, Caribbean immigrants sought financial improvement through self-help organizations. In any case, they thought that eventually they would return to their home country.

Politics, particularly after Marcus Garvey's failure, did not greatly attract their interest during these early years. There were, however, a few exceptions. Particularly in the first two decades of the twentieth century, New York City's Harlem community was a center for political ideas and activism. A number of English-speaking Caribbean immigrants felt attracted to this intense climate of debate, street agitation, and publication and joined what nevertheless were primarily efforts by African American individuals and groups to establish a political presence. Apart from the United Negro Improvement Association (UNIA), the African Blood Brotherhood (ABB) and a local branch of the Socialist party (the 21st Assembly district branch, or 21st AD club) were among the most active groups. For the Caribbeans involved in these activities, there were three main points of participation: (1) their political and economic adjustment to the United States, (2) mutual benefit organizations and (3) organizations which promoted economic and social development in and relations with the homeland (Turner and Turner 1988). In fact, like Garvey's UNIA, the ABB was one of the many responses of the day to the need to organize blacks at the national level and to bring greater international unity to people of Africa and African descent.

One of the more radical perspectives was propounded by the 21st AD club to which socialists like the African Americans A. Philip Randolph and Chandler Owen, and Jamaican-born Wilfred A. Domingo or the Barbadian Richard B. Moore actively or, like Cyril V. Briggs from Nevis, as sympathizers belonged. Moore, once described by a Department of Justice undercover agent as one of the "most outspoken, daring and radical among all the other negro 'Reds' in Harlem," was highly visible in politics (Turner and Turner 1988). He was active in both the Socialist party and the ABB. Moore was also associated with the prominent publication *The Emancipator*. However, when it became clear that rivalries between Garvey and other prominent organizations and its leaders led to their pressuring the government to deport

Garvey, Moore split with his former associates, illustrating the perceived political differences and allegiances between African Americans and West Indian immigrants.

By and large, however, the early West Indian immigrants were not active in politics. But in the 1970s, three distinct types of political leaders emerged: (1) a group of leaders (most of them middle class) seeking to align themselves and the Caribbean American community in various alliances in order to improve their political leverage, (2) a group that in the past has been called ethnicity entrepreneurs, and (3) a group of younger, second-generation leaders who are starting to pursue politics as a professional career and often begin with radical politics, who can be termed *radicals*.

The most prominent member of the middle-class Caribbean American community leaders is Lamuel Stanislaus from Grenada's offshore island Petit Martinique. A dentist by training, he arrived in the United States during the 1940s and since the mid-1950s has been involved in community affairs in Brooklyn and New York City. Although he did not really assume leadership positions in any of the numerous benevolent West Indian societies established in New York City, he has nevertheless often taken influential background roles in community organizations while leaving the more immediate leadership issues to others. Stanislaus's relative lack of direct leadership was a direct result of his perception that within the Caribbean American community, there were many organizations that competed with each other and did not try hard enough to come together as a united force. Through this involvement and his personal friendship with Herbert Blaize, a former prime minister of Grenada, Stanislaus's influence in the West Indian community has grown steadily. During the 1960s he became closely involved with the state assembly election campaign of Congresswoman Shirley Chisholm, whose parents are from Barbados, and he served as an organizer and fund raiser. In 1977 he organized Caribbeans for Percy Sutton, a group supporting the former Manhattan borough president's attempt to run in the mayoral primary. Although Sutton was an African American candidate, this was probably the first time that English-speaking Caribbean immigrants in the United States were seen as a political bloc. But their support for Sutton did not yield the expected increased influence, and subsequently Stanislaus shifted his support to New York City's mayor, Edward Koch (Clifford 1978). Koch appointed him to the Commission on Black New Yorkers, which helped to formalize and expand his role as official representative of the community.

Stanislaus's political involvement also demonstrates that political influence often works both ways: Caribbean political traditions exert influence on Caribbean immigrant political contents and styles, and Caribbean migrants have an influence on the political affairs of their home countries. Due to his friendship with Blaize, an influential member of the political opposition during the 1970s, Stanislaus became more closely involved with the political affairs of his home country, particularly during the end of the 1970s, when the overbearing government of Eric Gairy started to erode. Blaize formed an alliance with the New Jewel Movement (NJM), which in 1979 wrested power from Gairy but did not include Blaize and his party in the government. The NJM subsequently failed to legitimize this takeover with elections and in 1983 disintegrated in a bloody coup, which led to the assassination of Maurice Bishop, the prime minister. Stanislaus, like many other U.S.-based Grenadians, supported the subsequent U.S. invasion which ended the NJM's rule in Grenada. When his friend Herbert Blaize became prime minister in 1984, Stanislaus accepted the ambassadorship to the United Nations. When he retired from his ambassadorship, Stanislaus was replaced by another long-time New Yorker.

Somewhat different from this middle-class group of postwar English-speaking Caribbean immigrants are those with a mostly working-class background who arrived here after 1965. Realizing the growing appeal of ethnic politics, they are strongly banking on the political appeal that the Caribbean community's ethnicity has in other political circles. They rely less on patronage and are engaged to a great extent in effective community work. For these reasons they have been called *ethnicity entrepreneurs*.

One prominent representative of this group is the Grenadian Roy A. Hastick, who came to the United States in the 1970s. He has organized several organizations directed at community development and established contact with city councilman Ted Silverman. Silverman appointed Hastick to the Community Planning Board, where he was soon elected to chair its Public Safety Committee and in 1983 became its first vice president. As a former member of the Grenadian police force, he was also organizing Grenadian ex-police in Brooklyn and working as a security consultant. Hastick also founded a community newspaper, *The West Indian Tribune*, although it had a short life. However, the Tribune Company became an umbrella organization for his community activities as a self-described ethnic "ombudsman."

Like Stanislaus, Hastick had not been involved with Grenadian politics during the Bishop years. However, after the Blaize government assumed power, Hastick joined Stanislaus and others in forming a support committee in New York for Blaize's party. In 1985 Hastick made a public call for a Caribbean community press. Many community leaders had been surprised by the lack of attention that Washington and the New York press afforded the sudden death of the Barbadian prime minister Tom Adams, who died on the same weekend as the Soviet premier Konstantin Chernenko. The meeting Hastick convened called for greater support from advertisers doing business with the Caribbean community and the New York press. In particular, the black press, which had also failed to cover Adams's death, was taken to task for this and other perceived neglect of English-speaking Caribbean immigrants. The event led to great publicity for Hastick. As this example demonstrates, there is a close relationship between community leaders such as Hastick (who stage events and provide "news") and the community press (which covers such events, and thereby lends publicity and confers respectability on the featured community leaders).

During the 1980s, the cutbacks of public funds highlighted the existing political void for West Indian business owners in the United States. To fill this void, Hastick spearheaded an effort to organize such entrepreneurs under a common umbrella. With the help of a number of financial and political supporters within and notably outside of the West Indian community, he founded and funded the Caribbean American Chamber of Commerce and Industry, (CACCI), which continues to be based in Brooklyn. Boasting support in the white and Jewish communities as well as from African American supporters, CACCI has become a major instrument for English-speaking Caribbean businesspersons, as well as for Hastick's own continued involvement in community affairs. Through his leadership, CACCI has won several awards, most recently the Ronald H. Brown Business Services Award, from the Brooklyn borough president, the US SBA Distinguished Service Award and the NYS Federation of Hispanic Chamber of Commerce Chamber of the Year Award.

Another important political player in New York City is Councilwoman Una S. T. Clarke who was born and raised in Jamaica. Clarke's political involvement goes back to the days when her children attended school and she participated in PTA meetings. In the late 1950s, when she came to New York on a scholarship to New York City Business College, she experienced some of the discrimination that blacks are often faced with—an experience she wanted to save her children from. From the springboard of community involvement and school activities and in the bristling political climate of the civil rights movement, Clarke started to attend political meetings and become acquainted with politicians and their ways of operating. She then served as a senior consultant on early education with the New York City Agency for Child Development, as an adjunct professor at Medgar Evers College, and on the boards of numerous professional institutions. She also held leadership positions in various political and advocacy organizations, including the Caribbean American Political Organization and the Caribbean Action Lobby.

She has been honored with scores of awards and commendations by community and professional organizations, including the Congressional Brain Trust on Education and the Martin Luther King Commission.

In 1988 she participated in the nomination of the Rev. Jesse Jackson as the presidential candidate in the Democratic party. Clarke entered the New York City political arena in 1991. Since that time she has led an organization, Friends of Una Clarke, which each year recognizes the contribution to community development of black women in New York City. In 1993 she was returned to office for four more years with a record 93 percent of votes cast in the general election. She has fought successfully for the adoption of more stringent standards enforcement in group and family daycare centers throughout the city and spearheaded the establishment of the Immigrant Transition Institute for newly arriving students in the public school system.

Apart from this, she worked hard to motivate and mobilize Caribbean people living in the United States to become citizens and vote. As she puts it, "I see Caribbean people as one people, separated by water" (Plummer 1994: 46). She is noted too for her activism on behalf of Haitian refugees fleeing political repression at home. Despite her focus on the Caribbean American constituency, she reaches out to other people as well. Thus, she is very keen on bridging gaps between American and Caribbean blacks. Referring to the term African American, she remarks: "It's a term used to exclude other blacks. Ethnically we are all the same, so why is it that in a room crowded with all black people, the term African-American is used? When I came to America, it was negro, then it was black, now it's African-American; and we can't get any place without each other" (Plummer 1994: 46).

Another English-speaking immigrant from the Caribbean who contributes to improving the affairs of New York City is the Rev. Dr. Lloyd Henry, who was born in Belize. In 1978 Henry migrated to the United States to work for the Episcopal Church, where he served for three years as chaplain tutor and curate of schools in Crown Heights. In 1981 he was called to be rector of St. Augustine's Episcopal church, where he succeeded in building a comparatively small congregation into what is now the largest in the diocese of Long Island, with a membership of approximately 3,000 and a budget of over $1 million. In 1988 he received the master of divinity degree from the New York Seminary and in 1991 he earned the doctor of ministry degree from the same institution. Serving on the New York City Council since 1994, Henry is the chair of the subcommittee on immigration and serves on the general welfare, civil service, and labor and environmental protection committees of the city council. He is a member of several organizations (e.g., the NAACP, Kiwanis Club, Jaycees International, Episcopal Commission for

Black Ministries Ecclesiastical Court, and the Ecclesiastical Court) and has received numerous awards. Henry demonstrates that leadership in the church and in political affairs remains a feature of Caribbean American life, as it also does in the case of African Americans.

Finally, New York Assemblyman Noah "Nick" Perry, born in Jamaica, needs to be mentioned. He was drafted into the U.S. Army in 1972 and served on active duty for two years and inactive reserve for four years. Assemblyman Perry began community involvement on his graduation from college in 1978 and worked as a volunteer in many election campaigns, including Percy Sutton for mayor, David Dinkins for mayor in 1989, Jimmy Carter for president, and Jesse Jackson for president in 1984 and 1988. However, Perry does not particularly identify himself as a Caribbean person, nor does he work very visibly on behalf of the Caribbean American population. Nevertheless, he serves on various assembly standing committees and subcommittees and has given his time and advice to a great variety of community boards and councils. Perry is a graduate of Brooklyn College, where he earned a B.A. in political science, and later studied for an M.A. in public policy and administration. Among his membership in organizations, Assemblyman Perry is a life member of Disabled American Veterans (DAV).

The third group mentioned here, the radicals, is a loose group of community activists known for leftist, often anti-American, convictions and an interest in black empowerment. Despite their involvement in community affairs, its members have not been able to establish themselves as leaders of the community because their concerns tend to resonate well with Caribbean Americans only when there are extraordinary events affecting their communities. In addition, New York's establishment is less receptive to their kind of leadership than to those of Stanislaus or Hastick (Kasinitz 1995). One of the prominent members of this group is the Guyanese-born Colin Moore, who served as an attorney for a defendant in the 1989 Central Park jogger rape case. Moore strongly identifies with African American issues, although he has also criticized their leaders for taking the Caribbean community for granted. Moore is one of the cofounders of the Caribbean Action Lobby, which was established in 1980 in order to have an organization speaking for the entire community of Caribbean Americans.

REFERENCES

Afflick, Martin. 1989. "Caribbean Immigrant Consumer Behavior and Attitudes." In *Establishing New Lives: Selected Readings on Caribbean Immigrants in New*

York City, ed. Velta J. Clarke and Emmanuel Riviere, 193–223. Brooklyn: Caribbean Research Center, Medgar Evers College, CUNY.

Afflick, Martin. 1990. *Caribbean Immigrants and Economic Adaptation: "A Caribbean Business Survey."* Brooklyn: Caribbean Research Center, Medgar Evers College, CUNY.

Ashmeade, Roy. 1990. "A Critical Investigation with a view to Address Tension between African Americans and Caribbeans at the Brooklyn Temple Seventh-Day Adventist Church." D.Min. dissertation, Drew University.

Bonnett, Aubrey. 1981. *Institutional Adaptation of West Indian Immigrants to America: An Analysis of Rotating Credit Associations.* Washington, D.C.: University Press of America.

Campbell, Horace. 1990. *Rasta and Resistance: From Marcus Garvey to Walter Rodney.* 3rd ed. Trenton: Africa World Press.

Caribbean Research Center. 1997. "Oral History Project." Unpublished interview with Rev. George A. Lloyd, conducted by Wayne Jones, August 22.

Carnegie, Charles V. 1999. "Garvey and the Black Transnation." *Small Axe. A Journal of Criticism* 5 (March): 48–71.

Clifford, Paul. 1978. "Reminiscing, Reluctance, Rhetoric, Radicalism and Rastafarianism: The Political Participation of English-Speaking West Indians in Central Brooklyn." Senior paper, Trumbull College.

Conway, Dennis, and Ualthan Bigby. 1992. "Where Caribbean Peoples Live in New York City." In *Caribbean Life in New York City: Sociocultural Dimensions,* ed. Constance Sutton and Elsa M. Chaney, 70–78. New York: Center for Migration Studies.

Etzioni, Amitai. 1993. *The Spirit of Community.* New York: Crown.

Foner, Nancy. 1992. "West Indians in New York City and London: A Comparative Analysis." In *Caribbean Life in New York City: Sociocultural Dimensions,* ed. Constance Sutton and Elsa M. Chaney, 108–120. New York: Center for Migration Studies.

Green, Charles, and Basil Wilson. 1990. "Socio-Political Relations between African-Americans and African-Caribbeans in New York City." In *Political Behavior and Social Interaction among Caribbean and African American Residents in New York,* ed. J. A. George Irish and E. W. Riviere, 125–138. Brooklyn: Caribbean Research Center, Medgar Evers College, CUNY.

Henke, Holger. 1998. "The Granite Pampa: Notes on the Perception of Hemispheric Flows of Migration." *Wadabagei: A Journal of the Caribbean and its Diaspora* 1, 1 (Winter/Spring 1998): 85–110.

Ho, Christine. 1991. *Salt-Water Trinnies: Afro-Trinidadian Immigrant Networks and Non-Assimilation in Los Angeles.* New York: AMS Press.

Holder, Calvin. 1998. "Making Ends Meet: West Indian Economic Adjustment in New York City, 1900–1952." *Wadabagei: A Journal of the Caribbean and Its Diaspora* 1, 1 (Winter/Spring 1998): 31–84.

Irish, J. A. George, and Albert Murphy. N.d. *Demographic Profiles of: (1) Persons of*

Caribbean Ancestry: A Basic Demographic Social and Economic Profile Based on 1990 Census Data (2) Jamaicans in Major Cities of the United States. Brooklyn: Caribbean Research Center, Medgar Evers College, CUNY.

Kasinitz, Philip. 1995. *Caribbean New York: Black Immigrants and the Politics of Race.* 3rd ed. Ithaca, NY: Cornell University Press.

Marshall, Paule. 1987. "Black Immigrant Women in *Brown Girl, Brownstones.*" In *Caribbean Life in New York City: Sociocultural Dimensions,* ed. Constance Sutton and Elsa M.Chaney, 81–85. Staten Island: Center for Migration Studies of New York.

Miller, D. W. 1999. "A Ghetto Childhood Inspires the Research of a Yale Sociologist." *Chronicle of Higher Education,* March 19, A15–16.

Model, Suzanne. 1991. "Caribbean Immigrants: A Black Success Story?" *International Migration Review* 25 (Summer): 248–276.

Newton, Kenneth. 1997. "Social Capital and Democracy." *American Behavioral Scientist* 40 (March–April): 575–586.

Payne, Anthony J. 1988. *Politics in Jamaica.* London: Hurst & Co.

Plummer, Dawn. 1994. "Una Clarke: New York City's Feisty Politico." *Everybody's Magazine* 18 (November): 40–46.

Portes, Alejandro, and Julia Sensenbrenner. 1993. "Embeddedness and Immigration: Notes on the Social Determinants of Economic Action." *American Journal of Sociology* 98 (May): 1320–1350.

Pragg, Sam. 1999. "Children Hardest Hit in Migration Wave." Available at Internet Newsgroup reg.carib.

Putnam, Robert D. 1995. "Tuning In, Tuning Out: The Strange Disappearance of Social Capital in America." *PS: Political Science & Politics* 28 (December): 664–683.

Reid, Ira De A. 1939. *The Negro Immigrant: His Background, Characteristics and Social Adjustment, 1899–1937.* New York: AMS Press.

Sunshine, Catherine A., and Keith Warner, eds. 1998. *Caribbean Connections: Moving North.* Washington, D.C.: Network of Educators on the Americas.

Sutton, Constance, and Susan R. Makiesky-Barrow. 1992. "Migration and West Indian Racial and Ethnic Consciousness." In *Caribbean Life in New York City: Sociocultural Dimensions,* ed. Constance Sutton and Elsa M. Chaney, 86–107. Staten Island: Center for Migration Studies of New York.

Toney, Joyce. 1989. "The Changing Relationship between Caribbean Men and Women in New York City." In *Establishing New Lives: Selected Readings on Caribbean Immigrants in New York City,* ed. Velta J. Clarke and Emmanuel Riviere, 65–83. New York: Caribbean Research Center, Medgar Evers College, CUNY.

Turner, W. Burghardt, and Joyce Moore Turner. 1988. *Richard B. Moore, Caribbean Militant in Harlem: Collected Writings, 1920–1972.* Bloomington: Indiana University Press.

U.S. Maritime Service Veterans. 2000. *African-Americans in the U.S. Merchant Ma-*

rine and U.S. Maritime Service. Available at www.usmn.org/african-americans.html

Vickerman, Milton. 1999. *Crosscurrents: West Indian Immigrants and Race.* New York: Oxford University Press.

4

West Indian Cultural Traditions: Continuity and Change

The first opportunity for English-speaking Caribbean immigrants to make their cultural mark on American society presented itself with the emergence of a new cultural phenomenon in the United States in the 1920s, the Harlem Renaissance, a great outburst of creative activity among African Americans in all fields of art. The geographical focus of this activity was Harlem, in New York City. The movement celebrated the black heritage, and African Americans were encouraged to transform themselves into the "New Negro," a term coined in 1925 by sociologist Alain LeRoy Locke in a landmark anthology of black writers by the same title.

The Harlem Renaissance was a watershed in American history that allowed African Americans to assert themselves in U.S. culture and society. It brought forth great writers, musicians, political movements, and so on who sought to claim their stake in this country. It is not always acknowledged, however, that within this large movement, black immigrants from the Caribbean found a harbor for self-expression and assertion of their presence in black America and the larger society.

In the remarkable cultural ferment of this period, Caribbean people felt the opportunity and need to make their voices heard. Perhaps the most telling example of the extraordinarily creative spirit of this time is given by the story of Lieutenant Hubert Fauntleroy Julian, a Trinidadian who had enlisted in the Royal Canadian Airforce during World War I. In Harlem he became an officer in Marcus Garvey's UNIA and a community celebrity. In late October 1923, Julian parachuted from a plane over Harlem, blowing his gold-plated saxophone on the way down. Julian's jump was not only an entertaining show, but also an avant-garde expression of art and a political statement. It gives a vivid impression of the spirit that permeated Harlem during this time and inspired countless African Americans and black West Indians.

Many immigrants from the English-speaking Caribbean had an impact on their communities in quieter ways. They were active in their churches and community work. This chapter explores some of the mechanisms through which they achieved influence within the wider American society.

CHURCHES, RELIGIOUS MOVEMENTS, AND BENEVOLENT ASSOCIATIONS

During the first decades of the twentieth century, New York's Harlem and Brooklyn were the center of African American and West Indian social activity. In both areas, a great number of societies, clubs, and churches provided a focus for these minority groups and served to integrate them into the American mainstream. The benevolent associations and the churches formed a network through which the migrants were able to gain employment and achieve social status. A number of churches and societies became centers of political and social involvement and activism.

Churches

As it was for African Americans in the South and North, for West Indian immigrants the church became the social center of their life. Because they generally belong to denominations without established churches in the United States, the early West Indian immigrants often joined other black churches or even churches that were predominantly white. But they often did not feel at home, and they even faced discrimination. One author wrote about a family of Barbadian immigrants who changed their church several times before settling down in a Caribbean-led church in Brooklyn:

[They] felt unwelcomed at the predominantly native-born black St. Augustine and later joined . . . a newly organized Christ Church Cathedral, located at Atlantic and Classon Avenues. This church, headed by Barbadian Rev. Reginald Grant Barrow, served the Caribbean-immigrant community. It later became affiliated with the African Orthodox Church. This pattern may have been followed by other immigrant families, especially members of the Anglican Church, which did not have its counterpart in the United States. (Watkins-Owens 1996: 57)

With the increase in English-speaking Caribbeans living in the United States, there was a perceived need for more Caribbean clergy and churches.

Particularly after 1900, Caribbean clergy played a more significant role in the church and community affairs of the African American population in Harlem and Brooklyn. Relative to the American black churches, however, the Caribbean churches had comparatively little economic and political position. Although most black churches were headed by American-born blacks, a number of West Indian ministers also rose to leadership. One of them was a native Antiguan, Bishop Derrick of the African Methodist Episcopal (AME) church. Derrick was a supporter of the African American educator Booker T. Washington and a source of political influence for the small immigrant community.

West Indian-born persons became particularly prominent in the AME churches. Between 1890 and 1920 they were also prominent as Episcopalian ministers along the eastern seaboard and were sought after in Presbyterian churches. In September 1900 the bishop of the AME New England Conference and the presiding elder and secretary were West Indian (Watkins-Owens 1996). The pastors of the second largest AME church in New England, at Newport, Rhode Island, and of the much sought-after church in Greenwich, Connecticut, were both from the West Indies. Around 1910, the Guyana-born Dr. Yearwood was a popular pastor in Hartford, Connecticut. Earlier, the AME presiding elder in New Jersey had been a West Indian. In these positions English-speaking Caribbean ministers served both West Indians and native black congregations.

An example of this cross-ethnic appeal is Charles Douglass Martin, a native of St. Kitts who established a Moravian church on West 104th Street in 1908. Although most of his church members were African Caribbean, he developed close ties with the African American community as well. In 1917, Martin, a member of the Negro Society for Historical Research, together with the African American historian and sociologist W.E.B. Du Bois, helped to spearhead the famous Silent Protest Parade during which about 15,000 black New Yorkers marched to the dramatic muffled sound of drums down Fifth Avenue in order to protest increasing violence against blacks in the city.

Establishing their own churches was not easy. Evelyn John, a native Guyanese and founder of a 99 percent Guyanese church, the New Life Center of Truth in New York City, recounts her experience: "It was difficult in the form that, two years after we came, we had to get a building because we were a day-care school. And we got this place and this place was just a warehouse, a carpet warehouse, and I did not know you had so much to do with a building. So that was a little difficult" (Caribbean Research Center 1995).

In these instances, however, the church communities usually draw on their faith and simply trust in the future. Endowed with optimism, they often overcome great obstacles to establish their own organizations, groups, and churches.

It is important to realize that for English-speaking Caribbean immigrants, as well as for African Americans, churches had (and continue to have) a larger significance than worship and the creation of a religious community. In a very real sense, the churches became a piece of home or built a link with home. As a space within which island culture was preserved and through which Caribbean-type celebrations (for example, harvests, Christmas, and New Year) and ceremonies (for example, Emancipation Day) were organized and held, the church assumed a much larger role in the life of the immigrants than it does today for most of mainstream American society. Weddings and funerals were also important events which promoted island culture with the help of the local church. These celebrations assumed a distinct social function as they reflected upon the social societal standing of a family: the higher the status of a family, the more extravagant the celebration. Strict etiquette, highly formal dress codes, and often hundreds of invited guests created a (sometimes misleading) impression about the importance of the involved families. These rigid functions, however, have to some extent been rejected by the younger people, who have become accustomed to more easy-going ways of celebrating. It is not surprising therefore that the second generation of Caribbean immigrants has distanced itself from such high-profiled societal affairs.

In spite of belonging to an economically weak community, the pastors of Caribbean immigrant parishes were often politically active. The Jamaican-born pastor of Harlem Community Unitarian Church, Ethelred Brown, is a good example. In fact, not unlike the African American Rev. Al Sharpton in the 1980s and 1990s, he was probably better known as a political leader and major figure in the Jamaican independence movement in New York. In the 1920s Brown was a frequent speaker at political gatherings in the New York City area and one of the major orators of the Socialist Speakers Bureau. He had cordial relations with the African American leader and later Congressman Adam Clayton Powell, Jr., and his father, and he was frequently invited to preach at the Powells' Abyssinian Baptist Church in Harlem.

From the early days of West Indian immigration, Caribbean churches and West Indian priests have also always provided a space for the younger generation. Churches helped young people to gain confidence and learn about the demands of real life. As the Reverend George A. Lloyd, an Antiguan who is a prominent community leader, points out:

The young people in the parish that I served, one of the things that I always tried to do was to impress on them that they were important people. Because the society seemed to ingrain a defeatist attitude on them and I thought that the church was a place to help correct that. . . . Last night I was at a meeting and I met a young woman who was a youth at my church. She is now assistant dean at a college. I told her how proud of her I was. . . . I feel that the youth is important and that they have a lot to offer. And we have to do all we can to try to correct some of the negative things that society puts in their heads. Because they are the future and if they don't have some sense of worth where are they going to end up? (Caribbean Research Center 1997)

Evelyn John adds her view that "because the parents have to work, the youths nowadays are open to so much out there" (Caribbean Research Center 1995). Both ministers stress the importance of education.

Although churches and religion have lost some of the appeal they had to the earlier English-speaking Caribbean migrants, they have never lost their central role in community life. In addition to the common Christian holidays, which are widely celebrated, there are additional occasions where religion is carried out of the church and celebrated in the streets. In this way religion becomes a public manifestation of the immigrants' faith. Indeed, in a sense, one can say that English-speaking Caribbean immigrants pray not only with their soul but also with their body through these processions. A particularly grand celebration in the parishes of East Flatbush (Brooklyn, New York) is the Corpus Christi procession, which attracts about one thousand marchers and starts with a special service in the parish church (Trabold 1990). Elaborately decorated altars are carried through the streets and then returned to the church amid songs and celebration. Religious gatherings and marches of this kind are not just a manifestation of religious fervor, but also a tool by which the immigrants reconnect with their island cultures and create community.

Santeria and Shango

As mainstream religions gradually lost their attraction, folk religions and religious movements gathered new followers among West Indians in the United States. An important movement is Santeria, which is popular in Cuba and the Dominican Republic and now also attracts English-speaking Caribbeans and African Americans, among others. Santeria has its roots in the Yoruba culture of West Africa but also incorporates Christian elements. In

Cuba, the Spanish word *santos* (saints) was merged with the Yoruba word for spirits, *orishas*, and that usage gave rise to the term *Santería* (way of the saints). For immigrants from the Caribbean, including West Indians, participation in a "house of Ocha," as the Santeria temples (usually at a Santeria priest's residence) are called, can be an important way to compensate for the loss of immediate interaction with their immediate and extended family, and illegal immigrants can find social support in such groups (Gregory 1992).

Santeria resembles another religious movement rooted in African culture, the primarily Afro-Cuban Shango sect, which is also known in Trinidad and Tobago. Shango was once the fourth king of the African Yoruba people and is immortalized as the spirit of thunder and lightning. He is represented by a double-headed axe, a symbol of balance, and the fiery color red. As the regulator of rules, Shango reminds practitioners not to lose control. Symbols of his power—calabashes, crowns of beads, thunder rattles, and the double-headed axe—announce his presence and the message of God's moral judgment. Shango is legendary across the African Atlantic world. Shango's storms and lightning are believed to bring a purifying moral terror, which is symbolized by the assertiveness and immediacy of his art and altars. Given the close similarity between Santeria and Shango, it can be assumed that in the United States Shango also coexists with Santeria. Indeed, an important institution that regularly brings together practitioners of various African-based religious movements in the United States is the LePeristyle Haitian Sanctuary in Philadelphia. A number of web sites about Shango, several of them based in the United States, also suggest that there are practicing followers of this religious sect in the United States.

Santeria has an uneasy coexistence with established churches. Although some churches in New York City have become more multicultural, they also find themselves exposed to the undercurrents from these traditional Caribbean religious movements. Father Edward Smith of St. Matthew's Catholic Church in Brooklyn admits: "I'm always putting out voodoo candles in the chapel or finding a chicken with its head cut off stuffed behind the statue of St. Anthony. If our magic doesn't work, they go to their magic" (Sanders 1997). As in the Caribbean, balancing Christianity with African concepts serves many believers as a counterweight against the power and dominance historically symbolized by and exerted through Christianity. The continuing existence of such belief systems is a vivid testimony to their endurance and importance to the people from the region.

Others, however, particularly those with higher education, feel more ambiguous. Hilton White, a Trinidadian scholar and community worker who is close to—albeit not a member of—the Spiritual Baptist movement, points out a difference between the Spiritual Baptists and Shango: "I do not have dealings with the Shango people. It is devil. Blood and fire. . . . Spiritual Baptist is as neat as Presbyterian is now. They have kept some of the African traditions. . . . In the traditions there are a lot of things like water throwing, lighting of candles. Those are traditional things. They are not evil. But it can be used as that and people can get the wrong impression" (Caribbean Research Center 1996).

Followers among Caribbean immigrants of the traditional religious movements are by no means representative of the entire community. To regard them as the representative religion(s) of English-speaking Caribbean immigrants would be a serious misrepresentation of the complexity and diversity of this community.

Caribbean Hindus

Caribbean immigrants of East Indian descent have established temples in order to sustain their culture. Although the Trinidadians built the biggest and most beautiful temple in New York City, the Guyanese have set up over forty. Considering that there are about 200,000 Guyanese in the United States (mostly in Queens), this is a great number of houses of worship, and they are usually filled to capacity. This represents a significant development in terms of solidifying Indo-Caribbean religion in the United States. An Indo-Caribbean immigrant who has been in the United States for eighteen years points out, "When I came, there were no temples, and prayers were conducted in the houses."

Guyanese and other Indo-Caribbean Hindus are a minority subgroup and thus threatened by the influence of a largely nonreligious society. Indo-Caribbean Hindus in the United States are generally more religious than those in Guyana or Trinidad. In the words of Prakash Gossai, a teacher and community leader in New York, "They get changed to the religious side once they come here. When I was in India, I was surprised to see people even in small villages were not doing pujas [i.e., the acts of showing reverence to a god or to aspects of the divine] as regularly as I would have imagined; they were taking religion for granted. The same thing in Guyana: religion is taken for granted. But here I have seen men and women who have never gone to a temple in Guyana very actively involved in the temple life. As they grow older, they turn more toward the spiritual life" (Melwani 1995). In residential areas like Richmond Hill in Queens, where many Indo-Caribbeans live, Indian flags are common, and fasting, praying, and pujas are as much a part of their lifestyle as the traditional Indian music, dance, and food (Melwani

1997). One reason for this interest in their religion derives from the fact that while the Hindus in Guyana and Trinidad are surrounded by their religion, in the United States they are not. Their religion thus becomes more appreciated.

Ironically, immigrants from India shun the Indo-Caribbean population in the United States, and there are few formal links between both communities. The reason is that the Indians from India think of themselves as being "purer" than the Indo-Caribbeans, whom they regard as "polluted" by their Caribbean life. In much the same way, however, Indo-Caribbeans keep a considerable social distance from the Afro-Caribbean population in New York City and do not very actively participate in the major West Indian event, the Caribbean-American Carnival Parade on Labor Day (Strozier 1997). Relatively few Indo-Caribbeans reside in predominantly black West Indian neighborhoods. Indeed, most of them prefer to settle in Queens, some distance from Brooklyn. It has been said that there hardly exists an Indo-Caribbean community beyond the religious activities in which they participate (Ramadar 1993). Thus, the Indo-Caribbean population does not participate actively in politics. The comparatively politically passive character of this West Indian group can probably best be understood in the context of their disappointing political experience in their home countries, Guyana and Trinidad and Tobago. In both countries the East Indian population for many years was forced to play a relatively minor role in public affairs and perceived economic and social setbacks at the hand of political parties predominantly directed by Afro-Caribbeans.

The Hindu community among the English-speaking Caribbean immigrants in the United States is concerned about the waning interest in Indian tradition and culture among youth. As one teacher puts it: "The ideal Guyanese Hindu family is very concerned about dress and behavior, but in New York influences of television, the streets, and the schools we see our children slowly drifting away from what we like to consider a very rich culture. When the parents realize this, then they make the response of coming to the temple" (Melwani 1995). To address this concern, many temples offer cultural programs such as dance, religious chant, and lectures for children. Thus, religion and cultural preservation of their culture are intimately related.

By learning more about their culture and religion, many young Indo-Caribbeans learn how to define themselves and their place in the United States, how to relate to others, and how to respond to challenges to their identity from their peers. Consequently, religion is not just uncritically accepted by the younger generation, but once they get involved in community and cultural programs, young people often ask for more information and show great interest in this aspect of their heritage. The teacher Prakash Gossai observes: "It is a very inquiring world, and children when asked to perform a puja want to know the reasons behind the rituals, why do we sip water, why do the murthis [the visible form of a deity] have so many hands, and so on. . . . But I find that once the children are made aware of the symbols and their application, we find them very, very willing to participate in these functions" (Melwani 1995). Unlike in Guyana or Trinidad, where people of East Indian descent are the majority and they consequently become immersed in their culture almost subconsciously, the process of handing down traditions, customs, religion, and language becomes something that both the immigrant parents and the local Hindu communities actively need to sponsor. Hindu cultural centers, festivals, and dress codes are therefore not a question of cultural seclusion or an expression of cultural superiority to others, but simply reflect the wish of the older generation to help their children find and define their place in the larger scheme of things.

Rastafarianism

The most successful, popularly recognized, and influential African-based religious movement from the English-speaking Caribbean is Rastafarianism. Rastafarianism, which originated in Jamaica during the early twentieth century, has influenced much of Western popular culture, from music to fashion and hair styles. With the growing popularity of reggae music, this cultural phenomenon has spread throughout the Caribbean to North America and Europe, as well as to the African continent itself. Indeed, as reggae megastar Bob Marley prophetically sang at the beginning of the 1980s, "Reggae's on Broadway." This growth and spread of the movement has stemmed from a variety of factors, including reggae musicians and the efforts of traditional Rastafari elders from Jamaica to promote their culture and way of life. Also, many African Americans and West Indians who have become Rastafari outside Jamaica now make pilgrimages to Jamaica to attend religious ceremonies known as Nyabinghi. Despite the fact that Rastafari continue to be widely misunderstood and even stigmatized outside Jamaica, the movement embraces a nonviolent ethic of universal peace and love and pursues a disciplined code of religious principles.

There are probably several tens of thousands of Rastafarians living in the New York metropolitan area alone (Redeker Hepner and Hepner 1999). This is the largest community of Rastas outside Jamaica, and possibly even the largest in the world. Although the large majority of members are not organized or affiliated with Rasta organizations or churches, there has been a move in this direction. In the New York City area, for example, a number of sizable Rastafarian groups and institutions—churches, community and daycare centers, political associations, Sunday school classes—have developed. Among them are the Twelve Tribes of Israel, the Nyabinghi Order of Divine Theocracy, the Ethiopian Orthodox Church, the Church of Haile Selassie I, the Ethiopian World Federation, and the Itefayo Cultural Arts Facility. Obviously there is an appeal similar to the other early churches in Harlem and Brooklyn, and one can sense the same institutional vibrancy that characterized that period.

Since the 1980s the Rastafari movement has become more international. Music groups like the Fugees (featuring the dreadlocked Grammy winner Lauryn Hill, of Jamaican parentage) and the multiracial Rastafarian group Big Mountain (from California) have done their share to popularize the Rasta movement in the United States. In July 1999, the lead singer of the Fugees, Wyclef Jean, was a soloist at the private memorial service in New York City for John F. Kennedy, Jr., singing Jimmy Cliff's reggae anthem "Many Rivers to Cross." Rastafarians are increasingly having an impact on the wider public and established institutions of the mainstream society. In 1997 the Economic and Social Council of the United Nations approved the consultative status of the International Rastafarian Development Society, thus conferring significant legitimacy on one of the organizations within the Rastafari movement. Prior to this, in 1992, the British Rastafarian reggae group Steel Pulse had received a special invitation to play at President Clinton's inaugural party.

Another indicator of the mainstreaming tendencies of Rastafari, its music, and its messages is the fact that the musical theme of a popular television series for small children—"Arthur" on PBS—is performed by Bob Marley's children—Ziggy Marley and the Melody Makers. Few parents know or would even recognize this.

There has been a considerable diversification and the emergence of new voices within the movement, which are transforming certain aspects of Rastafarianism in the United States and other countries in the industrialized world. Most notably this evolution has occurred with regard to gender issues and in the field of music and music production. More and more women from the Third World are assuming an active and vocal role in the fight against discrimination, domestic violence, and underdevelopment (Turner 1994). Traditional (i.e., Jamaican) Rastafarianism assumed a patriarchical and, more often than not, sexist form in the relations between men and women within the movement. Some of the roles ascribed to Rastafarian women in this traditional scheme include their expected contentment in being the mothers for Rastafarian men's children, their secondary role in matters of Rastafarian beliefs and practices, their characterization as "unclean" (particularly during menstruation) and as a distraction to the spiritual dedication and connection of Rastafarian men to Jah (i.e., God), and their required modesty in matters of attire and fashion. The origins of this subordinate role of Rastafarian women lie both in a specific (i.e., male) interpretation of the Bible and Jamaican folk beliefs, which themselves are based on African and colonial British practices (Homiak 1998).

These traditional roles for Rastafarian women have been increasingly challenged, mainly by Rastafarian migrants in the United States, Canada, and the United Kingdom. There is a growing belief that Rastafarian patriarchy is itself a reflection of colonial oppression. Given this new consciousness, increasing numbers of younger Rastafarians, male and female, are beginning to challenge the theory and practice of patriarchy and sexism within the movement. For example, one male follower of the Twelve Tribes of Israel based in Queens, New York, has said:

In everything sometimes you have to bend. In the Catholic Church right now they're bending rules, rules that are 200 or 300 years old. They're bending to accommodate the times. You have to somewhere along the line give in. You have brothers who want the separation between men and women, but the separation between man and woman is not really necessary. With Rastafari, we need to be a family, because in the family unit comes strength. (quoted in Redeker Hepner and Hepner 1999: 20)

However, Rasta-womanism, as it should be more appropriately called, is not simply a reflection of the feminist movement. In important aspects it also stands in opposition to it. Feminism is widely regarded as the domain of white privileged women who locate their oppression mainly in the realm of motherhood and childrearing and are less concerned than their black counterparts with issues of "race" and class. Rastafarian women, however, increasingly use motherhood as a tool of power. As one of them put it, "My daughters and sons will make a difference because they've seen the struggles of their mothers and fathers, and they are more advantaged than we were when we came into Rasta. My hope is in the youth, not in trying to change the brethren" (quoted in Redeker Hepner and Hepner 1999: 26). This emerging opposition to outmoded forms of gender definition in the long run can only strengthen the overall appeal of Rastafarianism, since it gives its resistance to all forms of human oppression a more coherent basis in the movement's own practice.

Although the internationalization of the Rastafarian movement has led to greater knowledge about and acceptance of Rastafarians, it has also meant a watering down of its essential beliefs. Some of this stems from the ambiguity of some of the Rastafarian movement's symbols and iconography. For example, when the Ethiopian flag is juxtaposed to outline maps of Jamaica or Bob Marley images, this seems to be opposed to the sacred art of orthodox Rastafari. Also, the features of the Ethiopian emperor, the central icon in the Rastafarian belief system, do not conform to black stereotypes (Yawney 1994). Even in the movement itself such issues are not beyond dispute and can be regarded as both proof of its openness to external influences, as well as dilutions of its traditions. Without a doubt, some Rastafarians will decry the cooperation of Rastas with the United Nations system as a surrender to "Babylon," "the system," the anti-Christ, and great confuser of humanity. Others will say that cooperation is part of a growth process the movement has been experiencing and that recognition by international bodies such as the United Nations reflects a new stage in its development.

Rastafarians have increasingly become part of the cultural tapestry of the United States. Like in their home countries, they have become subject to prejudice, discrimination, and harassment by the authorities. In fact, in the early 1980s, the police department of at least one American city used a film to instruct its cadets on the perils of the Rastafarian movement (Lewis 1993). In this film Rastas were depicted as dangerous criminals without respect for law or law enforcement officers. "Rastafarians are not to be taken lightly, especially those that appear docile. They will use any means necessary to get away, even shoot you. They have no qualms about firing on an officer. . . . Keep in mind that you are dealing with a wanted fugitive. That will guarantee you that you will come home the same way you came to work," the film warns. Thus, police recruits and trainees were prodded to increase their fear of Rastas, and the film actively promoted stereotypes about them.

The Rastafarians themselves tend to interpret their role as targets of police observation and action through a religious lens. In their view, this targeting is a reflection of Baylon's wickedness and proof of the Rastafarians' righteousness and the correctness of their way of life. One could say that their interpretation of American society and their role within it resemble a reliving of a historical memory that captures their passage from Africa (and freedom) to the West Indies (and slavery). Thus, all contemporary events are passed through this filter, which gives fundamental importance to the crime of slavery. In this way, Rastafarians often tend to mythologize their conflicts with authority and public opinion in general and the state authorities in particular. In this interpretation, the Rastafarians will ultimately prevail: "Just as Moses led Pharaoh's troops to destruction in the sea when they pursued the Chosen People, so will it be for all of Babylon's forces" (Lewis 1993: 101). Drug raids by the police on their legitimate businesses are a regular feature in this drama, and in the view of the Rastafarians they only are one aspect of the evil of Babylonian society.

It is true, however, that many Rastafarians regard *ganja* (marijuana) as an integral part of their attempt to become one with Jah (God). Although not all Rastas use it, it is widely regarded as the herb of wisdom of which (in their interpretation) even the Bible appears to speak. Rastafarians have established businesses in a number of trades (e.g., crafts, records, and leather work), and some owners condone the use and sale of *ganja* on their premises. This has led to repeated conflicts with the authorities, who do not distinguish between the ritual and any other use of illegal drugs. Unlike in Jamaica, where their lifestyle finds at least limited acceptance, particularly in civil society, Rastafarians in the United States face less acceptance and stricter enforcement of antidrug policies.

With the growing acceptance and visibility of members belonging to the Rastafarian belief, their symbols and styles have been appropriated by mainstream culture. But in many instances, this appropriation involves misrepresentation or even prejudice. A number of Hollywood movies, for example, depict Rastafarians as figures more or less central to the plot. Often these Rastas pose as drug pushers or gangsters but, for the most part, these films do not portray Rastafarians in exhaustive detail. One of the most openly anti-Jamaican films is *Marked for Death* (1990). It features action actor Steven Seagal as a Chicago police officer in his usual macho pose trying to run a crack-selling Jamaican gang out of town. In the course of the film, several very broad, and even racist, stereotypes are used. The most ridiculous scene in this regard occurs when the film has the Rastafarians—especially their leader, "Screwface"—practice magic resembling Santeria. Obviously this is a huge distortion, since Rastafarians shun such practices. Other examples of such movies include *Predator II* (1987), *Only the Strong* (1993), *Water* (1986), *Club Paradise* (1986), and *The Mighty Quinn* (1989). Without a doubt, the strangest film to feature a sustained Rastafarian character is *The Adventures of Buckaroo Banzai: Across the 8th Dimension* (1984). In this movie with its bizarre, cartoonlike, sci-fi plot, a Rastafarian who assists the protagonist in busting the bad guys plays an extraterrestrial. Despite its weird story and unsophisticated finish, reminiscent of the old Batman and Robin movies, *Buckaroo Banzai* almost instantaneously became a cult classic.

On many Caribbean islands, mostly in Jamaica, so-called beach boys and dreadlocked youths known as rent-a-dreads—young, healthy looking, and physically fit black men working on the beaches around the popular tourist resorts—provide sexual adventures for female tourists. Another popular book and movie, *How Stella Got Her Groove Back* by Terry McMillan, has led to a marked increase of African American women spending their holidays in Jamaica and other Caribbean islands in search for such adventures. While African American women are, reportedly, more interested in long-term relationships than their white European and American counterparts, they too are following stereotypes of the natural and healthy Rasta perpetrated by the media, music industry, and sometimes the locals themselves. This aspect of sex tourism provides a temporary income for these young men; however, the ultimate goal of many of the rent-a-dreads and beach boys is to obtain a highly coveted U.S. green card (a visa allowing residency and employment) (Albuquerque 1999). Real Rastafarians scoff at these frivolous and promiscuous outgrowths of the Rastafarian popularity and recognition.

Although misrepresentations as in these examples of popular culture are regrettable and avoidable, they are evidence of the growing internationalization of the movement. They speak to the increasing recognition that Rastafarians have become an integral part of U.S. society.

Obeah

One of the most secret religious practices of English-speaking Caribbean immigrants in the United States is the Jamaican spiritualist movement obeah, a belief system with roots in West Africa; in fact the original Asante word for sorcerer (*obayifo*) is preserved in the term *obeah* (Alleyne 1989). Although far less known in the United States than the voodoo culture of Haitian origin, obeah is commonly seen as a sort of witchcraft in which obeah men or obeah women are regarded as a kind of medicine man, witch doctor, or sorcerer. The obeah man or obeah woman is usually frequented by clients who are seeking to cast an evil spell or receive a protective spell against spiritual or worldly forces. Some of the tools used by the obeah man are amulets, fetishes, grave dust and other powders, gourds, trinkets, and jumbies (ghosts).

More women than men seem to become clients of an obeah man or obeah woman, often in order to get out of a bad relationship or to ward off potential rivals. In many instances, an obeah spell, or "medicine," is supposed to inflict harm. Thus, it is often considered to be a negative and evil spiritual practice. However, quite often it is also applied to protect from obeah spells which the client feels himself or herself to be suffering from. Since obeah can also cast protective spells (e.g., against other obeah spells), it is not entirely correct to dismiss it as an evil practice. In fact, another important aspect of obeah is healing through the application of herbs and other natural medicines. Moreover, obeah men are consulted to promote fortune in love, personal and business pursuits, and employment. During slavery obeah was directed against members of the white ruling class and considered widely beneficial. Many obeah men and obeah women were leaders responsible for leading revolts among the slaves. In the Haitian Revolution, for example, obeah men played an important role in preparing slaves for the battle against their oppressors. In addition, one has to remember that in Africa, good and evil are not always clear opposites. Consequently, where obeah is directed against (perceived) oppression, it occupies a gray area between good and evil.

Nevertheless, obeah was in colonial times and remains outlawed, although this is not strictly, if at all, enforced in countries like, Jamaica. In the United States, however, obeah is both illegal and being persecuted. Indeed, in the late 1990s, several arrests were made in Brooklyn of persons accused of this practice. For this reason, obeah is an underground practice and only whispered about. Not many Caribbean people admit to knowing about it or are even prepared to talk about it, because for them as devoted Christians (or Hindus or Muslims, since obeah also has followers among East Indians), there is a strong social stigma attached to it. This makes it extremely difficult to get a precise picture of the extent of this practice in the United States.

Although there are many "spiritual healers" and card and palm readers readily available and advertising their services in local and ethnic newspapers, in reality there are probably only a handful of real obeah men or obeah women conducting their business in the Caribbean immigrant communities in the United States. In many instances, there are free-riders trying to capitalize on the obvious demand for such spiritual practices. Most likely they will advertise their services publicly and under the guise of mainstream spiritualist activities (see Figure 4.1).

One of, the possibly best-known obeah men in the United States is Reverend Brown. Indeed, he is the third generation in what has developed into a family business. His father, John Brown, also a well-known obeah man in Jamaica, assumed some fame in 1970 when the largest Jamaican newspaper reported about a curious incident that occurred in downtown Kingston, when an unguided, three-wheeled coffin with three crows dressed in coats was reportedly seen driving through the streets (Wint 1970). The incident

Figure 4.1
Newspaper Advertisement by a West Indian Spiritualist

```
┌─────────────────────────────────────────┐
│  In the name of Almighty God              │
│                                           │
│                                           │
│     SPIRITUALIST &                        │
│                                           │
│               MYSTIC HEALER               │
│                                           │
│                                           │
│   Mr. Dalli is available to remove evil spells. │
│                                           │
│   We handle mostly difficult cases.       │
│                                           │
│   We work for all nationalities.          │
│                                           │
│   References available.                   │
│                                           │
│                                           │
│                    CALL FOR APPOINTMENT   │
│                                           │
│  WE ONLY HEAL      718-XXX-XXXX           │
└─────────────────────────────────────────┘
```

sent a big crowd running through the streets for a glimpse of this strange spectacle. According to one witness, one of the crows asked a bystander if she knew John Brown. Subsequently, this bizarre event was taken up in a song by Lee "Scratch" Perry, the dominating music producer and artist in Jamaica at this time, and the song—simply called "Mr. Brown"—was later made famous by reggae superstar Bob Marley.

The Reverend Brown, according to informants, divides his time between Jamaica and different destinations in the United States where Jamaicans and other Caribbeans are living in greater numbers (e.g., New York, Florida, California). To get an appointment with this obeah man is extremely difficult; he works through informal channels. A person interested in contacting the obeah man has to "hear around" for people who know him or work with him. After this first contact, nothing may happen for a long time, but eventually the contact person for the obeah man may call or send a letter to the customer in which an appointment is made. For this appointment, an assistant of the obeah man may set up an informal interview to meet the customer and hear about his or her problem. If both parties agree to proceed further, the customer will—again after a waiting period—be contacted and informed about the scheduled appointment.

Although obeah is a clandestine aspect of Caribbean culture in North

America, in recent times it has appeared in movies. The movie *Meet Joe Black* (1998), starring Anthony Hopkins and Brad Pitt, has a scene set in a hospital in which Pitt—playing the dual role of death and lover—is challenged by an old woman who appears to be a Jamaican. The sick old woman recognizes Pitt (death) and utters the words "obeah, obeah." Pitt, swiftly switching to Jamaican dialect, answers her that he has not come for her and that she does not need to worry. The old woman asks Pitt to free her of her pain and take her with him. Obeah is depicted correctly here as a sort of witchcraft, although the film attributes more power to it than this practice can claim in reality. It is remarkable, however, that this relatively unknown West Indian religious practice has made it into a film which caters to American and international audiences.

Benevolent Associations

There are a large number of associations with the word *Caribbean* or any of the islands' names in it, and they have existed from the earliest presence of West Indian migrants. In fact, compared to the influence of the established churches, these benevolent associations and other voluntary organizations had a greater impact on the formation of communities (Watkins-Owens 1996). A few of these societies were organized to reflect social status. Most others provided a number of useful services to help newcomers find jobs, get assistance of various kinds, and participate in some form of social life. Meeting fellow islanders was important given the fact that West Indians came from small, closely knit societies with an intense social life. Thus, the quick walk in their home country to the street corner to hang out or to the local bar for a drink and a friendly chat with neighbors were not easily replaced in U.S. cities.

Most of the benevolent societies were active at organizing social events, allowing their members to convene and meet both formally and informally. Activities included boat and bus rides, trips, picnics, holiday programs, educational forums, and musical and literary programs. These activities were organized for the mutual improvement and relaxation of the members and invited guests. They were also meant to bring together older and more recent immigrants. Sometimes these functions were designed to raise funds or for charitable purposes.

For many members, the more immediate and important benefit of being involved with the benevolents was to supply funds for special purposes and emergency situations. For example, they gave money to members who had burial expenses or had fallen sick. In the case of the Bermudian Association, sick members were eligible on presentation of a doctor's note for three dollars a week and regular payments each week during the illness. Ill members could even expect a visit from other members—a "sick committee." The Grenada Mutual Association would pay upon the death of any member one hundred dollars—a very helpful amount for the times—to the relatives to assist with funeral costs. There is no doubt that these small donations were often needed and gratefully accepted. The Montserrat Progressive Society with its 750 members in 1925 paid $1,200 in such sick benefits.

Some of the financially better endowed benevolent associations provided benefits and sponsored larger undertakings that individuals would have found impossible to pay—loans for mortgages, political contributions, and general welfare. In this way they both provided mutual aid to their members and contributed to the economic stability of the larger community. In many instances this extended, according to their means, even to the associations' respective home countries. For example, in 1902, the Bermuda benevolents sent ten dollars to Martinique for relief after a volcanic eruption there, and in 1927 the St. Lucia United Association collected three hundred dollars to donate to victims of a fire that destroyed parts of a town in St. Lucia. Thanks to its wealthy president, the Virgin Islands Congressional Council in the 1920s was able to send thousands of dollars in charitable contributions to the Virgin Islands and other Caribbean locations. Frequently the benevolent societies would collect bundles of clothing and send them home to needy families and friends.

The societies were dominated by men, but most of them had women auxiliaries, which provided women opportunities for leadership. In 1917 the American West Indian Ladies Aid Society (AWILAS) was formed and assumed leadership in Harlem. While this society responded to various calls for assistance by the other, male-led, societies, it was also involved in radical political activity and reform movements in the Virgin Islands. Elizabeth Hendrickson, president of the society, was a moving force behind this activism and well known as a street corner speaker at political rallies. In the 1920s she was also involved with the Harlem Tenants League, a militant group that attempted to unite residents against unfair treatment such as outrageous rent increases and evictions.

Benevolent groups active today are focused on providing assistance to their home societies, organizing social affairs to keep the community of islanders at home and abroad connected, and providing a forum for the display of their social status. One example of the continuing tradition of providing service to their community is the Trinidad & Tobago Working Women's Association (T&TWWA), which sponsors an annual scholarship for college-bound youth. In recent years this initiative has been supported by the CACCI's new Educational Foundation, which raises money among its members. It is by no means uncommon that a Caribbean country's ambassador, prime minister, or even governor-general becomes involved in fund-raising events and graces them with his or her presence. Thus, in October 1998 Grenada's governor-general, Sir Daniel Williams, and his wife attended a fund raiser in Brooklyn to help the Grenada Needy Children Foundation raise money for local and international scholarships and other direct assistance to the youth of Grenada.

At all levels of social organization, English-speaking Caribbean immigrants have found themselves to a greater or lesser extent thrown into some form of political activity. This high level of activism is a reflection of not only the ferment of the early decades of the twentieth century but also shows that they were eager to establish networks and societies that could be of support in their quest for economic and social improvement.

LITERATURE

Oral and written literature is one of the most important art forms in the Caribbean. The people of the English-speaking Caribbean have given the world some of its literary giants. Among them are Derek Walcott, Edward Kamau Brathwaite, V. S. Naipaul, C.L.R. James, George Lamming, and Wilson Harris. Influential writers from the region have lived and worked in the United States, and some continue to do so. Apart from James, Lamming, Brathwaite, and Harris, Claude McKay is probably the most influential English-speaking Caribbean writer who lived in the United States. A number of writers less known to the general public are Jamaica Kincaid, Paule Marshall, and Merle Collins.

Claude McKay (1890–1948), born in Jamaica, is often called the most important figure of the Harlem Renaissance, the black literary "movement" at the beginning of the twentieth century that proclaimed the arrival of the "new Negro" (the race-conscious black without an inferiority complex). When McKay came to the United States in 1912, he was already known in his home country as a poet. His name was known even in London since he had published two small books of poetry there, *Songs of Jamaica* and *Constab Ballads*. In 1918–1919, he made a long journey to Europe and the Soviet Union, where he was celebrated as a representative of the black Left in the English-speaking world. Between 1919 and 1934, he lived only temporarily in the United States. In fact, his novel *Home to Harlem* (1928) was written abroad. In this book, the reader finds the protagonist, Jake, in pursuit of a girl named Felice, which can be read as a grand, and typical, American metaphor for the pursuit of happiness.

When McKay came to the United States, he first settled in Tuskegee and Kansas City. Two years later he moved to New York City where he opened a restaurant at West Fifty-third Street (not in Harlem). Probably because he was a socialist, McKay had difficulty obtaining U.S. citizenship. In his autobiography, *A Long Way from Home* (1937), however, he renounced socialism and three years later became a citizen. Soon after he also became a member of the Roman Catholic church, a rather atypical development for a black intellectual of his time.

Better known for his poetry than his fiction, McKay wrote a number of works that remain important for understanding Harlem in the 1920s. Apart from J. B. Moreton, McKay was the first West Indian poet to bring the everyday language, creole, into the literary tradition. His pioneering also worked the other way around, however, and "he was the first to weave into Caribbean poetry the strand of North American experience which has come to dominate the diaspora in more recent years. As an indication of the way in which the Caribbean's frame of reference was changing, his 1920 poetry collection was the first from the region to be published simultaneously in both London and New York" (Burnett 1986: lii).

Another West Indian author connected to the Harlem Renaissance is Eric Walrond (1898–1966). Like McKay, he lived most of his life outside his native Guyana and returned only for occasional visits to the Caribbean. In 1918 he arrived in New York City, where he joined the circle around Langston Hughes, a central figure of this literary movement. For some time, he closely collaborated with Marcus Garvey and in 1926 published a collection of short stories, *Tropic Death*, which brought him instant fame. In this book, his last fictional work, Walrond critically depicts the precarious social conditions of the lower classes in Guyana and other Caribbean islands, as well as the slums of the West Indian workers in Panama.

Louis Simpson (b. 1923) was born in Jamaica, the son of a lawyer of Scottish descent and a Russian mother. He came to the United States in 1940 and served between 1943 and 1945 with the U.S. Army in France, Holland, Belgium, and Germany. He produced some of the finest poetry to come out of World War II. After the war, he attended Columbia University and the University of Paris and worked for several years as an editor before turning to academic teaching, in which he has had a distinguished career at Columbia University, the University of California at Berkeley, and the State University of New York at Stony Brook. Simpson won numerous literary awards, including the Prix de Rome, the Hudson Review Fellowship, and the 1964 Pulitzer Prize for poetry. Living in Setauket, New York, he is a U.S. citizen and is often thought of as an American poet, but he has always continued to draw on his Jamaican experience in his work.

The most famous contemporary author from the English-speaking Caribbean is the St. Lucia–born Derek Walcott (b. 1930). Walcott currently divides his time between Trinidad, where he has his home as a writer, and Boston, Massachusetts, where he works as a professor of creative writing and literature at Boston University. In 1992 Walcott was awarded the Nobel Prize for literature. As a poet he made his debut at the age of eighteen, but his widespread recognition as a poet came with a collection of poems, *In a Green Night* (1962). After his education at St. Mary's College in St. Lucia and the University College of the West Indies in Kingston (Jamaica), Walcott moved to Trinidad in 1953, where he has worked as a theater and art critic. In 1958–1959, he studied theater in New York City and after his return to Trinidad founded the Trinidad Theatre Workshop, which produced many of his early plays. Walcott has traveled extensively; however, he has always felt himself to be deeply rooted in Caribbean society with its disparate elements of African, European, and Asiatic cultures and peoples. Walcott has written in both standard English and West Indian dialect, and his plays are influenced by creole and folk tradition. Thus, his work is a direct reflection of his own identity. Against the background of West Indian settings, Walcott explores the connections between historical awareness, everyday life, and folk activities like song, dance, and storytelling.

Another accomplished Caribbean poet currently residing in the United States is the Barbadian Edward Kamau Brathwaite (b. 1930). At age nineteen Brathwaite won a scholarship to Pembroke College at Cambridge University in England. In the late 1960s he earned a Ph.D. in history at the University of Sussex in England with a study about the development of creole society in Jamaica. Brathwaite has lived and worked several years in Ghana and Togoland. After his return to the West Indies in 1962, he worked as a lecturer in history at the University of the West Indies. In the early 1990s he moved to New York, where he currently lives and works at New York University.

His extensive travels made Brathwaite sensitive to the rootlessness of the Afro-Caribbeans. As he explains:

I had, at the moment of my return, completed the triangular trade of my historical origins. West Africa had given me a sense of place, of belonging; and that place . . . was the West Indies. My absence and travels, at the same time, had given me a sense of movement and restlessness—rootlessness. It was, I recognized, particularly the condition of the Negro of the West Indies and the New World. (quoted in Magill 1984: 211)

The curious gap between the sense of belonging and uprootedness in terms of personal and historical existence has become the theme of Brathwaite's subsequent work as historian, poet, and literary critic.

Brathwaite draws on both classical European sources (for example, Greek drama) and African religious practice (for example, chant or invocation). He is equally indebted to the Euro-American literary tradition through the influence of T. S. Eliot and the Afro–West Indian tradition through the work of Aimé Césaire. In addition, his poetry draws from musical forms such as jazz, blues, calypso, reggae, spirituals, and shango hymns. Brathwaite's poems build on the oral folk tradition of Claude McKay, Louise Bennett, and other Caribbean authors who grounded their work in the lives of the people about and for whom they wrote. Brathwaite's poetry is highly original and innovative, and the quality of his work makes him a contender for a future Nobel Prize in literature. His best-known works are *Rights of Passage* (1967), *Masks* (1968), *Islands* (1969), *Other Exiles* (1975), and *Black & Blues* (1976).

A prominent representative of the younger generation of West Indian authors living in the United States is Jamaica Kincaid (b. 1949). Despite her name (which is a pseudonym for Elaine Potter Richardson), she is not from Jamaica but was born in Antigua. In 1965 she was sent to Westchester County, New York, as an au pair. Having completed her secondary education in Antigua, she went on to study photography at the New York School for Social Research after she left the family for whom she had worked. In her writing Kincaid angrily expresses her disappointments with colonialism and her view that conditions in Antigua worsened after independence. Thus, in her book *A Small Place* (1988), she blames Antiguans for imitating colonial behavior by, for example, turning themselves into tourist attractions. In other novels she explores how the mother-daughter relationship influences the development of a female identity in a male-dominated society. Probing the ideas of love, affection, hostility, and death and their effect on the individual, Kincaid critically examines the role of cultural expectations and her mother in the novels *Annie John* (1986), *The Autobiography of My Mother* (1996), and *At the Bottom of the River* (1992).

Authors of West Indian origin born in the United States sometimes write about their encounter with the world of their parents and their conflicts with these traditions. For example, in the story "To Da-duh, in Memoriam" (1983), Paule Marshall, who was born in Brooklyn to parents who emigrated from Barbados during World War I, tells the story of a little girl who visits her grandmother in Barbados. A tense relationship develops between the girl and the grandmother, and in one particularly telling scene the generational and cultural conflicts between the two come to a head when the little girl challenges her grandmother's knowledge about heights:

> "What's the name of that hill I went to visit the other day, where they have the police station?"
> "You mean Bissex?"
> "Yes, Bissex. Well, the Empire State Building is way taller than that."
> "You're lying now!" she shouted, trembling with rage. Her hand lifted to strike me.
> "No, I'm not," I said. "It really is, if you don't believe me I'll send you a picture postcard of it as soon as I get back home so you can see for yourself. But it's way taller than Bissex."
> All the fight went out of her at that. The hand poised to strike me fell limp to her side, and as she stared at me, seeing not me but the building that was taller than the highest hill she knew, the small stubborn light in her eyes (it was the same amber as the flame in the kerosene lamp she lit at dusk) began to fail. (Marshall 1983; see Sunshine and Warner 1998: 103)

In these few lines Marshall expresses the fundamental rift that develops between the Caribbean migrants and their children and the society they left behind. In many cases it requires a visit to or extended residence in the "home country" to recognize the colonial folly of learning to sing Christmas carols about snowed-in landscapes in the tropical heat of the Caribbean. Marshall therefore allows us a small glimpse at both the desire to reconnect and the difficulty of doing so.

The literature of the migrant West Indians broadly corresponds to the development of West Indian literature as a whole. This development occurred in several distinct phases. Up to about the 1920s or 1930s, West Indian literature reflected the ideals, values, and worldviews of the British colonialists. In this picture, Caribbean people of East Indian or African descent played only minor, subordinate roles, and the texts adhered to the standards of and literary forms common in European literature. Consequently, West Indian novels and poetry were written in standard English and did not reflect the creolized English commonly spoken in the region. If this dialect was depicted at all, it was used to demonstrate the inferiority of those who used it and to ridicule their culture.

This approach changed during the 1930s when C. L. R. James and others started to portray the life of the common people in a more naturalistic way. Other authors, some of whom had lived in Europe and Africa, also published in this period and started to promote a new appreciation for the African roots of Caribbean culture. Claude McKay, who falls into this category, played an important role in the development of Caribbean literature. It is important to realize that West Indians first had to leave their Caribbean home countries and travel to the colonial "mother country" to discover their own culture and its relation to European culture. As one black Trinidadian author describes it vividly, upon arrival in England or the United States, "you discovered that you were no part of them either, you were very different; in fact you wished you would be even *more* different, as different, for example, as the Africans who could hold conversations in the midst of their hosts without being eavesdropped upon—the same Africans you had heartily despised (without ever having met one in the flesh) but whom you now respected and rather envied" (Hodge 1980: 27). As the English-speaking Caribbean countries started to prepare themselves for political independence in the 1950s, a whole flurry of literature emerged which picked up these new experiences and tendencies and broadened the appreciation of Afro-Caribbean culture among both writers and the reading public.

During this period also, many writers explored what it meant to be a Caribbean person, what the nature of the creolization process was, and how society and culture resembled and differed from that of other regions—in short, what the essence of West Indian life is. Different authors found different answers to these fundamental, and complicated, questions. By about the mid-1960s Africa had lost its appeal and given way to an appreciation of the complex and multifaceted reality that the Caribbean is (Rohlehr 1980).

This more refined concept of the Caribbean as a complex space full of contradictions, differing traditions, and competing value systems has not yet been fully absorbed by the masses of people who are of African descent and therefore still (and justifiably) preoccupied with the appreciation of their African-ness. Nor has it been absorbed by the economic and political elites in the Caribbean who remain committed to European values and institutions. In fact, their promotion of Caribbean and African- or Indian-derived culture becomes highly suspect. Thus, often West Indian elites patronize only those aspects of folk culture that support tourism (for example, carnival), thereby neglecting and oppressing the most creative and dynamic sectors of artistic production (for example, steel pan music). In other countries of the region politicians are found guilty of manipulating the religions of the oppressed and the symbols of folk culture in order to keep themselves in power (Rohlehr 1980). In light of this and the often economically desperate situation for artists, it is no surprise that some of the most talented West Indian writers (e.g., E. Kamau Brathwaite) seek "cultural asylum" in countries like the United States. As one writer criticizes this situation:

> Today the wealth is not sugar, or cocoa, it's the best of our creative genius creamed off and borne away to other societies. An appalling number of our creative artists live outside of the region. Caribbean artists function in exile, apart from their native culture of renewal and continuity. The folk arts cannot properly develop in isolation from what might be called the intellectual arts. Without the regenerative effect of creative expression taken to its highest possible peaks, the folk arts are in danger of standing still, turning into museum exhibits in a glass case. (Hodge 1980: 30)

Given this dimension of West Indian migration to the industrialized countries, it is easy to appreciate how this outflow of intellectuals and artists affects all levels of society and national development of these countries negatively.

MUSIC

Probably best known and best liked for their contribution to culture are the musical traditions from the English-speaking Caribbean: reggae, calypso, and soca. Caribbean music, in particular reggae and dub music, has decisively influenced the development of American music styles such as hip-hop and rap.

Largely forgotten today is one of the America's outstanding pantomimists and comedians who also recorded music, Bert Williams. Williams, who came to the United States in 1885 from the British West Indies at age eleven, rose to become the probably most widely revered vaudeville performer. Vaudeville was a theatrical form of entertainment that can be most closely compared to the stand-up comedy of our times. It was usually made up of several individual acts by a single entertainer or group of entertainers, such as acrobats, musicians, comedians, jugglers, magicians, and trained animals. It was the most popular form of American entertainment during the early twentieth century. Williams, a light-skinned creole, had to perform in the style of the day, blackface makeup, which emphasized his racial background. He never poked fun at his "race," but rather found hilarity in situations that might apply equally to any poor folk. Williams was the only black vaudevillian who could appear on an all-white bill in Washington, D.C., and in 1904 he played a command performance before King Edward VII. In his art he was very

much a pioneer and, in the judgment of one observer, of all the black performers who followed him, "none has the appeal or the personality of the
man who made vaudeville audiences accept black performers and, coinci-
dentally, proved they could be better than many white entertainers of the
era" (Slide 1994: 556).

Reggae

Without doubt, the most influential Caribbean music has been reggae
music. Interestingly, the origin of reggae owes a lot to American music.
Reggae's immediate predecessor, ska music, developed in the 1950s from a
Jamaican folk music style called mento and rhythm and blues (R&B), with
calypso, jazz, ballads, rock 'n' roll, Latin American dance music, and other
Jamaican folk music playing important supporting roles (White 1980). Particularly important at that time was the influence of U.S. musicians like Fats
Domino, Little Richard, Otis Redding, and Carla Thomas. In the 1960s,
under the increasing influence of the Rastafarian movement, ska developed
a slower tempo. This style, now also using Rastafarian protest and antisystem
lyrics, evolved into what became known as rocksteady.

Out of the already slower rocksteady beat developed in the late 1960s the
now typical reggae rhythm with delayed and overlapping rhythmical patterns,
using heavier bass and more pronounced drum lines:

Basically in reggae a half-note is added to the classic afterchord—one-
and-two-and-three-and-four-and becoming "one-anda-two-anda-three-
anda-four-anda." . . . Something like this had been done by U.S. R&B,
and rock and roll artists but the Jamaican drummer, continuing a rocksteady pattern, falls in between the beats, a more "sinuous" and less
"jumpy" rhythm being thereby produced. At the same time a piano or
organ often provides a ska or a mento effect playing at a quicker tempo,
one then has both slow and quick beats. Add a rocksteady bass rhyth-
mically developed, oftentimes operating contrapuntally to the vocal line
with more running and a dramatic observation of rests and the effect
is as if rhythm after rhythm were overlaid on one another. The
"croaking-lizard" second rhythm guitar often harmonizes and brings
into a closer relief the syncopated notes of the bass. Shakers, graters,
triangles and other percussion instruments complete the rhythm section. (White 1980: 9)

In recent years a variation of this elaborate styling, the dub style, has developed, which emphasizes the drum and bass, thereby turning the music into almost pure rhythm. These are often accompanied by disc jockey rhymes and poems, which closely resemble American-style rap music.

An indication of reggae's impact can be heard in Paul Simon's "Mother and Child Reunion," Johnny Nash's "I Can See Clearly Now," the J. Geil's Band's "Give It to Me," Stevie Wonder's "Master Blaster," Blondie's "The Tide Is High," and many other covers and originals by U.S. and British bands and artists like the Rolling Stones, Lauryn Hill, Ry Cooder, Grace Jones, Joan Armatrading, the Clash, the Police, the Fugees, and the Specials. In the 1980s and 1990s reggae got a boost in the United States from hits by widely recognized artists such as Big Mountain (a California-based multiethnic reggae group), Ziggy Marley and the Melody Makers, Shabba Ranks, Ini Kamoze, and Inner Circle. In the 1990s reggae also started to fuse with American indigenous music, notably Hawaiian music. In Hawaii this fusion is called Jawaiian reggae (the contraction for *Jamaican-Hawaiian*), reggae with a distinctly Hawaiian flavor. Most of the Jawaiian songs are remakes of recent and old songs done by local or British artists. In most cases, the quality of the music and the interpretation of the originals are good, and there appears to be a significant audience among the youth in Hawaii, as is the case in other Pacific countries.

The popularity of reggae in the United States has given rise to reggae and ska music festivals, some of them held annually. A popular festival guide lists about a dozen reggae festivals for the U.S. Northeast alone. Among these are the Sugarloaf Reggae Ski Bash in Kingfield, Maine, in early April; the Vermont Reggae Fest in Johnson, Vermont, in mid-July; the Reggae Festival in Washington, Massachusetts, in early September; and the Reggae on the Hudson in Kingston, New York, in mid-July. One particularly popular and growing regional event is the New England Reggae Festival in Escoheag, Rhode Island, which has been presented annually since 1990.

Although ska and reggae music have had some popularity in the United States, particularly as a cultural phenomenon spread by the late Bob Marley, they have never enjoyed the mass enthusiasm they have found in Europe, Africa, and South America. In many African countries, members of the Marley family enjoy a quasi-royal status and are hosted with diplomatic honors when touring or visiting. In the United Kingdom, the reggae scene is infinitely more vibrant and creative than in the United States. Surprisingly, even African Americans never fully subscribed to this musical form from the Caribbean. Similar to the rap music market, where they constitute a considerable portion of the target audience, reggae music is much more widely enjoyed among middle-class white American youths than among their black contemporaries. This lack of mass appeal may also explain why, unlike in Britain, in the United States—although there are a number of "home-grown" bands—there has not yet emerged a number of internationally known reggae bands such as the British bands UB40, Aswad, or Steel Pulse. Caribbean reggae artists such as Millie Small, Desmond Dekker, and Jimmy Cliff have each had one U.S. Top Forty hit, but by and large this music seems to have been more eagerly absorbed by other artists and musicians than by the general public.

Rap music, which emerged in the mid-1970s in Brooklyn and the South Bronx, New York, has become a much more popular musical genre. Not many people realize that it owes a lot of its development to the dub style and the Jamaican disc jockeys' (DJs) singing or reciting lyrics ("toasting") to it. However, in the United States they used the funkier styles of James Brown, Funkadelic, Sly and the Family Stone, and Chic over which they spoke in fast rhyming couplets. Originally inspired by early Jamaican sound-system DJs and dub producers such as U-Roy and Lee Perry, who experimented with and talked over reggae rhythms, South Bronx DJs Loveby Starski, Kool Herc, and others created an Americanized version of the music that drew more from these sources than from reggae. Nevertheless, the basic structure of the tunes closely resemble the Jamaican dub DJs.

Originally the role of the rapper was to keep the beat going with hand claps while DJs changed the records. Soon rappers developed extensive routines with lines of lyrics, slogans, double-dutch (jumping rope) rhymes, and call-and-response exchanges with the audience. By 1980 the hip-hop/rap culture crossed racial lines, as white acts like Ian Dury, Blondie, the Police, the Clash, and Tom Tom Club incorporated rap styles into their tunes. Later this cross-over was carried by such white groups as Aerosmith, the Beastie Boys, and Vanilla Ice. In the 1990s, Jamaican artists became influenced by the vitality of the rap style, which, like the dub style, progressively developed into a musical form dominated more by drum and bass. The influence of Jamaican DJs like Shabba Ranks, Shinehead, and Beenie Man speaks to this development.

As the posthumously released Doo-Bop, a jazz/hip-hop collaborative project between the late jazz legend Miles Davis and rapper Easy Mo Bee, proved, Afro-Caribbean styles have arrived in the most American of all music: jazz.

Calypso

One of the most recognizable musical styles from the English-speaking Caribbean is calypso music and, more recently, its somewhat faster offspring, soca. The word *calypso* itself possibly derives from "kaiso," which has its West African origin in the Hausa language, where it roughly means "bravo!" Calypso evolved as a mode of song during slavery, and its immediate origin lies in the sugar fields. Slaves were forbidden conversation in the fields, but allowed to sing because the overseers discovered that this increased their productivity. The slaves found that through the songs they could converse, plot revolts, voice their grievances, or simply spread gossip since their language was not understood by the overseers. Later the songs were sung during carnival time, when slaves were allowed to celebrate and dress up (masquerade) as comic versions of their masters and to mock the ruling elite.

In the first two decades of the twentieth century, calypso assumed all of its main features. Calypso singers took extravagantly boastful names like the Mighty Panther, Attila the Hun, or the Roaring Lion, and they often sang humorously about politicians, current events, and well-known public figures. They often retained a level of double meaning, ribald puns, and sarcasm, which were common during slavery times when songs were the only way of criticizing the masters with impunity. Since the 1930s calypso music has also been connected to the invention of the only original new instrument of this century, the steel pan, an instrument made from the top and/or bottom part of large metal oil drums.

In the 1930s Trinidadian calypso music spread to the United States. Paul Whiteman, an American jazz band leader, had a big hit with the calypso "Sly Mongoose." In the 1940s *National Geographic* magazine wrote about the popularity of this song: "Hum this song to an expatriate West Indian in New York's Harlem and watch his face light up at the voice from home" (Marden 1942: 740). Trinidadian calypsonians Attila the Hun and the Roaring Lion went to New York in 1934 to record for the record company Decca and received grand receptions by singer-actor Bing Crosby and Rudy Vallee, who played Lion's "Ugly Woman" on national radio.

During World War II calypso increased in popularity as a large number of GIs were based in Trinidad and had a chance to get to know the culture better. Among Trinidadians this presence was viewed with some ambivalence. In his song "Rum and Coca-Cola" the calypsonian Lord Invader commented on some Trinidadian women's response, and sang about both mother and daughter working for the American dollar, which was ironically made into a major hit in the United States by the white Andrew Sisters. Invader had to take the American entertainers to court to obtain composer's royalties. Rejection, however, worked both ways. In 1953 one writer described calypso as "primitive" and "less sophisticated" than the Brazilian samba (Allmon 1953: 64).

The artist most responsible for popularizing calypso among Americans is the singer and actor Harry Belafonte. At the age of eight, Belafonte, born in Harlem in 1927, moved from New York City to Kingston, Jamaica, where his mother had come from. Of these years in Jamaica, Belafonte has said: "I still have the impression of an environment that sang. Nature sang and the people sang too. The streets of Kingston constantly rang with the songs of piping peddlers or politicians drumming up votes in the lilting singsong of the island. I loved it" (Shaw 1960: 26). Nevertheless, Belafonte's years in Kingston were far from idyllic. In fact, he was often at odds with his schoolmates who ridiculed his clothes and foreign accent. Often he sat in class without listening to a word his teachers said.

He returned to New York City in 1940, now acutely aware of race and color discrimination. Upon his return, the family lived in a predominantly white and Hispanic community in New York City. To avoid unnecessary questioning by other children in the neighborhood, Harry and his lighter-skinned brother pretended to be from countries that the children did not immediately associate with black people. Belafonte explains their ploy the following way: "Here we were two Negro kids in a white neighborhood. The desire to belong was there. My brother . . . used to say he was Greek or Spanish. I said I was from Martinique. The kids nicknamed me 'Frenchy' " (Shaw 1960: 26–27). Nevertheless, he ended up in many street fights and soon ended his deception. Four years later Belafonte left school and served in the U.S. Navy from 1944 to 1946. Following that time he worked in New York's garment district, pushing dress carts in order to earn his living. Belafonte then went on to study acting at the New School of Social Research. His life's direction changed in 1949 when the owner of the Royal Roost, a Broadway jazz club, signed him for a two-week singing engagement, which was extended to twenty weeks. In mid-1950 he changed his song repertoire and investigated folk music at the Library of Congress, which led to his interpreting traditional melodies from Jamaica, Africa, Asia, and America. By 1956 Harry Belafonte was at the forefront of the calypso craze that gripped the country.

Belafonte's interpretations of calypso music between 1956 and 1959 won him great success and marked the height of his career. Some of his early hits included "Jamaica Farewell," "Mary's Boy Child," and his classic folk-based hit "Banana Boat Song." In 1956 his *Calypso* became the first album ever to sell 1 million copies, and it spent thirty-one weeks at the top of the musical charts in the United States. In fact, between 1956 and 1962 Belafonte's music was almost never absent from the album chart. For his successes and his promotion of calypso music, Belafonte is often called King of Calypso, a crown he wore only reluctantly despite the fame it won him. Although this is understandable from an American point of view, in the home country of calypso, Trinidad, this title would not be bestowed on him, since his lyrics and music are not typical calypsos, but just commercialized versions. In fact, in Trinidad and throughout the Caribbean a singer called "The Mighty Sparrow" is considered the currently undisputed ruler over the musical dominion of calypso.

Calypso music has found a permanent place in the cultural tapestry of the United States. This is clearly evident when it is used in popular children programs like Sesame Street.

Steel Pan Music

One of the few, and perhaps the only acoustic (not electrically amplified), new instruments invented in the twentieth century is the steel pan. Today this instrument can be found all over the United States; there are even steel pan ensembles in Japan.

The pan, as a steel pan is often referred to, is a rather unique instrument. Invented in Trinidad, it is cut off from the top of a 55-gallon oil drum. The bottom is hammered down like a pan, which is divided into sections, each of which gives a different pitch when played with a short drumstick.

The history of the instrument is as intriguing as its bell-like sound, which can be used to play jazz and classical music too. When the colonial government in 1884 outlawed the use of drums for fear of their power to call together and organize large groups of people in protest, Trinidadians developed the so-called "bamboo tamboo" bands. The instruments of these bands were bamboo poles of different sizes that the players would pound on the ground, thereby creating distinctive rhythms that identified each band. The Bamboo Tamboo bands were banned in the late 1930s for similar reasons as the drum, but under the pretext that they damaged the road surfaces. Deprived of their traditional rhythmic instruments, Trinidadians started to use any objects they could find—old car parts, empty oil barrels, and even garbage can lids. They used these materials and instruments to form the so-called iron bands that marched, especially during carnival time, down the streets playing distinctive rhythms.

In the late 1930s, during a particularly rough iron band session, it was discovered that a dented section of barrel had produced a tone. Winston "Spree" Simon and Ellie Manette are usually credited with inventing the steel pan. In fact, Manette was the first to dish out a pan and give it its mature form. Today, studies have been conducted at the University of the West

Indies on how to improve the sound of the steel pan. The best instruments are still made by hand.

As in the Caribbean, steel pan bands are particularly in demand during the carnival season, playing calypso and other music. But, it is by no means unusual to find a single steel pan musician playing Christmas carols in public (for example, in the subway stations of New York City).

Punta Rock

Perhaps the cultural achievement of Garinagu people with the widest reach is punta rock music, a rich and creative blend of all the cultural traditions to which the Garinagu are heir. In addition to the Amerindian and African elements, early French, Spanish, and English folk music contribute to this musical heritage. Other Afro-Caribbean peoples, such as Haitians, Jamaicans, and Barbadians, have also contributed to the Garifuna musical stock. As a musical style, punta rock reminds the listener of other styles such as merengue, salsa, calypso, and reggae. Hundreds of popular songs are sung by the Garifuna today, and most are accompanied by particular dance forms and drum beats. The most popular dance, performed at wakes, holidays, parties, and other social events, is the punta. Dancing as couples, men and women try to outdo each other with their sexy dance movements and style. The song lyrics are usually written by women. Punta rock, a derivative of the traditional dance, has a particularly strong market in Los Angeles and is riding along with the current revival of Latin music in the United States. Los Angeles–based distributors are benefitting from growing sales, dances, shows, and radio and television promotions.

The well-known Belizean punta rock singer Andy Palacio has recorded more songs than any other artist in Belize and Central America and is the largest-selling Belizean musical artist in Los Angeles and Belize. Other punta rock artists who have become big hits in Los Angeles are Mohobob Flores and Brother David Obi. The 1997 Belizean album *Celebration* features contributions by various artists.

FESTIVALS

In the mainstream press and in much of the public, Caribbean people are often described one-dimensionally as "happy-go-lucky." Without doubt, this is a way of misrepresenting others. Like any other group, West Indians like to celebrate, and like many other immigrant groups, they have also made their mark on American society with their festivities and parades.

Carnival

One of the best-known events organized and celebrated by West Indian immigrants to the United States are the carnival celebrations. There are over sixty Caribbean carnivals worldwide, and at least forty cities in the United States (among them Atlanta, Baltimore, Boston, Cambridge, Chicago, Dallas, Detroit, Hartford, Houston, Jacksonville, Miami, New York, Oakland, Orlando, Philadelphia, Rochester, San Francisco, Tallahassee, Washington, D.C., and Westchester) hold annual carnival celebrations which imitate the festival held in the carnival capital of the Caribbean, Trinidad and Tobago (Nurse 1999). Some spectators even travel from carnival to carnival, and for musicians and performers the increasing number of carnivals offers an opportunity for more or less permanent employment.

This festival has a long history. There are claims that it has roots in ancient Egyptian celebrations (Nehusi 2000). In medieval Europe, the Catholics engaged in feasting and revelry before the annual fast of Lent that begins on Ash Wednesday in February. These traditions were transplanted to the Caribbean, where they evolved into a festivity that both celebrated life and subtly criticized slavery. African-derived traditions of masking and parading were emulated and blended with the fancy masked balls of the Lenten festivals in Catholic Europe. Since 1962, the Trinidadian government has officially recognized the festival and supports it financially as an expression of national culture and a major tourist attraction.

The largest, most spectacular, and best-known Caribbean-style carnival in the United States is the annual West Indian Labor Day Parade in Brooklyn, New York. With hundreds of thousands, possibly as much as 2 million, spectators, the parade is one of the largest regularly scheduled street events in North America. Trinidadians and other West Indian immigrants brought with them the carnival tradition when they came to New York. In Harlem in the 1920s, they would get together to celebrate the event in houses and ballrooms. As its popularity grew during the following decades, these events became bigger as well. On one occasion over 5,000 revelers crowded the Renaissance Ballroom in Harlem, and many others had to be turned away for lack of space. Eventually organizers planned an outdoor festival and shifted the event from the pre-Lenten period in midwinter to the warmer months. The first street carnival was held in Harlem on Labor Day in 1947.

In 1964, after a small disturbance, the parade permit was revoked. Under the leadership of Rufus Gorin, a Trinidadian, a new attempt was made to revive the parade in Brooklyn, where large numbers of West Indians had settled. In concert with a small committee he headed, he was able to obtain a parade permit from the City of New York in 1967. The small committee evolved into the West Indian American Day Carnival Association (WIADCA), which today organizes and sponsors not only this parade but calypso, reggae and steelband, and music competitions, as well as a "kiddie carnival" behind the Brooklyn Museum.

Unlike most other New York ethnic festivals, the Caribbean carnival does not rely on a centralized structure. Although WIADCA obtains the permits, it operates more as a facilitator and coordinator than as a leading organizer. The various bands in the parade are organized privately, and, in fact, often their leaders are at odds with WIADCA about details. The bands are completely independent of and in competition with each other, and they form specifically to participate in the parade.

The band members in the parade dress in elaborate and colorful costumes and dance and prance to loud calypso and soca music as they proceed down Eastern Parkway, the parade route. Usually they are following a flatbed truck that carries a steelband, calypso group, or sound system playing recorded music. On and behind these trucks, people dance to the music. Each band may number between several dozen and up to about a hundred revelers, and each also features at least one or two (sometimes more) fantastic outfits, which are often small, one-person floats. In general, all costumes are coordinated, and the bands are loosely organized around themes. Thus, they may run under mottoes like "Caribbean Freedom," "Galactic Star Wars," "Splendors of the Islands," "Arawak Renaissance," or similar themes. All bands are judged by a panel of judges.

Nevertheless, the parade is not primarily a competition or even a race. In fact, the structure of the parade reflects the lack of a central authority involved in its planning. Usually it starts at about noon with a group of dignitaries (business leaders, sponsors, politicians) and city officials, who march down the route. They are followed by a group of beauty contest winners. Neither of these groups is the main attraction of the parade, and they are largely ignored by the spectators, who are busy mingling, eating, and drinking. The action starts when the bands and the flatbed trucks arrive. They move in a stop-and-go fashion, sometimes changing their directions, while everyone keeps on dancing. Depending on the energy that flows from the bands and the music, the crowd of spectators becomes involved through dancing and cheering the bands. Unlike other ethnic parades, the carnival is rather informal and rarely promotes any individuals (e.g., politicians, community leaders) or any political interests of the West Indian community. Although the other parades are largely about leadership, the dramatic structure of the Caribbean Carnival in Brooklyn is essentially leaderless (Kasinitz 1995). Nevertheless, political leaders such as Ed Koch or Jesse Jackson have made brief appearances at the periphery of the carnival—a way for WIADCA to pay tribute and express gratitude to political supporters of the event.

For English-speaking Caribbeans, the carnival is an important tool for creating ethnic identity in the United States and marks the presence of black West Indians from various countries. Although it is dominated by English-speaking Caribbean immigrants, it also offers space for participation by other Caribbean language groups (e.g., the Haitians and Dominicans). Attempts have been made to broaden the essentially Trinidadian character of the carnival by adding reggae nights and a Haitian night during the week and the weekend preceding the parade.

Although the main event is largely neglected by the mainstream media, for the Caribbean American community, this is the most important statement of its pan-Caribbean identity—that is an event uniting all the different nationalities of the region. Both the relative inability or unwillingness of the carnival parade to lend itself as a political platform and its status as a pan-Caribbean event underline that it stands apart from the everyday experiences of the West Indian community. In other words, more than any other ethnic minority, West Indians use their parade to proclaim and celebrate their difference rather than use it to claim their recognition as a legitimate part of U.S. society. In this attitude lies a profound and peculiarly mixed sense of modesty and self-awareness.

Phagwah

In a number of U.S. cities with large Caribbean populations of Indian origin, *phagwah* has emerged as a major public celebration. *Phagwah*, known in India as Holi, marks the beginning of new year in the Hindu calendar and also stands for the victory of good over evil and the conquest of sensual values by spiritual values. The festival falls on the first full moon in March and involves traditions such as people dusting each other with colored talc powder (*abeer*) and dowsing each other with scented water to symbolize the color and fragrance of the new season. The *phagwah* parade in New York, organized in 1986, brings together over 50,000 Indo-Caribbeans singing and marching with banners proclaiming "Victory to Shri Ram." It is the biggest Indo-Caribbean contribution to New York's many parades and, arguably, to all cultural events in the city in general. Indeed, in 1991 Queens borough president Claire Shulman pronounced March Phagwah Month. Although the New York parade is the biggest, cities such as Jersey City in New Jersey also feature annual *phagwah* parades.

The New York *phagwah* parade is held in the Richmond Hill section of Queens and proceeds from 133rd Street and Liberty Avenue to Smokey Park. Two hours or so before the parade's start, the assembly of the street performers and floats begins in front of the popular Guyanese bakery and restaurant Sybil's. At Smokey Park the parade dissolves into a program of music, dance, and drama featuring various aspects of Indo-Caribbean arts and culture. Similar to the carnival parade, the *phagwah* parade also features about fifteen colorfully decorated floats. Dusting each other with *abeer*, men and women dance on the street, mixing *phagwah* songs and other Indian rhythms. The parade transforms Liberty Avenue into an open air arena, and the mood becomes so festive that at times even the police abandon its own parade rules. At its peak, the parade becomes an undulating sea of color with thick, colorful dust clouds hovering over the revelers. Indeed, *phagwah* in New York has become such an enticing event that even Indians from India express their admiration. As the well-known Indian film director and producer Ajay Sharma in his message to the cheering crowd gathered for the 1991 parade put it: "When I left Bombay a few days ago I thought I would miss Holi, but today, playing Phagwa with you I feel totally at home" (*Global Times* 1991: 19).

Since the parade always occurs in March, the weather often stands in contrast to the cotton and silk fineries that many of the revelers wear in disregard of the cold. This parade adds color to the gray, wintry March days in New York and allows everybody to look ahead to spring.

Garinagu Festivities

Most Garinagu festivities occur in very private settings and lack the bright and public splendor of carnival or *phagwah*. Their religion, like others from the Caribbean, is a form of ancestor remembrance, respect, and even worship. Its roots are not African, but Amerindian, although there is a strong influence from contacts with African-derived cultures in the Caribbean and later the United States. Their religion serves to unite families, even after death, and to preserve some of the values concerning behavior, to monitor that behavior, and to give psychological support when people are under stress, including serious and terminal illness, when other treatments are ineffective. Some of the music and dance related to their religious rites survive in New York, although much of the original ceremony has been altered.

CONTINUITY, CHANGE, AND FUSION

Unlike with many other ethnic minorities in the United States, several aspects of the culture of the English-speaking Caribbean population do not seem to get assimilated (in the sense of diluted), but they seem to become even more pronounced. One of these aspects is the sense among West Indians that they are part of a larger region. Most English-speaking Caribbean immigrants arrive in the United States with only a national consciousness. If they are aware of or informed about other Caribbean countries, it is mostly other English-speaking Caribbean islands. However, in the process of meeting other Caribbeans and through pan-Caribbean events, they gradually come to appreciate the cultural and ethnic closeness of other Caribbean migrants in the United States, including those from the Dutch-, Spanish-, or French-speaking countries. Another example of what might be called ethnic reinforcement can be seen in the fact that a large portion of the Indo-Caribbean population turns to religion and the preservation of Indian traditions in a way unprecedented in their Caribbean home countries and India itself.

Much of this ethnic reinforcement may have to do with the fact that Caribbean people in the United States face a double invisibility—they are both foreigners and dark skinned. In addition, they find themselves in a land that, despite all the rhetoric to the contrary, is deeply steeped in nonreligious ways of life. Both factors join forces in denying West Indians in the United States equal opportunities and recognition of their ethnic difference. A return to traditional value systems and the emergence of a pan-Caribbean identity therefore appear to be the natural way for them to compensate for this double invisibility.

REFERENCES

Albuquerque, Klaus de. 1999. "In Search of the Big Bamboo." *Transition* 77 (March): 48–57. Available at www.cofc.edu/~klausda/bamboo.htm.

Alleyne, Mervyn. 1989. *Roots of Jamaican Culture*. London: Pluto Press.

Allmon, Charles. 1953. "Happy-Go-Lucky Trinidad and Tobago." *National Geographic* (January): 35–75.

Burnett, Paula, ed. 1986. *The Penguin Book of Caribbean Verse in English*. London: Penguin.

Caribbean Research Center. 1995. Oral History Project. Unpublished interview with Ms. Evelyn John, conducted by Wayne Jones, May 18.

Caribbean Research Center. 1996. Oral History Project. Unpublished interview with Dr. Hilton White, conducted by Wayne Jones, June 12.

Caribbean Research Center. 1997. Oral History Project. Unpublished interview with Rev. George A. Lloyd, conducted by Wayne Jones, August 22.

Global Times. 1991. "Phagwa Celebrations in N.Y. Makes Milestone Proclamation." *Global Times* (March-April 1991): 18–19.

González, Nancie L. 1992. "Garifuna Settlement in New York: A New Frontier." In *Caribbean Life in New York City: Sociocultural Dimensions*, ed. Constance R. Sutton and Elsa M. Chaney, 138–146. Staten Island, NY: Center of Migration Studies.

Gregory, Steven. 1992. "Afro-Caribbean Religions in New York City: The Case of Santería." In *Caribbean Life in New York City: Sociocultural Dimensions*, ed. Constance R. Sutton and Elsa M. Chaney, 287–302. Staten Island, NY: Center of Migration Studies.

Hodge, Merle. 1980. "Articulating a Caribbean Aesthetic: The Revolution of Self-Perception." *Caribe* (Report: Caribbean Expressions Festival I): 24–31.

Homiak, John P. 1998. "Dub History: Soundings on Rastafari Livity and Language." In *Rastafari and Other African-Caribbean Worldviews*, ed. Barry Chevannes, 127–181. New Brunswick, NJ: Rutgers University Press.

Lewis, William F. 1993. *Soul Rebels: The Rastafari.* Prospect Heights, IL: Waveland Press.

Magill, Frank N., ed. 1984. *Critical Survey of Poetry.* Vol. 1. Englewood Cliffs, NJ: Salem Press.

Marden, Luis. 1942. "Americans in the Caribbean." *National Geographic* (June): 723–758.

Melwani, Lavina. 1995. "What Are over 200,000 Guyanese Hindus Doing in New York State?" *Hinduism Today* 95–08 (August).

Melwani, Lavina. 1997. "No Place Called Home." *Little India* (October).

Nehusi, Kimani S. K. 2000. "The Origins of Carnival: Notes from a Preliminary Investigation." In *Ah Come Back Home: Perspectives on the Trinidad and Tobago Carnival*, ed. Ian Isidore Smart and Kimani S. K. Nehusi, 77–103. Washington, D.C.: Original World Press.

Nurse, Keith. 1999. "Globalization and Trinidad Carnival: Diaspora, Hybridity and Identity in Global Culture." *Cultural Studies* 13 (4): 661–690.

Ramadar, Frankie B. 1993. "First Generation Caribbean East Indian Americans and Voluntary Community Participation." In *The East Indian Diaspora: 150 Years of Survival, Contributions and Achievements*, ed. Tilokie Depoo (with Prem Misir and Basdeo Mangru), 137–144. Cypress Hills: East Indian Diaspora Press.

Redeker Hepner, Tricia, and Randal Hepner. 1999. " 'Take These Shackles Away, Lord'—Gender, Community, and Change among the Rastafari of New York City." Paper presented at the West Indian Migration to New York: Historical, Contemporary, and Transnational Perspectives Conference, Research Institute for the Study of Man, April 16–17.

Rohlehr, Gordon. 1980. "Articulating a Caribbean Aesthetic: The Revolution of Self-Perception." *Caribe* (Report: Caribbean Expressions Festival I): 7–15.

Sanders, Etta. 1997. "N.Y. City Home for a New Immigrant Church." *National Catholic Reporter* (January 17).

Shaw, Arnold. 1960. *Belafonte: An Unauthorized Biography*. Philadelphia: Chilton.

Slide, Anthony. 1994. *The Encyclopedia of Vaudeville*. Westport, CT: Greenwood Press.

Strozier, Matthew. 1997. "West Indian Day Parade: Indo-Caribbeans Play Minor Role." *India in New York* (September 5). Available at www.indiain newyork.com/iny090597/celebrations/westind2.html.

Sunshine, Catherine A., and Keith Warner, eds. 1998. *Caribbean Connections: Moving North*. Washington, D.C.: Network of Educators on the Americas.

Trabold, Robert. 1990. "A Festive Caribbean Immigrant Community in New York City: A Self Image." *Migration World* 18 (1): 18–23.

Turner, Terisa E. 1994. "Rastafari and the New Society: Caribbean and East African Feminist Roots of a Popular Movement to Reclaim the Earthly Commons." In *Arise Ye Mighty People! Gender, Class, and Race in Popular Struggle*, ed. Terisa E. Turner, 9–55. Trenton: Africa World Press.

Watkins-Owens, Irma. 1996. *Blood Relations. Caribbean Immigrants and the Harlem Community, 1900–1930*. Bloomington: Indiana University Press.

White, Garth. 1980. "Reggae—A Musical Weapon." *Caribe* (December): 6–10.

Wint, Carl. 1970. "Hundreds Seek the Coffin and Crows." *Daily Gleaner*, October 29.

Yawney, Carole. 1994. "Rasta mek a trod: symbolic ambiguity in a globalizing religion." *In Arise Ye Mighty People! Gender, Class, and Race in Popular Struggle*, ed. Terisa E. Turner, 75–83. Trenton: Africa World Press.

Woman in Carnival costume. Courtesy of Akira Tomita.

Carnival band. Courtesy of Akira Tomita.

Caribbean barber shop in Queens, New York.

Colin Powell giving a speech at the University of the West Indies fundraising Gala Dinner 2000, New York City.

Caribbean restaurant in Queens, New York.

Steelpan players. Courtesy of Akira Tomita.

Patrick Ewing (right), Jamaican-born basketball player for the New York Knicks.
Photo: Everybody's/Mitchell Layton.

Organizer of the annual Labor Day parade Carlos Lezama and publisher Hermann
Hall. Photo: Everybody's/Hayden Roger Celestin.

Marcus Garvey depicted on a stained-glass window in St. Mark's Church, Brooklyn, New York. Photo: Everybody's/Lloyd Patterson.

New York Councilwoman Una Clarke, Jamaican Prime Minister P. J. Patterson, and guests. Photo: Everybody's/Donovan Gopie.

The Roaring Lion (left) receives the Lifetime
Achievement Award from Trinidadian American
actor Sullivan Walker at the 1993 Everybody's
Caribbean Magazine Calypso Awards held
in New York.
Photo: Everybody's/Lloyd Patterson.

Congresswoman Shirley Chisolm and President Jimmy Carter at Camp David, 1979.
Photo: Everybody's.

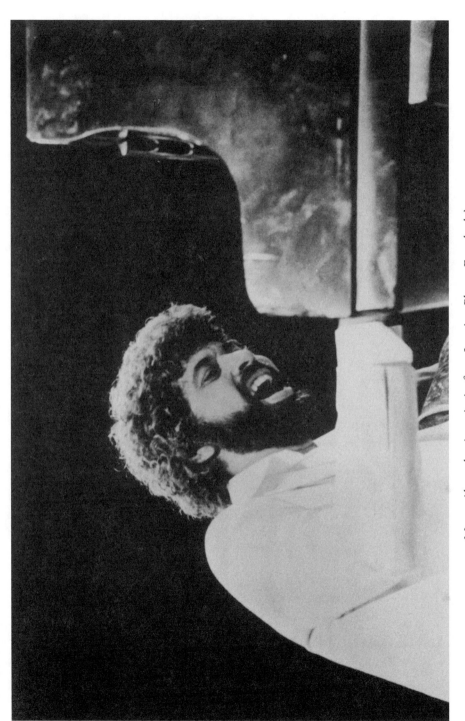

Monty Alexander, jazz pianist from Jamaica. Photo: Everybody's.

Phagwah Parade 2000, Queens, New York.

West Indian variety store in Queens, New York.

Singer/Actor/Philanthropist Harry Belafonte at a fundraising dinner for the University of the West Indies. New York City (2000).

Rastafarian reggae singer Luciano during a concert in New York's Central Park, with elaborate stage decoration depicting Rastafarian iconography.

Calypsonian "The Mighty Sparrow" and a young admirer, New York City.

Labor Day Carnival parade on the Eastern Parkway, Brooklyn, New York.

Children continuing the tradition during
Carnival, Brooklyn, New York.

Children Carnival behind the Brooklyn Museum, Brooklyn, New York.

5

Family Networks

The decision to migrate often requires that families are, at least temporarily, separated from each other and only after some time find it possible to reunite. This chapter explores the various consequences of this separation and the ways West Indian migrants have grappled with such a situation.

FROM HOUSEHOLDS TO NETWORKS

Generally as people move from one place to another, they experience dislocation of a material or psychological nature. Almost always it has an influence on their relationships. There may be a disruption in the family structure, for example, or a loss of financial resources and psychological consequences. They may have to leave a house or car behind when moving. Psychological costs of the migration experience may occur in feelings of powerlessness and alienation. The sudden absence of friends, relatives, or other social relationships can cause severe traumatic effects, particularly on younger children.

In most cases, West Indian families moved not as complete units to the United States, but with perhaps the father or the mother going first and the child or children following eventually. As a consequence, the head of families changes in about a third of all Caribbean migrant families from the male to the female (Barrett 1985: 56). The fact that women often found it easier to secure employment meant that in many cases the husband was not the major breadwinner, a situation that easily results in feelings of loss of self-esteem. In other cases, when husbands are not able or willing to follow their wives to the United States, the separation becomes permanent and can lead to divorce. A father without enough money may feel that his children no longer need him. In other cases, however, adjusting to the new environment can strengthen the relationships. The need to do things together as a family unit can forge stronger relationships.

Another dimension in which the family structure can be affected concerns the relationship between parents and children. While the parents may worry about leaving the support of their extended family, the young immigrants appreciate the new-found freedom of a more open and diverse society. For them, migrating may mean new options for self-expression and self-improvement.

The American social welfare system may work against the traditional norms of child rearing. Many parents are accustomed to physically disciplining their children; the fact that this is not accepted in the United States can become a serious point of conflict and estrangement between child(ren) and parent(s) (Mathelier 1990). Not knowing how to deal with their child's disobedience in any other way and not daring to risk the involvement of the authorities (e.g., police or social service) may leave some parents with a feeling of powerlessness and lack of control over their children. Still, we should not overestimate this problem since about 60 percent of Caribbean immigrants claim that they have a better relationship with their children in the United States, although 63 percent in one survey also said that their children were better behaved in the home country (Barrett 1985).

Some children are left behind in the home country because their parents are too poor to support them. In such cases, the children often stay behind for extended periods of time. And some even abandon their children, leaving them in the care of a grandmother or uncle in the home country. Tanya Williams, a twenty-five year-old Jamaican woman, expresses the psychological scars that result from such abandonment: "I was a small child [when my mother migrated] and I just couldn't understand why [she did not visit]. She only got a chance to come back when I was a teenager when I no longer felt any attachment towards her" (quoted in Pragg 1999). Small children often experience such a devastating situation as betrayal and this may become a lifetime burden for them. Worse, the kin in whose care a child is left may not be capable and some children even run the danger of being sexually molested by such caregivers.

Separation stress must not be underestimated. Bernice Frazer of the Department of Child and Adolescent Psychiatry at Kings County Hospital in New York City points out, "Ninety-five percent of the children we see have migrated from the West Indies. They are from homes where one or both parents are absent" (quoted in Pragg 1999). The children resent the separation and are unwilling to subordinate themselves to the guidance of parents who left them. The psychological costs of migration have not yet been explored and are often unacknowledged or misdiagnosed (Duval-Harvey 1990).

Nevertheless, kinship relations in West Indian "international families" ought to be understood in terms of a social network rather than a household, divided or not. In the English-speaking Caribbean, "families" are flexible, fluid forms of kinship rather than stable "nuclear families" with firm boundaries as they are commonly known in the United States. Consider the following scenario, which shows how international kin connections work (cf. Ho 1993).

This family—let us call them the Browns—has family members throughout the United States, but particularly in New Jersey, New York, and Texas. Steffanie Brown left St. Lucia for Washington, D.C., in 1969. At that time she was twenty-three years old and had two children (ages one and two) from her first marriage, which had ended in divorce. The father of her two children did not support her, and although she had completed her secondary education, the bleak job prospects in St. Lucia compelled her to migrate. While living with her oldest brother, a dental surgeon, in Washington, D.C., she worked as a domestic for an American family and through evening classes got a secretarial degree and found work with the St. Lucia Tourist Board in New York City, where another of her brothers lived.

Although her decision to migrate made good economic sense, it disrupted her family life considerably. She was not able to take her two children with her, and she was able to migrate only because her parents agreed to "mind" them for a while. Five years went by before she was able to send for them. Around this time, in 1975, Steffanie met Gene Brown, a Barbadian who had been in the United States for almost ten years. Gene, who had a business degree from New York University, at that time considered a job offer as an investment banker in Los Angeles and hoped to persuade Steffanie to move there with him. In 1976 they moved to Los Angeles and married; Steffanie later gave birth to their daughter, Michelle. A few years later, while Michelle was still young, Steffanie decided that she needed to acquire a degree in business administration to improve her earning power. Since she could not leave Michelle in the care of her other two children, she had to organize another "child-fostering" or, as West Indians often call it, a "child-minding" arrangement. Gene's mother, grandmother, and younger sister, Barbara, agreed to raise Michelle for a while. Although Barbadian, Gene's kin lived in the U.S. Virgin Islands, where they had migrated several years before. Michelle moved to the Virgin Islands where she was doted on by her paternal great-grandmother, grandmother, and young aunt.

The situation changed yet again six years later. Steffanie's two other children were almost finished with school, and Steffanie needed someone in the home to be responsible for Michelle while she and Gene were pursuing demanding full-time jobs. At the same time, Barbara, Gene's younger sister in the U.S. Virgin Islands, wanted to pursue an education as a nurse in the United States. Thus, Barbara was invited to migrate from the Virgin Islands and to live in the Brown household in Los Angeles, where she attended school and looked after Michelle.

This example of the Brown family network gives a good idea about the intensive and extensive nature of family relations. Migration and international family networks are part of Caribbean people's life. Contact between the different branches and members of such a transcontinental network are regular, either by mail or, more often, by phone, email, and travel. In some instances, the contact may even be direct and personal, as in this example:

> We lived on New York Avenue. A close family member lived two doors down with her husband. Across the street lived a couple of West Indians, and at St. John's Place my aunt and uncle lived with their son. . . . Down the block lived my other aunt . . . and half a mile away . . . my uncle and his wife and their three children. It was very much a family atmosphere. We used to gather together and play. (quoted in Olwig 1999: 14)

Here the neighborhood and the host country became almost a new home country, with close attachments.

Nevertheless, it is important to realize that there are notable differences in their social life between New York City, where the largest group of Caribbean immigrants lives, and other cities in the United States, where only smaller West Indian communities exist. Life in New York is dense in kin relationships and relationships with "home-fellows." Social life in Los Angeles is much less intense, at least as far as mingling with family members or fellow West Indians is concerned. As one Trinidadian migrant now residing in L.A. explains it:

> One of the reasons I left Brooklyn was my circle of friends was becoming too large. They were taking up all my time, and I didn't have time for other pursuits. I like to write. Short stories. I was doing too much socializing. My house was always open. . . . People would call me up

in the night and come across. So, I came here [to Los Angeles] to cut down on socializing. But I like to know it's there. I wouldn't have come out here unless I knew there was a West Indian reference group. I mightn't mix with them as often as I did back home in Brooklyn, but . . . (quoted in Ho 1991; 112)

Another West Indian resident in Los Angeles makes a similar observation about the intensity of West Indian social life in New York:

"Fetes" have always been a way of life for me. I'm a partying type of guy. In fact, in New York, we used to give parties to the point where I was thinking seriously of quitting my job. I used to make good money throwing parties. New York is a partying place. It's a way of life. . . . If you give a party out here and the neighbors complain, the cops come and close down the party in a minute. Because you find that people out here do not have that partying spirit they do back East. (quoted in Ho 1991: 113)

What these quotations also demonstrate is the extent to which the private lives of many West Indian migrants are determined by their social lives. While one of them changed his location to an environment less densely populated with other Caribbean migrants, the other actually considered making his pastime of partying into a profession.

West Indians also travel back and forth between their home country and the United States for various reasons: serious illness or a funeral of a close relative, a wedding, or a family reunion, for example. Under normal circumstances, however, English-speaking migrants return to the home country to get back in touch with their roots and "recharge" themselves in ways that they do not find possible in the United States. For the Trinidadians, for example, the carnival and Christmas seasons are favorite times to visit home. As one of them observes, in Trinidad there are certain freedoms not available in the United States, especially for a black man—for example, joking with the police or even teasing them is possible in Trinidad, but not in the United States. In Trinidad, no one is arrested for drinking in the streets or other minor infractions, particularly during the carnival, when everybody is in a partying mood. That kind of personal freedom and relaxation is important for West Indians, who generally grow up in a more carefree society: "I go home every Carnival. How you mean? I can't miss dat! You know any medicine de doctor could give me to make me happy besides dat? Dat's the greatest ting in the world, man! You making joke or what? Talking about

Carnival in Trinidad, boy? Sweet too bad! Rum drinking and ting!" (quoted in Ho 1991: 124). The exuberance with which these and most other West Indian migrants praise the recreational effects of visiting their home country and the excitement that grips most of them when they travel back home speak volumes about this experience.

Because the United States and the Caribbean are so near, traveling is often much more affordable than has been the case with South American, African, or Asian immigrants. For Caribbean immigrants, the proximity of "home" and their more marginal position in this country leads to an ambiguous situation. In their case it is therefore often more appropriate to speak of circular or repeat migration (cf. Pessar 1997). They are, in other words, less likely than other immigrant groups to establish a new life independent and irrespective of their roots.

For countries in the Caribbean the regular visits by their expatriates have become important sources of income. The Trinidad carnival, for example, attracts between thirty and forty thousand visitors each year. Both tourists and expatriates spend an estimated $30 million during the carnival (Nurse 1999).

An almost carnevalesque exuberance can be seen when West Indians are traveling back home—to their "yard," as Jamaicans say—before, during, and after the flight. While the large majority consists of decent and hard-working people, often there are also a number of travelers who display a loud and cheerful attitude, which can be seen in their entire outward appearance, sometimes clearly overdressed for a journey, or decked out with ostentatiously displayed and often oversized gold jewelry, carrying technical gadgets or hi-fi equipment for relatives back home and an obligatory cellular phone on the waist. While still humbly lining up at the check-in counter at the U.S. airport, some get increasingly worked up as they approach their home island, which upon disembarkation or while waiting in the customs inspection line may end in half-loudly uttered complaints about the "bad service," the "unnec-essary hold-up," or even the heat. The locals, half-disgusted and half-agreeing, usually, dismiss such attitudes as foreign-mindedness and interpret it as a measure of alienation from the ways in the home country.

REMITTANCES AND RETURN MIGRATION

Given the frequency with which they travel "back home," it is not sur-prising that a large number of English-speaking Caribbean migrants return to their home country permanently to retire. Often they have acquired prop-erty in their home country to build a house, or they make sure that an already existing home remains within the family. Remittances (e.g., money sent back home) and return migration show the extent to which immigrants from the English-speaking Caribbean regard their residence in the United States as temporary. In addition, many move back and forth between the United States and their home country. Thus, they become members of a new kind of community, one with a "home" in more than one country.

Remittances were a feature in the Caribbean from the very beginning. During colonial times, they usually came from the Caribbean and were profit transfers to Britain. It is worth remembering, though, that even then, the direction of remittances was not always out of the Caribbean. In the eighteenth and nineteenth centuries, people spoke of the "remittance man," usually a ne'er-do-well who was sent to the colonies to straighten out his life. In these cases, the embarrassed families sent money from England to maintain and, probably, keep him in the colonies.

Since English-speaking Caribbean people started to migrate within and out of the region, a long-standing tradition has developed that those who go abroad to work or improve themselves through education occasionally remit money or goods to their relatives at home. Between 1868 and 1875, for example, 5,654 money orders totaling almost $48,000 were sent from British Guiana to Barbados (Richardson 1985). At least £550,000, possibly much more than £1,000,000, were remitted from Panama to Barbados between 1906 and 1920. These monetary contributions were presumably sent by temporary migrant wage laborers who had found work. Eventually the postman's arrival in West Indian villages became a significant and eagerly awaited event, and even today the elderly occasionally grumble if their children who have gone abroad send back an "empty letter" (i.e., one not containing any money). On many islands the postal authorities are suspected of stealing money from envelopes, therefore those living abroad sometimes send cash to friends or neighbors with instructions to pass it on to someone else in order to prevent such theft.

Even now considerable amounts of money are sent back to relatives in the islands each year by West Indian migrants living in the United States, Canada, and the United Kingdom. These remittances are of great importance to a large number of people and are the primary source of currency on several of the smaller islands. In 1960 the value of remittances to Montserrat, for example, amounted to almost four times the earnings from cotton, Montserrat's main cash crop at that time (Bascom 1991). Over 35 percent of households on this island derived 70 to 100 percent of their income from cash from kin overseas. A similar situation existed in Nevis. To give a better idea of the magnitude and intensity of this flow of remittances, Table 5.1

Table 5.1
Remittances to Barbados and Jamaica, Selected Years
(millions of dollars)

Year	Barbados	Jamaica
1977	27.7	50.5
1979	35.3	94.6
1981	56.8	162.7
1983	41.0	128.5
1985	36.3	191.4
1987	43.1	–
Avg., 1977–85	39.5	120.0
Avg., 1980–85	43.8	147.2

Source: Bascom (1991:85).

documents the data for two islands, Barbados and Jamaica. In the 1999/2000 budget debate, Jamaica's minister of foreign affairs noted that the country earns $600 million per year from overseas Jamaicans (*Jamaica Gleaner* 1999). The amounts transmitted speak eloquently of the migrants' commitment to their home country. In recent years, the growth of the funds seems to have slowed somewhat.

There is an ongoing debate about whether these remittances improve the long-term perspectives of the recipients and if they help to develop the home country. Arguments can be found for both views—those who say there has been development due to remittances and those who say that most of this money is spent on immediate consumption. Indeed, most of the money appears to go to nonproductive expenses, for example, special events, luxuries, or day-to-day maintenance. As one author argued in the case of a St. Lucian fishing village he researched, these immediate expenses have created the "appearance of prosperity." However, this impression "is illusory, for the new houses and bright paint are not the result of economic growth in the area, but of remittances from London-based villagers" (quoted in Brana-Shute and Brana-Shute 1982: 281). In addition, remittances may create a psychological dependence that prevents people from assuming responsibility for their own life.

Some of this money is also invested in buying small land plots and building houses on them. This is important since owners of freehold plots are no longer under the former exploitative labor relationships. Along with these remittances a new sense of the real value of labor was also transmitted. Remittances have made a critical contribution to social change. Although migration is often debated only in terms of its effects on the host society, the issue of remittances and social change accompanying them demonstrates the extent to which its effects are also felt in the English-speaking Caribbean.

Even when these goods or money are not invested or saved, they still can make a valuable contribution to the everyday lives of the recipients. Particularly where unemployment is high and fertile land scarce, remittances can make the difference between abject poverty and relative survival. Thus, it has been estimated that on the tiny island of Saba between 1945 and 1965 an average of $3,000 per year per person was received and even this relatively large sum may only have been half of the total value of remittances received (Brana-Shute and Brana-Shute 1982).

Remittances are also a way of establishing a nest egg in the home country for the time that migrants decide to return home. In the case of Jamaica, it has been found that about half of the sources used as start-up capital in a local business venture are from overseas. In fact, personal savings made in the host country are the single largest source of start-up capital. Relatively little start-up capital is needed in most of the new businesses. Thus, in the tourist areas on the north coast, about half of the new ventures have a capital base of just $340–$7,400, and in the country's capital Kingston about half of the businesses started with only up to $1,100 (Chevannes and Ricketts 1997: 184). Establishing a business back home both strengthens and prepares the economic base for an eventual return, permanent or not, to the home country.

The remittances of West Indian and other immigrants in the United States have given rise to a small industry that transmits this money abroad. Particularly in the large metropolitan areas in New York, Florida, Texas, and California, hundreds of such businesses have been established. They are meeting a need that is not fulfilled by the domestic banking service or larger firms such as Western Union, American Express, or Deak International Limited, which apparently are not very interested in setting up branches in economically depressed neighborhoods.

Family reunions, an intermediate form between travel and permanent return, have become more popular and more elaborate. They provide an opportunity for both branches of a family network to meet back in the home country and to strengthen bonds and a sense of belonging.

RETURNING RESIDENTS

Return migration—the temporary or permanent settlement in their country of origin (or even in another Caribbean country)—has been an often overlooked aspect of migration from the beginning. Since the days of the construction of the Panama Canal, West Indian migrants returned in significant numbers to their homeland. For example, 28,000 Jamaicans returned from Central America between 1928 and 1934, and some 52,000 left the United Kingdom between 1965 and 1968.

In recent years, more returnees have been counted. In particular, those who moved to the United Kingdom in the 1950s and early 1960s and have now reached retirement age are returning home in large numbers. The same is true of those who have moved to the United States since the mid-1960s. As the number of returnees grows, they have started to receive attention from governments and scholars. Many West Indian countries have set up special units to facilitate this return, and in many countries the enormous increase in home building is explained in part by the latest wave of returnees.

Return migration picked up in the 1980s and 1990s. Between 1993 and mid-1999, for example, over 14,000 returning residents had registered with the Jamaican government's Returning Residents Facilitation Unit. Of these, 6,149 returned from the United Kingdom and 5,442 from the United States. However, because of the stipulated registration requirements the real number is certainly higher than this, and it is estimated that indeed over 20,000 returnees arrived in Jamaica over this time period. Jamaica's minister of foreign affairs pointed out in his presentation to the budget 1999/2000 debate that returning migrants are "a significant reservoir of financial and human resources, including scarce skills, which still remain in large measure, untapped" (*Jamaica Gleaner* 1999).

Almost all West Indian migrants will say that they are only temporarily in the United States. Indeed, when asked, perhaps 90 percent or more will say that they intend to return to their home country. Of course, not all of them will do so. Indeed, to some extent the intent to return home is simply a nostalgic impulse that creates a "myth of return" (Rubenstein 1982: 23). Nevertheless, the number of returning citizens is significant. According to one estimate, around 60 percent of all Caribbean emigrants will eventually return (Strachan 1983: 126).

It is interesting to take a closer look at those who return. A number of reasons can account for why an immigrant from the English-speaking Caribbean returns to his or her home country. In many cases, there seems to be a close emotional connection with their home country, sometimes because of a lack of acceptance in the host country. One interviewee asked if he felt different in the United States replied, "Yes, a foreigner. The U.S. has room for foreigners. It amazes me to see a Black Spanish speaking person be more accepted than a well educated Black American. The latter is not accorded the same treatment. There is some respect, but the person is not socially accepted" (quoted in Olwig 1999: 18). Apparently there is a certain exotic appeal in a black person with a different language or ethnic background, which is not seen in the case of African Americans and other English-speaking blacks.

Although initially emigration is a burden to the sending country, particularly when educated and wealthy individuals leave, many migrants who return improved their education and skills levels in the United States. A study of Guyanese return migrants found that 65 percent acquired a new skill or received a diploma or a degree; in fact, 22 percent completed a degree, 23 percent received a diploma, 11 percent a professional training, and the remaining 8 percent learned either nursing or a trade (cf. Strachan 1983: 130ff.). Of those who had returned, a relatively high number were dissatisfied because of food and other shortages, the political situation, the poor job situation, and/or the high cost of living. It is hardly surprising that nearly two-thirds of all return migrants intend to go abroad again.

CONCLUSION

West Indian migrants are more appropriately identified as birds of passage than as permanent and persistent resident aliens or even (i.e., if they assume U.S. citizenship) as resident citizens. This questions the common view of immigrants as a group that will gradually "become American," that is, become adapted to the American way of life and eventually be integrated into U.S. society. If English-speaking Caribbean immigrants remain attached to their home country and remigrate in relatively high numbers, a high identification with the American way of life is unlikely. Indeed, it may precisely be that a high degree of success (i.e., successful social and economic integration) becomes a motive to return to the home country, because it may allow the individual to live there comfortably despite the permanent economic crisis which may prevail.

Another important aspect is the question whether, in the face of the current and persistent economic crisis in many countries of the English-speaking Caribbean, returning migrants can play an influential and meaningful part as agents of development. The question is not only if they are able to ignite savings and investments that go beyond simple consumption of goods and services, but more fundamentally whether they will return to the Caribbean at all in sufficient numbers. The other question is whether, given their improved qualifications and job training, their skills will be in demand or whether they essentially will remain idle as overqualified applicants. In other words, it is good to have a trained brain surgeon around, but if there is no job opening, this person is unlikely to make a difference, notwithstanding the excellence of his or her achievement and training.

REFERENCES

Barrett, Ina R. 1985. "The Impact of the New York Immigration Experience on the Structure and Interrelationships of the Caribbean Immigrant Family." In *Establishing New Lives: Selected Readings on Caribbean Immigrants in New York City*, ed. Velta J. Clarke and Emmanuel Riviere, 44–64. Brooklyn, NY: Caribbean Research Center.

Bascom, Wilbert O. 1991. "Remittance Inflows." In *Migration, Remittances, and Small Business Development: Mexico and Caribbean Basin Countries*, ed. Sergio Díaz-Briquets and Sidney Weintraub, 73–99. Boulder, CO: Westview Press.

Brana-Shute, Rosemary, and Gary Brana-Shute. 1982. "The Magnitude and Impact of Remittances in the Eastern Caribbean: A Research Note." In *Return Migration and Remittances: Developing a Caribbean Perspective*, ed. William F. Stinner, Klaus de Albuquerque, and Roy S. Bryce-Laporte, 267–289. Washington, D.C.: Research Institute on Immigration and Ethnic Studies, Smithsonian Institution.

Chevannes, Barry, and Heather Ricketts. 1997. "Return Migration and Small Business Development in Jamaica." In *Caribbean Circuits: New Directions in the Study of Caribbean Migration*, ed. Patricia R. Pessar, 161–195. Staten Island, NY: Center for Migration Studies.

Duval-Harvey, Jacquelin E. 1990. "Mental Health and the Caribbean Immigrant." In *Proceedings of the Caribbean-American Family Conference: Issues and Implications for Public Policy*, ed. J. A. George Irish and Veronica N. Udeogalanya, 45–68. Brooklyn, NY: Caribbean Research Center.

Jamaica Gleaner. 1999. "14,000 Returning Residents Registered in Six Years." June 24.

Ho, Christine. 1991. *Salt-Water Trinnies: Afro-Trinidadian Immigrant Networks and Non-Assimilation in Los Angeles*. New York: AMS Press.

Ho, Christine. 1993. "The Internationalization of Kinship and the Feminization of

Caribbean Migration: The Case of Afro-Trinidadian Immigrants in Los Angeles." *Human Organization* 52 (1): 32–40.

Mathelier, George. 1990. "Nurturing Parenting versus Child Abuse: A Growing Concern in the Caribbean Community." In *Proceedings of the Caribbean-American Family Conference: Issues and Implications for Public Policy*, ed. J. A. George Irish and Veronica N. Udeogalanya, 28–31. Brooklyn, NY: Caribbean Research Center.

Nurse, Keith. 1999. "Globalization and Trinidad Carnival: Diaspora, Hybridity and Identity in Global Culture." *Cultural Studies* 13 (4): 661–690.

Olwig, Karen Fog. 1999. "Global Family Networks: The New York Experience in Comparative Perspective." Paper presented at the West Indian Migration to New York: Historical, Contemporary, and Transnational Perspectives Conference, Research Institute for the Study of Man, April 16–17.

Pessar, Patricia R. 1997. *Caribbean Circuits: New Directions in the Study of Caribbean Migration*. Staten Island, NY: Center for Migration Studies.

Pragg, Sam. 1999. "Children Hardest Hit in Migration Wave." In Internet Newsgroup reg.carib.

Richardson, Bonham. 1985. "The Impact of Panama Money in Barbados in the Early Twentieth Century." In *Nieuwe West-Indische Gids* 59 (1, 2): 1–26.

Rubenstein, Hymie. 1982. "Return Migration to the English-speaking Caribbean: Review and Commentary." In *Return Migration and Remittances: Developing a Caribbean Perspective*, ed. William F. Stinner, Klaus de Albuquerque, and Roy S. Bryce-Laporte, 3–34. Washington, D.C.: Research Institute on Immigration and Ethnic Studies, Smithsonian Institution.

Strachan, A. J. 1983. "Return Migration to Guyana." *Social and Economic Studies* 32 (3): 121–142.

6

The New Challenges: The Second Generation of English-Speaking Caribbean Immigrants

IDENTITY PROBLEMS

The children born in the United States to parents who had migrated there grow up in two worlds: the world of their parents and the world of American society. Both worlds transmit different sets of values to these second-generation immigrants, and to sort out which are most useful and appealing to them can create serious identity conflicts.

The large majority of West Indians pass on to their children who are born in the United States a focus on education, hard work, achievement, respect for elders, discipline, and a desire to maintain a West Indian identity. Like their parents, these young West Indians of the second generation face a social environment that tends to lump together all people of African ancestry. However, in contrast to their parents, they do not grow up in a multiethnic West Indian society where racism is much less pronounced than in the United States. Without this experience, the younger generation of English-speaking Caribbeans are lacking a psychological fallback position their parents' generation was able to rely on when faced with discrimination and racism. In other words, they do not have the comparison their parents can make with life in a society where black people are the majority and not as openly discriminated against as in the United States. Also, they do not have the outside markers, such as accent, which easily identify them as Caribbean American or, at least, not African American.

Generally, there are three different identity options that second-generation West Indians in the United States are choosing from. Usually they either choose a black American identity (ca. 40 percent), or an ethnic identity (ca.

30 percent) that emphasizes their West Indianness, or an "immigrant" identity (ca. 30 percent) (Waters 1994, 1999). Each of these options has a specific and identifiable attitude towards the central values of their parents' generation. For the second generation, however, their reaction to "race" becomes the factor that determines the extent to which these values are absorbed and internalized. "Race," in other words, becomes the most important component in the second generation's quest for identity.

Among the first group, who prefers to describe themselves as American and black, there is a pervasive sense of pessimism, stemming from the perception that racism in America is an overpowering barrier for them. Often these teens are harassed by the police and store owners, or even attacked on the streets if they venture into white neighborhoods. As a boy born in Grenada asserts: "It's the same discrimination, but they are more careful of the way they let it out. It's always there. You have to be very keen to pick it up. But it's always there. But it's just on a lower level now" (quoted in Waters 1999: 10). Consequently this group tends to identify more closely with poor African Americans with whom they routinely interact and who exert great influence over them. For example, the boys may start wearing flattops, baggy pants, and certain types of jewelry. If, however, they work studiously in school or in college and please their parents, their peers may say they are "acting white" or "not acting black."

The second group, who chooses an ethnic identity, tends to differ notably from these views. Although they understand how pervasive racism is, they nevertheless see hard work, education, and ambition as important. They agree with their parents that there are strong differences between West Indians and black Americans. And they usually hold positive views of the United States and their chances of succeeding. As one young man from Montserrat explains: "I felt like an American when I went overseas to Europe and talking to people there. I probably have never felt prouder to be an American. I think most of the time I feel proud to be an American when I am away though. Or when America as a whole has done something great. Most of the time though I think of myself as a West Indian" (quoted in Waters 1999: 14). On the other hand, this group also holds stereotypes about African Americans. Like their parents' generation, they often believe that African Americans give the "race" factor too much importance and do not try hard enough to improve themselves.

The third group, who exhibits an "immigrant" identity, identifies so closely with West Indians that they are not worried about how they are seen by other Americans, white or black. They feel very secure in their West Indianness, and indeed are often recent immigrants themselves. In fact, through their clothing, behavior, and accent, they signal to others that they are foreign born. As one young woman born in the United States explained her preference for Jamaican men: "Actually I want my children to be able to identify themselves as, you know, being, or having some kind of Jamaican culture still. I want them to frequent Jamaica. I want them to go back and forth. At one point I saw that I was strictly attracted to Jamaican men. I guess it was subconsciously, you know, I wanted to hold on to that culture so bad, that I would not allow myself to be interested in any other guys that were not Jamaican" (quoted in Vickerman 1999: 21). As black people from the Caribbean, they share certain concerns with black Americans about "race," but still make a point of distinguishing themselves. By and large, however, they adopt a rather relaxed attitude toward the issue of racial identity.

The way in which a youth from the West Indies or of West Indian parentage is likely to decide which of the identity models fits most closely depends to a large extent on his or her family's socioeconomic position. (Of course, we are talking here about an unconscious decision, which is also influenced by gender and environmental conditions such as the school district and the peers a youngster is "hanging out" with. But the chief influence derives from the family's social class position.) Thus, poor West Indians in urban areas may face a bleak future, which overshadows the parent message on achievement and in effect blocks it. One study found that 57 percent of middle-class teens identified ethnically, while only 17 percent of the working-class and poor teens identified ethnically (Waters 1999). Also, parents with more education and income were better able to afford better schools for their children. Some of the middle-class families in this study had moved from inner city neighborhoods to middle-class or suburban areas with better schools that had higher academic quality and are more likely to be racially integrated. Another factor are the social networks of the parents. Regardless of social class, parents who work with ethnic voluntary organizations or are heavily involved in their church seemed better able to transmit a strong sense of ethnic identity to their children.

While not denying their racial identity as black, these middle-class second-generation youth distance themselves from the underclass image common among many African Americans. They tend to hold on to their parents' view of West Indians as a hard-working, ambitious, and ultimately successful minority in the United States—whatever the reality behind this image may be. Frequently the second-generation West Indians point out that their West Indian status gave them drive and helped them to hone a work ethic which gave them a sense that they were "capable of much more" than other Americans (Bashi and Clarke 1999). In doing so, however, they are more ambiguous than their parents were, since they are more aware of the existing glass ceiling.

Their parents' generation, who grew up in the West Indies, regarded changing jobs often or perhaps even regularly as a strategy to gain greater opportunities in life. The second generation, having been socialized in the United States, is more likely to regard career changes as a failure rather than the pursuit of opportunity and economic flexibility. While for their parents coming to the United States meant a step up that had them prepared to hold jobs that most Americans might look down on, the second generation is less likely to see these jobs as desirable. They are interested in pursuing jobs outside the typical immigrant network connections—jobs that require higher education. At the same time, however, these jobs outside the positions typically held by blacks in this country are also often characterized by greater hurdles erected by racism and stereotypes. In other words, they are faced with the typical dilemma of blacks in this country who, for example, want to become members in a golf or tennis club or other previously exclusively white institutions and old boys networks, but still have to fight and work twice as hard as whites to get accepted there.

The more ambiguous position of the second-generation Caribbean Americans is aptly summarized by a second-generation West Indian woman:

> We are affected by race 'cause a lot of people just see us as Black Americans. So we're affected, you know, we're treated as far as I know, the same ways Black Americans are treated because we're clumped in that category. But I think our own perception is different than that of a Black American because our parents had such a drive and a strive that other Americans did not have. We come from a totally different perspective of work ethic and a different perspective of, you know, their education. With, you know, my father's education is probably so much better probably than mine when I reached the level that he reached because of, you know, that British influence. You know, they far exceeded us in math and other areas. So I think we're affected because we are clumped in those categories, but I think that our perception is different. (quoted in Bashi and Clarke 1999: 34)

Second- and next-generation West Indians ultimately will have to decide between an identity that resembles that of African Americans or that of their West Indian parents. There seems to be little room for other alternatives, and to a large extent their choice is determined by their parents' social class status and their peer environment.

EDUCATION AND JOB OPPORTUNITIES

Education is a serious issue in the English-speaking Caribbean. Most West Indian families see education as the most promising way to a better life. This attitude is supported by the educational institutions in the region. Because of the relative lack of placement opportunities (in many countries there is only a limited number of available places in secondary schools) and the stiff competition among students for high school and college places, education is generally regarded as a privilege rather than as a basic right.

Traditional values of discipline, obedience, and diligence are greatly emphasized and almost part of the curriculum. Certainly the mandatory wearing of school uniforms can be seen as an outward sign of the rigid West Indian educational system. Upon their arrival in the United States, most, if not all, immigrant students immediately notice the difference in the American school system, particularly in U.S. cities. As one Jamaican student explains:

> In the United States students curse at the teacher. He is from India. He will try his very best to let every one understand, yet students misbehave by pushing chairs. Sometimes, five to six students are referred to the Dean. Students will curse teachers and tell them insulting things about their parents. I do not see this kind of bad behavior in Jamaica—that would not happen. In Jamaica, if I were to do these things, the teacher is going to flog me and when I get home I am going to get it again. I will get kicked out of school and maybe I will get expelled and not attend school again. I will not have an education. (quoted in White-Davis 1992: 105)

In the closely knit community of small English-speaking Caribbean countries, school is an important aspect of daily life, and therefore one can find a greater harmony between school, family, and the local community. In other words, school in the Caribbean becomes a sort of home away from home. In contrast, public schools in the United States are more tolerant than those in the Caribbean. Even if physical punishment, as it is still happening in many West Indian schools, is deemed unacceptable in the United States, most West Indian parents and indeed many students themselves (at least in retrospect) accept it as a tool to achieve order and discipline. Nevertheless, the existence of sanction should not be misinterpreted as reflecting a lack of affection in Caribbean classrooms. While there is sanction, most teachers in the region are deeply committed to their job as educators.

The coping abilities of second-generation English-speaking Caribbean immigrants have become an issue. In cities such as New York, Boston, Miami, and Hartford, entire schools are currently populated with mainly Caribbean American youth. In 1996, for example, roughly 25 percent of New York City public school children came from or were associated with the Caribbean (Thomas 1998: 30). It appears that in the urban centers of New York, Chicago, Miami, and other cities, a dismal picture of failure emerges, for several reasons.

We have seen that in the case of West Indian immigrants, migration is mostly achieved in steps: one parent left to establish an economic base in the United States, then perhaps the second parent followed, and then, finally, the child or children. When children are left in the care of relatives in the home country, they sometimes become depressed or lonely, abandoned, or even guilty. When the children finally follow their parents, they must leave their friends and readjust to parents who have been away and may even seem like strangers. In some cases, there may even be an even more traumatic adjustment to divorce and/or a new stepparent.

The confusion and possible feelings of rejection can result in anger or hostility, even in children who formerly seemed well adjusted. Such problems can create difficulties in adjusting that may have far-reaching consequences. This is one of the often-overlooked costs of migration. In fact, many second-generation immigrant children from the Caribbean are showing psychological stress disorders resulting from a separation they deeply resented. They may also resent their new environment and the demands imposed on them by their new way of life and school. It should be mentioned, however, that some studies show that separation did not result in significantly higher adjustment problems (cf. Höhn, Midlarsky, and Branch 1997).

Many parents, teachers, or fellow students do not understand the problems these second-generation immigrants face. Many of them arrive with inflated or distorted expectations about their new life and are shocked that their expectations do not coincide with reality. As one second-generation immigrant describes it: "In Jamaica, you are carefree. You are able to run up and down and neighbors would watch you. Here, people just look out for themselves. They are very unfriendly. I feel very uncomfortable. In Jamaica, people take care of you as if you are their own kids" (quoted in White-Davis 1992: 135). The community-centered lifestyle provided by the extended family and rural setting in the Caribbean contrast sharply with the impersonality and aggressiveness of an industrialized society. In many ways, the school reflects that society.

The first major disappointment for the Caribbean immigrant student may occur with school assignment. Students may not end up in schools that were their first or even second choice. And quite regularly students from the Caribbean are placed without any testing into grades below the level of their academic skills. Consequently they become bored and passive in class, which teachers and school authorities misinterpret as low performance. In such a situation, the student can easily become seriously frustrated with the new school experience and start to show dysfunctional behavior. A vicious circle has started to take hold of the student's education.

In addition to these new demands and challenges, peer pressures may arise, often the result of cultural misunderstandings. Many students from the English-speaking Caribbean report that they are teased in school for their accent—for example:

> I felt stupid in class. At that time I can't speak like the Americans can do. So sometimes I stayed at home and didn't come to school. Sometimes when I did go to school, I would put my head on the desk and pretend I wasn't interested. But I really was. At least the teacher didn't call on me and they [the students] didn't laugh at me and make me feel small. (quoted in Richards and Pratt-Johnson 1995: 12)

This statement shows how easily young Caribbean students can get trapped in academic failure.

In another case, a Jamaican student was attacked and beaten up by a gang on his way home because he was accused by another student for "messing" with his girl (cf. White-Davis 1992). According to the student, this girl had kept staring at him in class and he in turn stared back at her. In Jamaica, when someone stares at you, staring back is a way of telling that person to stop or to show that you are not afraid. In this case a cultural misunderstanding led to a dangerous situation. However, the opposite can also happen, that is, a Caribbean student unaccustomed to and unable to manage his or her newfound classroom freedom can lose control about his or her social behavior and "go crazy." In such a situation the student may completely misjudge his or her boundaries and become socially dysfunctional. To some extent, therefore, the reaction to the adjustment process also depends on the individual.

Despite, or perhaps because of, the adaptation problems of many younger

West Indians in the American school system, there are initiatives underway that address this problem. One project deserving mention is the Beacon Project in Flatbush, Brooklyn, New York. The Beacon Program was conceived by New York City's ex-mayor David Dinkins in 1992, and there were thirty-six such programs across the city in 1995. The Flatbush Beacon Program is the only one that primarily serves the Caribbean American population. This community center and safe haven has programs that help Caribbean youth to develop problem-solving skills and provides academic counseling, review of classwork, homework assistance, GED tutorials, self-esteem and family life workshops, and recreation. George Irish, director of the Caribbean Research Center at Medgar Evers College, which administers the Flatbush Beacon Project, emphasizes that the project's teaching approach is culturally sensitive: "You have to sell them math through culture. Like dance, choir. Sell them. Sell them" (quoted in Mark-Duruaku 1995: 20). Although the entire program has been threatened by the tight budget policies of the Giuliani administration, the Flatbush Beacon Program still exists and provides valuable service to about five hundred youth, with a waiting list exceeding this number several times. There are no fees, but there is a parents' advisory board to which all parents must give four hours monthly.

It needs to be pointed out that young Caribbean Americans, like their American and African American peers, often do not see the value of an education. There is a pervading sense that money can be made more quickly and in larger amounts without going through the lengthy process of acquiring an education.

Another trend that has to be kept in mind is that since 1965, the reasons for migrating have changed somewhat. For the parents' generation, job opportunities and education were the primary reasons to migrate; now a lot of migrants arrive primarily to be reunited with their families. For them, education is not their main reason for moving. Nor do they see their opportunities improving through education. In fact, a lot of young Caribbean Americans perceive the job market as biased, and therefore they are at a disadvantage even with an education. They see that people in certain industries and services (e.g., stock exchange daytraders, software development) can make a good profit at an early age even without a college degree. Although most of the younger generation still agree with their parents that education is important, they do not regard it as the highway to a golden future in the way their parents' generation did:

> I can have the same grades as a person in a University of Penn, to go somewhere, and just because he or she went to Penn and I went to

Virginia State, I would get overlooked with the quickness. . . . I feel like to be coerced to go to a predominantly white school or some other school because of a reputation—you know, I feel the person should speak for himself not the reputation of the school. . . . To me, I feel the way that was set up was a setback for me because I don't think I was able to really focus on my, you know, major first goal. Eventually, you know, I had to find ways to find out what else am I good at, what else I like doing. I don't take nothin' away from my school. . . . I think it's the society. (quoted in Bashi and Clarke 1999: 22–23)

While in this case the student observed the existing differences between the quality and reputation of colleges as making a difference, the next incident reflects on the perhaps racially motivated favoritism that can devalue an education and shatter the self-esteem of the young Caribbean American trying to pursue it (Bashi and Clarke 1999: 28). In this particular case, he and a number of other black boys in a racially mixed area of Queens had attempted to participate in Little League. However, it turned out that there were not enough coaches and about a dozen black kids were not chosen for team positions. As he recalls it, his friend's father decided to coach these kids as a separate team. However, he remains convinced that the choice was racially motivated and that the whole episode would have gone differently if the youth had been white.

However, despite the best efforts of many concerned people, second-generation Caribbean Americans are in serious danger of getting lost in a society that is new to them and often more complex than their home country. At the same time West Indian parents are under a great deal of stress, with single parents or both parents working and not being able to afford private babysitters, caregivers, or other daycare options. Perhaps more than ever before, Caribbean youth today are in danger.

THE TEMPTATIONS OF THE STREET: GANGS AND DRUGS

The process of migration and possibly temporary separation from parents can mean serious adaptation problems and stressful situations for young West Indian immigrants. If children are especially susceptible to such pressures, they may fall into a downward spiral of academic and personal failure. At that point they become vulnerable to negative influences. The vast majority of both legal and illegal West Indian immigrants, however, pursue noncriminal lives and work in (sometimes two or three) legitimate jobs. By focusing on drugs and gangs, I do not intend to cast a bad light on these honest and hard-working immigrants and citizens. In recent years there have been more high-profiled crime cases involving West Indians and these issues have to be addressed, because they speak of other social problems this immigrant group is facing.

In recent years gangs have been an especially vexing problem in Los Angeles and other major U.S. cities. Some young immigrants from the English-speaking Caribbean get entrapped in this underworld of crime and drug abuse. A number of gangs have attained a gruesome level of notoriety. In most instances these gangs are dominated by Jamaicans and are known as *posses*.

Members of posses, as one Jamaican puts it, "destroy more life than they help anybody. If you go bust shot, you gonna bust shot 'pon your own brother an' sister. If you gonna make war, go somewhere else. Why black haffi' make war 'pon black? Why Jamaican haffi' make war 'pon Jamaican? This posse so blind an' dumb an' ignorant" (quoted in Gunst 1990: 98–99).

Some writers suggest that the origin of the posses was the political warfare in the ghettos of Jamaica's capital, Kingston (English 1991; Griffith 1997). Others have said that this warfare to some extent was sponsored by the CIA (Stein 1999). It is true that Jamaica has a long history of political violence, which culminated in the late 1970s. At that time Jamaica was ruled by a social-democratic government, which had made several advances to the international communist movement, in particular Cuba, and had fallen from grace with the United States. Although there is no conclusive proof, many sources claim that the CIA was trying to undermine the Jamaican government. The level of violence sharply increased as the 1980 elections approached. Without question, a large number of weapons reached Jamaica illegally and possibly with the help of both the government and the opposition party, under the leadership of the Edward Seaga. Over 900 people were killed in the 1980 election, and Seaga, a favorite of the United States, won a landslide victory.

Following his election, there was a change in the priorities of the government. The new emphasis on reducing state expenditures made the distribution of political handouts, previously a feature of political patronage in the ghettos, almost impossible. The gangs that had formerly killed political rivals and terrorized voters into political obedience found themselves without the political protection they formerly enjoyed. In fact, they were now being persecuted by special police squads. In this limbo situation, there was a shift in gang activity from political violence to drug dealing. The drying up of resources from the political parties had to be addressed, and it was solved by making money with drugs. And the increasing pressure from the Jamaican state authorities apparently led a number of gang members to migrate to the United States.

The estimated number of posses operating in the United States varies; however, it is safe to say that there are at least thirty such gangs active in major cities (U.S. Department of the Treasury 1987). Miami is the main port of entry for most of the posse members (most of which are illegal aliens), and it is the entry point and distribution center for approximately 80 percent of the cocaine and 50 percent of the marijuana that is illegally imported into the United States. The estimated membership of the posses is 2,500 to 20,000 (Griffith 1997).

Although they are best known for trafficking in drugs and weapons, they have also been involved in robbery, kidnapping, documents forgery, and murder. In fact, during the 1980s the posses achieved a degree of notoriety for their ruthless killings of rival gang members and defectors. Swift and brutal violence has become a posse trademark. Between 1985 and 1992, almost 5,000 posse-related homicides were committed in the United States. As one anonymous posse member related to the press: "It's better off for the police to catch you with a weapon than for the opposition to catch you without it. They cut you into pieces in a bathtub. They dump you into Dempster Dumpsters all over town. All parts never get found. . . . We call it jointing" (*U.S. News & World Report* 1988; 34).

For the most part posses are not very structured, but typical roles within the posses include boss (top of the chain of command), manager (oversees operations of retail sellers), couriers (to transport drugs or money between managers and sellers), seller (distributes drugs at retail level), lookouts (protect sellers from law enforcement, competitors, customers), and steerers (directs customers to sellers). While only trusted workers are employed, enforcers are often required to keep discipline because of disagreements and confrontations that can lead to violence arising over profits, losses, and thefts. Posses are almost exclusively male. Female members served only as "baby mothers" (that is, mothers for children of posse members), couriers, and renters of cars or apartments. They have begun to fill some of the middle-rank roles, and there is allegedly an all-female group, the Classic posse, operating in the United States. After their high-profile activities in the 1980s and early 1990s, posses are now increasingly removing themselves from the violence and exposure to law enforcement entailed in the day-to-day operation of crack houses and street selling, focusing instead on supplying sellers with larger quantities of cocaine.

One of the most ill-famed posses during the 1980s was the Renkers posse (*renk* is the Jamaican term for a pungent stench, but can also mean to quarrel or be quarrelsome). When one of their main leaders, Delroy "Uzi" Edwards, was captured and tried in early 1988, many details of the inner workings of the posses became known. Edwards's criminal path is typical for the development of many other posses operating in the United States.

Born in Kingston in December 1959, Edwards arrived in New York on a tourist visa in early 1980, after working as a strongman for the Jamaican Labour party of Edward Seaga. In the apartment above his father's grocery store in Brooklyn he established himself as a small-time marijuana dealer.

By 1985 Edwards went into the selling of crack and cocaine. He was a shrewd drug dealer, luring customers with two-for-one days and holiday discounts. On a busy day, sales in some of his crack houses would reach $45,000, and thirty or forty addicts would line up to make their buys. As Brooklyn became swamped with crack in 1986, Edwards sought less competitive markets in cities like Washington, Baltimore, and Philadelphia. His couriers picked up shipments of cocaine in California, Miami, and the Bahamas, which they would smuggle into the United States. In Brooklyn, Edwards cooked the cocaine into crack and measured it into vials ready for selling.

The Renkers posse was loosely structured and had no fixed rules of conduct or a criminal code of honor. Edwards seemed to have an ability to attract young workers to his posse. In fact, of the fifteen former posse members who testified against him in court, only two were older than thirty. As one writer explains it: "Of course, paying tax-free salaries that ranged from $250 to $1,000 a week gave Edwards a recruiting edge over Burger King. But Edwards meant more than money to these high school dropouts. He offered a place to belong, if only temporarily" (Singer 1990: 56).

Considering the ruthless approach of the posses, it has to be noted that there is no Robin Hood–like nobleness in their actions. The posse members occasionally send back money or goods to friends and relatives in the Kingston ghettos, but these goods are acquired at a great cost—the destruction of drug addicts they are supplying with their daily or hourly fix, and a disregard for innocent third parties who might be completely uninvolved with their business. When Edwards was shot by a rival, he ordered one of his lieutenants to go to an area controlled by the rival and fire at anybody looking Jamaican. "I walked up to the store, and I seen three guys standing there," Edward's assistant later testified to the court. He shot one man in the back from a distance of just four feet.

Posses operate not only in the United States, but also in Canada, Britain, the Netherlands, and Germany. Some of the larger posses, such as the Shower

Table 6.1
Aliens Excluded, by Country of Birth and Total Caribbean, 1992–1996

	1992	1993	1994	1995	1996
Barbados	4	1	1	3	3
Jamaica	200	185	205	212	280
Trinidad/Tobago	39	15	31	28	28
Guyana	41	50	35	61	66
Belize	9	16	15	15	18
Total Caribbean	964	1,039	831	813	781

Source: Immigration and Naturalization Service (1997:178).

posse, have their own planes and pilots for smuggling, as well as various legitimate businesses through which they launder their money (Griffith 1997).

THE SPECTER OF DEPORTATION

Not all West Indians enter the United States legally or conduct themselves lawfully. Probably the most prominent Caribbean national who was deported from the United States was Marcus Garvey. Unfortunately, a disproportionate amount of public attention is spent on this minority among the larger group of honest, hard-working, and taxpaying West Indians living in the United States. Illegal migration and deportation have far-reaching implications for both the host and the home countries. A variety of reasons can lead to an alien's exclusion. First is illegal immigration. Illegal immigrants to the United States are either refused entry to the country or, if they are caught after entering, are deported. From the early to the mid-1990s the number of English-speaking Caribbeans prevented from entering the United States appears to have decreased, as Table 6.1 indicates. What this table shows, among other things, is the comparatively high number of Jamaican nationals who apparently attempt to enter the United States with insufficient or false documentation. Furthermore, although the trend for the entire Caribbean seems to point downward, the English-speaking Caribbean countries listed in the table seem to show a slight increase of excluded aliens.

The United States is an immigrant country. There have, however, been occasional waves of public anti-immigrant sentiment, and in the late 1980s and early 1990s, such a new cycle began. There were many calls from the public to curb immigration; they argued that immigrants pose an extraordinary burden on the public purse and are more inclined to criminal activity than are U.S. citizens. Regardless of the value of these opinions—and many cannot stand up to any evidence about the contributions made by current immigrants—the U.S. Congress and several presidents could not completely ignore this public sentiment. The result was tougher legislation to prevent entry and admission into the United States, as well as the forced removal (i.e., deportation) of people who had run afoul of the law after having been admitted. The most significant among these new legal restrictions, the Illegal Immigration Reform and Immigrant Responsibility Act of 1996, intends to reduce the flow of legal and illegal immigrants and limit their access to certain public services (i.e., education, health, and welfare). In addition, the act calls for an acceleration in the deportation of both legal and illegal immigrants convicted of felonies (including such comparatively minor offenses such as drunk driving) regardless of how long they may have lived in the United States. Consequently, it is not surprising that deportations among West Indian immigrants are on the increase—even if many of those targeted for removal are neither drug dealers nor killers.

As a consequence of the new legal situation and the apparently increasing and high-profiled illegal activities of some of its members, the English-speaking Caribbean community saw an increasing number of its nationals being arrested. Between 1980 and 1992 the number of arrests of Caribbean immigrants in New York City tripled from 8,902 to 24,545 (Noguera 1999). Many of these were deported from the United States.

Table 6.2 gives a comparative overview of the extent of deportations of West Indians in the 1990s. Although there was a clear increase in deportations for the entire Caribbean, the trend for the other regions and the selected English-speaking Caribbean countries is not as uniform. Rather, it appears that they experienced their highest level around 1992 and 1993, although in 1996 increasing numbers of Asians and Europeans were deported as well. Noteworthy is the high number of Jamaicans deported from the United States, which cannot be explained as a consequence of their numerical majority among all West Indian immigrants. Instead, it appears that they have been convicted for illegal activities in greater numbers than their fellow West Indians. Indeed, among the immigrants incarcerated in U.S. prisons, six Central American and Caribbean countries are included in the top sixteen countries, with Jamaica at number six on the list.

Table 6.2
Aliens Deported, by Region and Selected Country, 1991-1996

	1991	1992	1993	1994	1995	1996
Belize	84	97	114	83	55	88
Bahamas	37	60	56	53	59	62
Barbados	19	20	27	27	25	35
Jamaica	612	934	888	795	826	891
Trinidad & Tobago	87	107	123	104	118	156
Caribbean	1,717	2,458	2,502	2,315	2,573	3,084
S. America	1,360	1,784	1,635	1,717	1,666	1,688
Europe	450	626	673	733	713	831
Asia	457	590	547	585	519	609

Sources: Immigration and Naturalization Service (1996:171); Immigration and Naturalization Service (1997:184).

The rising numbers of deportees, many of them posse members, former posse members, or otherwise implicated in serious crime, have had an obvious effect on their home countries. For several countries, in particular Jamaica, Trinidad, and Guyana, this inflow of criminal citizens has had serious consequences. As Jamaica's minister of national security reported in 1993, "Nearly a thousand Jamaicans were deported from other countries last year, with over 700 coming from the United States. . . . Intelligence indicates that many of them become more involved in criminal activity here" (quoted in Griffith 1997; 129). In many cases, the deportees were involved in importing or using firearms, the drug trade, and money laundering. According to a recent editorial in a major Jamaican newspaper, between June 1997 and January 1999, Jamaican deportees were implicated in 600 murders, 1,700 armed robberies, 900 rapes, 150 cases of shoot-outs with the police, 200 cases of extortion, 30 cases of murdering witnesses, and 10 cases of arson (*Jamaica Gleaner* 1999).

Many of the deportees have been involved in serious crimes such as drug trade and possession of firearms. Table 6.3 gives an idea of the numbers

Table 6.3
Deportations by Cause and Selected Country of Nationality, 1996

	Criminal/ Narcotics Conviction	Related to Criminal/ Narcotics Violations	Entered without Inspection	Violation of Non-immigrant Status	Other	Total
Bahamas	58	–	2	2	–	62
Barbados	33	–	2	–	–	35
Jamaica	816	4	57	3	11	891
Trinidad & Tobago	147	–	7	–	2	156
Guyana	62	–	2	1	2	67
Caribbean[a]	2,632	10	368	11	63	3,084

[a]Without Guyana.

Source: Immigration and Naturalization Service (1996:188).

involved. Apart from the listed crimes, many have also served time for crimes ranging from fraud to murder. Noncriminal deportees are usually guilty of overstaying their time on a visitor's visa and often request voluntary deportation. The costs are usually borne by the individual, and they are not accompanied by a marshal. Criminal deportees, however, are subject to higher costs; they require a marshal for transportation and, if they are deemed too violent for other passengers to sit in close proximity to them, the authorities have to pay for the unoccupied seats. A flight from New York to Jamaica currently costs about $365. Deportation costs governments millions of dollars.

Even in the smaller territories of the Eastern Caribbean, the impact of the deportees is often felt, although their numbers there are respectively smaller. In these cases, size plays a role insofar as it appears to multiply the impact of a few hardened criminals on their communities. Given the fact that the American, British, and Canadian public and governments resent (and justly so) the immigration of criminals from third countries, it is questionable how appropriate the deportation of hardened criminals to the fragile and resource-constrained societies of the English-speaking Caribbean can be deemed. As one commentator recently put it: "It cannot be either fair or appropriate that the U.S. deports to Jamaica, at the age of 30, people who left here when they were seven years old and learnt their trade in the U.S. Such people don't even know where the Carib Cinema [a landmark in Kingston] is, and view their ejection into this alien society with as much distaste as we their untimely arrival" (Ritch 1999). For both the smaller Eastern Caribbean and the larger territories (e.g., Jamaica, Trinidad, and Barbados), the arrival of unwanted deportees has been highly disruptive, as a case study will demonstrate.

The dangers to both Caribbean societies and U.S. citizens living in the Caribbean that may stem from the dumping of deportees on the ill-prepared and resource-constrained societies of the region can be seen in the case of Cecil Connor, a.k.a. Charles Emmanuel Miller, a.k.a. "Little Nut." Connors, who grew up poor and orphaned on St. Kitts, developed a keen sense for economic survival. According to an American anthropology professor who met him as a child, Connors became involved early in the drug trade and used to shuttle between Kingston, Jamaica, and Basseterre, St. Kitts. At the age of fifteen or sixteen, he "graduated" from marijuana trade to cocaine when he became a member of the feared Shower posse in Kingston. In 1977 he was arrested for armed robbery and sent to a Kingston prison with three life sentences, plus twenty-five years, which was later reduced (cf. Stein 1999). In 1983 he escaped and flew to New York with false documents, but was returned to Antigua at his request after being stopped by immigration officers at New York's John F. Kennedy Airport. A few months later, he wound up in Florida on a visa obtained from the U.S. embassy in Antigua. In Miami he reconnected with the Shower posse. Here he became the right hand to the posse's co-leaders, Jim Brown (alias Lester Coke) and Vivian Blake. Connor was transporting 600 pounds of marijuana and a kilo of cocaine every week to Rochester, New York, which became his personal fiefdom. In early 1985 he was caught by the police, convicted, and sentenced to five years in prison.

The police were eager to strike a deal with Connors for inside information about the Shower posse, and after two years in prison Connors called them. In return for a number of mid-level posse members, Connors demanded immunity, a promise that prosecutors would fight any Jamaican extradition order, and resettlement in the federal witness protection program. All three requests were met, and Connors testified in court that he had stood guard at a Miami crack house in which Coke and Blake killed five people, including a pregnant mother. In 1991, Connors returned to St. Kitts.

Back in St. Kitts he changed his name to Charles Emmanuel Miller and with an estimated savings of perhaps as much as $200,000 bought several businesses. He also established friends in the Labour party. Connors saw his chance to pay old debts and make new profits when he discovered that Dr. William "Billy" Herbert, a well-off local businessman who had been ambassador to the United Nations and the United States until 1992, was involved in cocaine trade. With the help of a former acquaintance from the U.S. Bureau of Alcohol, Tobacco and Firearms (ATF), the retired agent J. J. Watterson, Connors planned to sell information about a major cocaine shipment to the U.S. Drug Enforcement Agency (DEA), but they did not show any interest in it (cf. Stein 1999). Neither did the British Scotland Yard. Following this failed attempt, Billy Herbert mysteriously disappeared on a boating tour in the Caribbean. Herbert and his five guests were never seen or heard from again. Two more people disappeared months later, and their bodies were found in a burned-out car in a sugarcane field. The victims were Vincent Morris, the son of a deputy prime minister, and his girlfriend. The investigating local police officer, who was shot and killed months later by a lone gunman, concluded that Morris had dug out from a beach a cache of cocaine that belonged to Connors. Within a few months nine people were dead and St. Kitts had a major problem.

On July 30, 1998, State Department officials declared that Miller had threatened "to murder at random U.S. citizen students at Ross Veterinary University in St. Kitts if the U.S. Government is successful in obtaining his extradition." The report was widely circulated in the press and on the Internet, and although "Little Nut" denied the threat subsequently, both the college administration and the State Department have taken it very seriously and installed additional security on campus. Both the school and the State Department informed parents about the threat and since then many students have chosen to leave St. Kitts. Florida prosecutors have been trying again to win Connor's extradition since 1995. In February 2000, the government of St. Kitts finally decided to extradite him since it perceived his conduct as detrimental to national security.

CONCLUSION

English-speaking Caribbean immigrants have often been considered to be a "model minority" in the United States: they were said to have a good work ethic, a high determination to succeed economically, great flexibility in their choice of jobs, respect for family and kinship, and a very high regard for formal education, which regularly translated to their pursuit of professional degrees and careers. Some commentators used the relative success of this group to contrast it with the performance of African Americans, who sometimes appeared to be lacking these successes. Caribbean Americans themselves gladly cultivated the notion of their being different from or even superior to other ethnic groups.

However, it has become obvious that a structural change is in process with regard to the socioeconomic composition of the latest generation of immigrants from the islands and that the second and following generations significantly differ from the first wave. Since the mid-1960s, the previous emphasis on middle-class members and professionals shifted to the legally endorsed reunification of families. In the 1970s and especially since the 1980s, an inflow of younger, rural, and typically not as highly educated Caribbeans occurred, which has started to transform the social and economic profile of the West Indian community in the United States.

In addition to this shift, the structure of the economy has changed in ways that make it more difficult to obtain good jobs without basic skills or some sort of specialized education. Younger Caribbean immigrants also often find it difficult to adapt to the demands imposed on them in the school system and in some cases find it difficult to make the transition to the new society. Combined, these factors can become a basis for structural unemployment and social problems (e.g., weakening of the family, teenage pregnancy). Cases like the Jamaican Colin Ferguson, who in the early 1990s shot several commuters on a Long Island train, are certainly the extreme, but they still point to the severity of the underlying problem. If public officials and administrators see the need to cut social and educational programs such as the Beacon Project or remedial courses at the City University of New York that (among others) are geared toward the West Indian communities in the five boroughs of New York City, this cannot be regarded as useful in the long term.

There are a number of ways in which a failing young immigrant can fall prey to the temptations of the streets. That this is a real possibility can be seen in the rise of the posses. The United States has the potential to integrate all different people into its society and the public ought to become aware of the long-term benefits of efficient social support mechanisms that work towards that end. What can happen when a society fails to integrate its immigrants can be seen in the case of France. Here millions of Algerians and other—primarily Muslim—immigrants from Africa have settled since the 1960s, but are essentially excluded from meaningful participation in their host society. The younger generation finds itself pushed aside, even though it might be more willing and prepared to participate and assume responsibilities than their parents' generation. Their frustration exploded in the summer of 1981, when they battled police for several days and nights in a suburb of Lyon. Lessons from this experience can be learned, and gang and individual violence can be decreased if responsible private sector entities and public officials find it important enough to promote integrative and adaptive mechanisms geared at its West Indian minorities.

REFERENCES

Bashi, Vilna, and Averil Clarke. 1999. "Perceptions and Realities of the Opportunity Structure for First and Second Generation West Indians." Paper presented at the West Indian Migration to New York: Historical, Contemporary, and Transnational Perspectives Conference, Research Institute for the Study of Man, April 16–17.

English, T. J. 1991. "Rude Boys." *Playboy* (October): 87–88, 98, 178–179.

Griffith, Ivelaw. 1997. *Drugs and Security in the Caribbean: Sovereignty under Siege.* University Park: Pennsylvania State University Press.

Gunst, Laurie. 1990. "Johnny-Too-Bad and the Sufferers." *The Nation* (November 13): 549, 567–569.

Höhn, Gabriela, Elizabeth Midlarsky, and Curtis Branch. 1997. "Emotional and Behavioral Functioning of Jamaican Immigrant Children: Preliminary Findings." Unpublished paper, Teachers College, Columbia University.

Immigration and Naturalization Service. 1996. *Statistical Yearbook of the Immigration and Naturalization Service, 1995.* Washington, D.C.: Government Printing Office.

Immigration and Naturalization Service. 1997. *Statistical Yearbook of the Immigration and Naturalization Service, 1996.* Washington, D.C.: Government Printing Office.

Jamaica Gleaner. 1999. "Monitoring Deportees." June 29.

Mark-Duruaku, Christine. 1995. "The Beacon Project. Leading Youth in Positive Directions." *Everybody's* 19 (December): 20–21.

Noguera, Pedro. 1999. "Exporting the Undesirable: An Analysis of the Factors Influencing the Deportation of Immigrants from the United States and an Examination of Their Impact on Caribbean and Central American Societies." *Wadabagei: A Journal of the Caribbean and Its Diaspora* 2 (Winter/Spring): 1–28.

Richards, Cynthia, and Yvonne Pratt-Johnson. 1995. "The Use of Jamaican Creole in the Jamaican Classroom and Educational Implications for the New York City Public School and CUNY Systems." Paper presented at the Evolving Patterns in Caribbean Migration: Impact and Challenges Conference, Medgar Evers College, October.

Ritch, Dawn. 1999. "Jamaica Sitting on a Time Bomb." *Jamaica Gleaner,* July 12.

Singer, Amy. 1990. "Uzi Disarmed." *American Lawyer* (March): 52–60.

Stein, Jeff. 1999. "The Caribbean Connection." *Gentlemen's Quarterly* (August): 164–171, 209–211.

Thomas, Bert. 1998. "Americanizing Caribbean Youth." *Everybody's* 22 (March): 29–31.

U.S. Department of Treasury. 1987. *Jamaican Organized Crime.* Washington, D.C.: Bureau of Alcohol, Tobacco, and Firearms.

U.S. News & World Report. 1988. "A Gang Member's Story. True Confessions." January 18, 34.

Vickerman, Milton. 1999. "Tweaking a Monolith: The West Indian Immigrant Encounter with 'Blackness.' " Paper presented at the West Indian Migration to New York: Historical, Contemporary, and Transnational Perspectives, Conference, Research Institute for the Study of Man, April 16–17.

Waters, Mary. 1994. "Ethnic and Racial Identities of Second Generation Black Immigrants in New York." *International Migration Review* 28 (4): 795–820.

Waters, Mary. 1999. "Growing Up West Indian and African American: Gender and Class Differences in the Second Generation." Paper presented at the West Indian Migration to New York: Historical, Contemporary, and Transnational Perspectives Conference Research Institute for the Study of Man, April 16–17.

White-Davis, Gerald E. 1992. "Adaptation of Jamaican Immigrants in American Schools: Problems and Possibilities." Ph.D. dissertation, Teachers College, Columbia University.

7

Conclusion

MAKING IT DESPITE THE ODDS?

About twenty years ago the first international music superstar from the so-called Third World, Jamaica's Bob Marley, prophetically sang a song entitled "Reggae's on Broadway." Not only has his vision become true today, but it is also possible to hear steel pan music in Manhattan subway stations and Times Square. The international reach of Caribbean culture can also be seen from the fact that recently the British Broadcasting Corporation adopted Bob Marley's reggae anthem, "One Love," as the official "millennium song," and as *Time* magazine recently wrote in an article about Marley, a Marley theme restaurant opened at Universal Studio's City Walk in Orlando, Florida (Farley 1999). Even Germany now has its own calypso singer, Chako, who competed in Trinidad and Tobago's World Calypso Monarch Competition. Caribbean music has thoroughly penetrated U.S. and Western mainstream music and culture. Few, if any, other Third World cultures can say that of themselves.

Caribbean immigrants have made a great contribution to the cultural diversification of black America. American household names of international acclaim like Malcolm X, Stokely Carmichael (later Kwame Turé), Grace Jones, Harry Belafonte, Sidney Poitier, Patrick Ewing, Colin Powell, and Shirley Chisholm all look back at a Caribbean heritage or point of origin. To speak about black Americans or African Americans when referring to black people living in the United States is a denial of this great diversity. With the arrival of Caribbean immigrants, this group and the whole country has been enriched by a mosaic of new traditions, religions, musical rhythms, hair and dressing styles, flavors, colors, and scents.

Unfortunately, however, while this growing cultural influence is taking place, Caribbean people continue to be pushed to the margins of mainstream society by social, political, and economic developments. This was brought into a strong focus in 1992 when many people in the West celebrated the 500th anniversary of Columbus's arrival in what was then called the New World. Little thought was given to the fact that "the quintessential observance duly set for 'celebration' means something quite different to millions of 'Americans,' starting with Native Americans, small branches of which continue to survive in the insular Caribbean as Caribs, though the majority of their ancestral kin died out early in the encounters with Europe's marauding hordes" (Nettleford 1993: 11–12). Indeed, from a Caribbean perspective, the arrival of this European adventurer meant the rather violent end of a lifestyle in great harmony with nature.

What manifests itself in a symbolic way also has its actual expression in the streets of U.S. cities and suburbs, where Caribbean citizens still face stereotyping and prejudice. The late 1990s witnessed the brutalization of West Indian and other people of color by many state authorities. The execution-style police killing in 1999 of an unarmed African immigrant in New York, Amadou Diallo, and the subsequent acquittal of officers charged with the killing, the sodomization by New York Police Department officers of a Haitian immigrant, Abner Louima, and the unjustified killing in New York City of another unarmed Haitian, Patrick Dorismond, are only the unfortunate tip of this iceberg of civil and human rights denial. If nothing else, in this major global city where over half of the population is not white and many are immigrants, this approach by a majority white police force is extremely bad public relations. From the perspective of those who are affected in their daily lives by it and with apologetic support of some politicians, such transgressions of the powers that be smack of political discrimination and fundamental injustice.

They are the political flip side of the economic discrimination that West Indians have experienced. For example, recent changes in the admission policies at City University of New York (CUNY) have the consequence of denying poorer people in the New York City area access to higher education. Undoubtedly, many West Indian immigrants (and others) are negatively affected by this development and as a result are practically sentenced to work in low-income jobs. Under New York City's so-called work experience program (WEP), thousands of welfare benefit recipients attending CUNY have been forced to abandon their education because they cannot combine a full schedule of study with twenty hours per week working off welfare benefits in assignments in sanitation, maintenance, or the Parks Department. These minimum wage assignments do not pay their expenses, take away valuable study time, and lead to lower grades. In addition, they do not develop their skills or minds and ultimately will not help them to get off their welfare rolls. Instead of getting a diploma, welfare students are forced to push brooms.

It is already quite difficult for West Indian students to make it through the dilapidated and substandard high schools many of them attend. As one study showed, the average expenditure per student in New York City was $5,500, while in the suburbs such as Great Neck and Manhasset (both on Long Island) students received twice as much funding (Kozol 1991). Thus, by their very location, West Indian students are in a situation that reproduces poverty rather than enables them to succeed economically and socially. It can be no surprise that their dropout rates are high and increasing.

And yet Caribbean people are uniquely equipped with a cultural "survival kit" that gives them a great advantage over many other people. While the rest of the world is only beginning to experience globalization, Caribbean people have been located at the center of this maelstrom for several hundred years. The necessity of survival in spite of slavery and after has engendered in their lifestyle a great propensity for improvisation and creative flexibility while other peoples (e.g., the Arawak Indians) before them had perished under the same pressures. Using their traditional problem-solving approaches and ways of making sense of the world, they became used to recombining these with other ways of living and the necessities dictated by working on plantations owned by men resident in London, Paris, or other European capitals. The art of make-believe, mockery, carnival, theater, and imitation became popular parts of West Indian everyday life, which continued to move to the distant sounds of the drum. Their inclination and instant preparedness to pack their suitcases and migrate is rooted in this experience of coping in a new environment and their profound sense of being displaced. The strength and weakness of the region can be described best in the following terms:

> The Caribbean is a region of options. Variety at the crossroads at worst spells confusion, periodically inviting self-doubt and equivocation. At best it engenders among individuals the capacity to operate on two or more levels, sequentially or simultaneously, in dealing with the quixotic, multi-faceted social phenomena characteristic of the crossroads where disparate elements meet and have their being. (Nettleford 1993: 3)

Because Caribbean immigrants in the United States come from a cultural background so familiar with ambiguity, multiple logics, and polyrhythmics (i.e., two or more separate rhythms superimposed over each other), the need to operate on several levels, and the knowledge of different ethnic and cultural value systems, they are well positioned (Simmons-Lewis 2000). Postmodernity and globalization increasingly will make the need for flexibility and creativeness evident. With this trend, this inherent quality of their culture should increasingly become an asset for Caribbean people.

MAKING CONTRIBUTIONS

Jamaicans and other West Indians have contributed in numerous ways to the United States, despite the fact that they also and primarily were engaged in everyday efforts to carve out an economic niche for themselves. As pointed out earlier, many of them had arrived after having helped to build the Panama Canal—a canal, President Rutherford B. Hayes announced in 1880, "under American control." There can be little doubt that the completion of the canal was a very important factor in the rise of the United States to the status of a military and economic superpower. It is equally true to say that black West Indians—those who helped to build the canal—made an enormous contribution to this American achievement in the twentieth century. Often forgotten, but no less important, are West Indians such as Marcus Garvey and C.L.R. James, who made outstanding contributions to the fight for liberty and justice in the United States and added their voices to the emerging civil rights movement's call for social justice and equal opportunity for all Americans. The American legacy has also been built with the sweat and blood of the people living in the United States' sister nations of the English-speaking Caribbean.

Caribbean men and women of lesser names who nevertheless made great sacrifices for causes that were not necessarily their own are legion. Despite their hardships, Caribbean immigrants were always among the achievers. In 1826, for example, Jamaican-born John Brown Russwurm was the third black to graduate from an American college (Bowdoin in Maine) as well as the first black to publish a newspaper in the United States (*Freedom's Journal*). In 1829, he moved to Liberia, in Africa, where he served as governor of a colony at Cape Palmas. Fellow Jamaican Robert Brown Elliot became attorney general of South Carolina in 1876. Elliot was elected to Congress twice and earned a reputation as an eloquent orator. As one recent example, 105-year-old Jamaican Eugent Clarke, in 1999 was awarded France's highest military honor, the Cross of the Legion of Honor, for his participation in the fight for liberty in France during World War I.

The Caribbean and Caribbean American quest for excellence continues and can be seen in Maurice Ashley, a Jamaican national resident in New York who made history by becoming the first black person to qualify as a Grand Master in Chess, and Jody-Anne Maxwell's determination in her successful quest to win the National Spelling Bee championship. At the time of writing, a New York City Council member of Jamaican background, Una Clarke, is preparing to run for a seat in Congress. Apparently there is a concerted effort among organizations and individuals in the Caribbean community to elect a representative of their community to this high office. As Clarke is about to vacate her seat as council member, the 2001 councilmanic races might well become influenced by ethnic considerations. In her quest for a seat in Congress, she will run against Congressman Major Owens, who is backed by the African American community in the 11th Congressional District but has little grounding among Caribbean Americans. Since Caribbean voters do not necessarily choose on the basis of a person's ethnicity, the challenge for Una Clarke is to build on her strong past achievements for the Caribbean American community while demonstrating that her agenda is superior to that of the congressman and can also speak to the concerns of African Americans and other ethnic groups living in the district. The race for this seat promises to be close and to a large extent will be determined by the professionalism and political shrewdness of the contenders and their support teams. Clarke's challenge to Major Owens has been criticized by Democrat assemblypersons, senators, and district leaders, who vaguely argued that her challenge "constituted a disrespect to colleagues" and jeopardized the "operational unity within our leadership and community" (*Weekly Gleaner* 2000: 13). The West Indian voters of the 11th Congressional District will perceive this open letter for what it is, and it might very well backfire in the subsequent election.

The expatriate communities of West Indian people are also of immense value to their home societies in the Caribbean. Jamaica, for example, has an estimated half of its population living abroad. Their increasing remittances in the form of money and goods are a vital lifeline for many families there. The $600 million of remittances by Jamaicans roughly equals the foreign exchange potential of Jamaica's entire tourism industry, which is probably a more volatile and less reliable source of foreign exchange than the expatriate community. Many retirees and young people with professional education eagerly wait for their opportunity to return. With great regularity, therefore, Caribbean prime ministers travel to major cities to meet with the overseas West Indians in order to keep them abreast of the developments at home and also to elicit their involvement. In most cases, children of West Indian parents can claim the citizenship of their parents' country of origin and have the constitutional right to hold dual citizenship. Whether the governments will be able to mobilize the full potential of the overseas West Indians remains to be seen.

THE CHALLENGES AHEAD

The beginning of the 1990s saw a number of developments in the United States that can be described as an anti-immigrant backlash. The passage of Proposition 187 in California and similar proposals in Florida, which were followed by federal legislation, made legal immigration more difficult and barred even legal immigrants from certain social assistance programs. In addition, U.S. deportation practice targeted not only illegal but also legal immigrants convicted of a crime (Noguera 1999). While many of these practises really were top-down initiatives, it is not surprising that, encouraged by such propaganda, similar sentiments were also expressed from the bottom up. In late 1999 anti-immigrant posters were plastered all over Queens, which held immigrants responsible for the loss of jobs and declining standards of living in the United States. Actually, however, the situation is more the opposite way; there are currently not enough skilled people in the United States, and if there are not enough well-educated migrants to fill such positions, many businesses will leave.

These anti-immigration sentiments and U.S. withdrawal from regional affairs (except drug trafficking and illegal immigration) have led to an unprecedented drive for citizenship applications among this population, which traditionally perceived itself as only temporary settlers. Yet a challenge remains for increasing political empowerment in the United States. Unfortunately, although many Jamaicans, Trinidadians, or St. Lucians living in the United States without much hesitation identify themselves as Caribbean, the truth is that the West Indian community remains organized along country lines. Indeed, no West Indian "Moses" has emerged yet who would be able to unite the different nationalities (Payne 1998). In addition to the geographic differences, the challenge of developing a unified voice has been hampered by ethnic divisions within the community. There remain considerable mutual suspicions and, indeed, prejudices between West Indians of African descent and Indo-Caribbeans, particularly in the case of Trinidadians and Guyanese immigrants. The distance between these two subgroups is exacerbated by their settlement patterns, which find, for example, Afro-Guyanese living in Brooklyn, New York, and Dade County, Florida, and Indo-Guyanese in Queens, New York, and Broward County, Florida. Similarly, people from Belize are divided geographically, with the biggest concentration found in Los Angeles. In addition, some Belizeans identify as Garifuna people first and as Belizean or West Indian second. As a consequence of these divisions the hundreds of thousands of West Indians celebrating carnival on Brooklyn's Eastern Parkway every Labor Day are just a potential—a potential that is yet to be unified politically.

It is not surprising that developing a West Indian lobby that speaks for the entire community has been difficult. While West Indians note with considerable pride their achievements in the world of entertainment, music, and sports, there is a need and will to excel in fields other than these somewhat stereotypical areas for black people in the Americas. In particular, there seems to be a need to press for a broader perception of common interests among both the community leadership and the business sector. Unfortunately, with regard to the latter there still exists too little preparedness to cooperate and venture into partnerships with other businesses in order to revive the fledgling Caribbean trade. Although it is easy to find statements claiming the opposite, when it comes to making strategic decisions about such joint ventures and networking efforts, most business leaders in the Caribbean community are slow to grasp such opportunities (Griffith 1998). Despite the great potential and market force that can be seen in the undulating mass of spectators along the Eastern Parkway during the Caribbean Carnival Day in New York, the West Indian community has yet to develop the common political will and entrepreneurial perspective to improve itself as a community (i.e., as opposed to as a group of individuals). This can be seen in the relative detachment and lack of support from within the community itself for vital Caribbean American institutions and services such as the Caribbean Research Center at Medgar Evers College or the Caribbean Women's Health Association in Brooklyn. The community is also far removed yet from a good measure of integration between Caribbeans of African and those of Indian ancestry. Interestingly, the need for more dynamic West Indian participation in the public institutional life is also felt in Canada (Doyle-Marshall 1994).

Another case in point is the question of a lasting heritage built by the generation of post-1965 immigrants to their children and grandchildren. The need, for example, for a major community center collecting, displaying, and celebrating the culture of all peoples and cultures in and of the Caribbean and their achievements and impact on U.S. society has not yet been fulfilled. This dream has also experienced setbacks because of internal dissent and competition for political and economic turf. Thus, following the 1991 riots in Brooklyn, Governor Mario Cuomo decided, after consulting with community representatives, that Caribbean Americans lacked a certain measure of communal identity, and he advocated the construction of a Caribbean cultural center. Money from the New York State was—and possibly still is—being committed to this project. However, soon after the project started to get off the ground, various factions started to claim the project as their brain-child and attempted to gain control of it, which halted its progress. In fact, at one point, rent was being paid for a building in Brooklyn that remained empty because of these problems and because it was not suited to host the new institution without renovation. The chairperson of this new institution, Lamuel Stanislaus, has not succeeded in overcoming the obstacles of infighting. As a consequence, to this day there is no Caribbean cultural center, despite the fact that New York state supported the idea.

Although leaders have emerged in the community, the community itself has not yet united to such a degree that self-interests among some of its leadership have become impossible. This is an accusation that, for example, has been leveled against the Caribbean American Chamber of Commerce. This organization has been quite successful in bringing together and organizing Caribbean businesspeople and has managed to elevate these entrepreneurs to a higher level of representation and organization. However, while the chamber claims to speak and act in the interest of Caribbean businesses, it has developed few programs. It has not yet managed to produce or sponsor the collection and analysis of data about business-related matters in the Caribbean community. Certainly more can and should be done by this organization and the members whom it serves as an institutional umbrella.

Other issues that pose challenges for the West Indian community in the United States are the question of how educational services for the younger generation can be improved in an environment that seeks to reduce public expenditures rather than improve education by investing in teachers and facilities. Caribbean immigrant children are an at-risk group that requires particular attention during their transition from their home country and the adjustment to a new school system in a new country. In New York, 50 percent of the immigrant children are from the Caribbean or Latin America. Similar problems may soon face rapidly growing Caribbean communities in urban communities in Florida, California, and New Jersey. Faced with the problems posed by immigration, it should be obvious that education is a two-way street that does not exclude the teacher. Thus, as one insider pointed out, there is a need to improve the information of teachers about the island societies regarding different ethnic, economic, social, and linguistic characteristics; to enhance student-teacher, teacher-teacher, student-student, and school-community interaction to improve the teaching-learning transaction; to develop strategies of development for bridging gaps of understanding, social distance, and discord across various student bodies (London 1995).

Many people in the Caribbean American community deny these problems. Some downplay the problems that new, young West Indian immigrants face in the American school system and the new cultural climate to which they have to adjust. A possible reason is that there is a desire to keep alive the notion of Caribbean excellence and achievement, even though it has been put into question by immigrants from the region who have less education to begin with when they arrive in the United States and who are less well equipped to cope with the intricacies of the education system in urban America. The failure or unwillingness to recognize the problem translates into a lack of attention from official sources in the private and public sectors and is therefore to be criticized in the strongest terms. It is without question a failure of the community's leadership to look after its own long-term interests.

The challenge for the future is not only for the leadership of the West Indian community to get elected to positions of local, regional, state, or national importance, but more fundamentally for the community to come together and realize its full potential. There is still too much one-upmanship keeping Caribbean Americans from joining forces as one political and economic community, similar to other ethnic groups such as Italian Americans or Jewish Americans. This challenge is to a large extent one that has to be picked up by the leaders themselves. However, the business community also has an important role to play in supporting individuals and organizations that provide vital services. There is still too much reluctance, particularly among Indo-Caribbean Americans, to perceive themselves as and unite as a political interest group. At the level of pure business, Caribbean American businesspeople by and large are still thinking in parochial local terms while in many of their communities (e.g., in New York, Los Angeles, or Miami) they are really uniquely positioned at the centers of what has truly become a globalized economy.

REFERENCES

Doyle-Marshall, William. 1994. "Scholar Challenges Canadian Immigration in Book." *Everybody's* 18 (April): 36–38.

Farley, Christopher John. 1999. "Marley's Ghosts." *Time*, November 29.

Griffith, Clyde. 1998. " 'Whither the Caribbean Community?' Score One for Assemblyman Nick Perry." *Everybody's* 22 (February): 10.

Kozol, Jonathan. 1991. *Savage Inequalities: Children in America's School.* New York: HarperCollins.

London, Clement B.G. 1995. "Suggested Curriculum Strategies for Caribbean Parents of Children Enrolled in United States' Schools." In *Caribbean Students in New York*, ed. J. A. George Irish, 73–90. Brooklyn, NY: Caribbean Diaspora Press.

Nettleford, Rex. 1993. *Inward Stretch, Outward Reach: A Voice from the Caribbean.* London: Macmillan.

Noguera, Pedro. 1999. "Exporting the Undesirable: An Analysis of the Factors Influencing the Deportation of Immigrants from the United States and an Examination of Their Impact on Caribbean and Central American Societies." *Wadabagei: A Journal of the Caribbean and Its Diaspora* 2 (Winter-Spring): 1–28.

Payne, Douglas W. 1998. *Emerging Voices: The West Indian, Dominican, and Haitian Diasporas in the United States.* CSIS Policy Papers on the Americas, Vol. IX, Study 11, Washington, D.C.: Center for Strategic and International Studies.

Simmons-Lewis, Suzanne. 2000. "Dip into Our Melting Pot: Caribbean Islands Are Light Years Ahead in Forging a Multi-cultural Society." *The Voice* 892 (January 24): 13.

Weekly Gleaner. 2000. "Should Una Run?" February 10–16: 13.

White-Davis, Gerald E. 1995. "Recommendations for Enhancing the Education of English-Speaking Caribbean Students in New York Public Schools." In *Caribbean Students in New York*, ed. J. A. George Irish, 133–143. Brooklyn, NY: Caribbean Diaspora Press.

Appendix A:
Migration Statistics

Table A.1
Caribbean Immigrants Admitted to the United States in 1997, by Country

Country	1996–1997
Barbados	356
Belize	326
Cuba	2,355
Dominica	390
Dominican Rep.	20,191
Grenada	360
Haiti	9,304
Jamaica	11,575
Trinidad & Tobago	2,813
Other Caribbean	1,386
Total Caribbean*	48,730

*May not add up precisely because INS lists Belize as a Central American country.

Sources: Immigration and Naturalization Service (1999); *Statistical Yearbook of the Immigration and Naturalization Service, 1997*, Table 11.

Table A.2
Caribbean Persons Naturalized, by Country of Former Allegiance

Country	Total Naturalized
Antigua-Barbuda	714
Bahamas	303
Barbados	1,873
Belize	1,280
Cuba	12,860
Dominica	535
Dominican Republic	19,450
Grenada	1,136
Haiti	15,667
Jamaica	18,746
St. Kitts & Nevis	540
St. Lucia	429
St. Vincent & Grenadines	737
Trinidad & Tobago	5,273
Total Caribbean*	78,263

*May not add up precisely because INS includes Belize as a Central American country.

Sources: Immigration and Naturalization Service (1999): *Statistical Yearbook of the Immigration and Naturalization Service, 1997*, Table 46.

Appendix B: Notable Caribbean Americans

Kareem Abdul-Jabbar (1947–). National Basketball Association player of Trinidadian descent. Abdul-Jabbar, born Ferdinand Lewis Alcindor, was the Michael Jordan of his days. From the time he stepped on the court at Power Memorial High School in his native New York City, to the time he retired as the NBA's all-time leader in nine statistical categories, the 7-foot 2-inch Abdul-Jabbar established himself as basketball's most talented and recognizable figure. In his first year of a stellar twenty-year career, the fiercely competitive seven-footer was named NBA Rookie of the Year after averaging 28.8 points per game and 14.5 rebounds for the Milwaukee Bucks. He became an instant force in the league, bringing finesse and agility to the center position, which had previously seen brute force and strength as the rule. In 1975, Abdul-Jabbar was traded to the Los Angeles Lakers, where his patented "sky hook" helped the Lakers earn a staggering five NBA championships (1980, 1982, 1985, 1987, and 1988). He picked up another three NBA Most Valuable Player awards (1976, 1977, and 1980), for a record total of six, and was named *Sports Illustrated*'s Sportsman of the Year in 1985. Upon his retirement in 1989, Abdul-Jabbar stood alone in nine NBA statistical categories. He has become a national spokesperson for Athletes and Entertainers for Kids and has been active in several humanitarian organizations, including C.A.R.E., RP International, and various literacy groups.

Monty Alexander (1944–). Jazz pianist, born in Jamaica. In the 1960s Alexander played with jazz greats like Milt Jackson and Ray Brown before forming his own trio. Alexander occasionally uses his West Indian musical background with impressive effects. On two of his albums in the late 1980s, *Ivory and Steel* and *Jamboree*, he successfully incorporated the jazz piano with a steel band.

Edward Kamau Brathwaite (1930–   ). Barbadian poet, historian, and essayist. Brathwaite is a prolific West Indian writer whose reputation rests primarily on several volumes of verse, including two trilogies. Throughout his career, Brathwaite has been concerned with exploring the Caribbean identity. After attending Harrison College in Barbados, he won a scholarship to Cambridge University, where he received a bachelor's degree in history in 1953 and a certificate in education the following year. The publication of *Rights of Passage* (1967), *Masks* (1968), and *Islands* (1969) introduced his poetry to a wider audience. This autobiographical series, collectively titled *The Arrivants: A New World Trilogy* (1973), examines Caribbean people's quest for identity. Around this time, Brathwaite studied at the University of Sussex in England, where he received a doctoral degree in 1968 for historical research later published as *The Development of Creole Society in Jamaica, 1770–1820* (1971). Brathwaite then returned to teaching at the University of the West Indies in Kingston, Jamaica, and continued to publish literary criticism, essays, and books, including *Folk Culture of the Slaves in Jamaica* (1970), *History of the Voice* (1984), and *Roots* (1986). He also released more of his own poetry in books and recordings. His second verse trilogy, comprising the volumes *Mother Poem* (1977), *Sun Poem* (1982), and *X/Self* (1987), investigates the issue of self- and peoplehood. In 1994 Brathwaite won the Neustadt International Prize for Literature. He is currently a professor of comparative literature at New York University. The quality of his work could qualify him for a Nobel Prize for Literature.

Stokely Carmichael (1941–1998). Black civil rights activist and writer. Carmichael left Trinidad at the age of eleven to come with his family to New York City. His parents encouraged him to excel in school, and Carmichael won admission in 1956 to the selective Bronx High School of Science. In 1960 Carmichael decided to attend Howard University in Washington, D.C., where he soon became active in the civil rights movement. After college, Carmichael became a secretary for the Student Nonviolent Coordinating Committee (SNCC) and worked in the campaign to register blacks in Mississippi to vote. In 1965 Carmichael moved to Alabama to work in the voting rights campaign and helped to organize the Black Panther party. In May 1966 he became chairperson of the SNCC. Carmichael's many speeches led many blacks to see him as a symbol of black radicalism and a worthy successor to Malcolm X, the black Muslim leader. Because of ideological disagreements, Carmichael resigned from the Black Panther party in 1969. During the same year, he began to work in Africa and eventually changed his name to Kwame Turé (or Touré), a name he derived from two popular African leaders, Kwame Nkrumah of Ghana and Sékou Touré of Guinea. Until his death he continued to work and live in Guinea, although he returned occasionally to the United States.

Shirley Chisholm (1924–). American legislator, who in 1968 became the first black woman elected to the Congress of the United States. Born in Brooklyn, Shirley Anita St. Hill Chisholm has been famous for her efforts to bring about greater justice for black people and women. At age three, she and her two younger sisters were sent to Barbados to live with the grandmother, to allow the St. Hills to save some money. The children stayed seven years, and this time became one of the most important periods of her life. Chisholm's father, an avid reader, was a follower of Marcus Garvey. Chisholm graduated from Brooklyn College and earned a master's degree at Columbia University. She taught nursery school and directed daycare centers in New York City. From 1959–1964, Chisholm was a consultant for the city's Bureau of Child Welfare. In 1970 she wrote a book called *Unbought and Unbossed*. She sought but did not win the Democratic presidential nomination in 1972.

Merle Collins (1950–). A poet and essayist born in Grenada, Collins is professor of comparative literature and English at the University of Maryland. She studied at the University of the West Indies and at Georgetown University and holds a Ph.D. in government from the London School of Economics and Political Science. Her publications include two novels, *Angel* (1987 and 1988) and *The Colour of Forgetting* (1995), as well as a collection of short stories, *Rain Darling* (1990). She has also published two volumes of poetry: *Because the Dawn Breaks* (1985) and *Rotten Pomerack* (1992). A specialist in Caribbean studies, her critical works include "Themes and Trends in Caribbean Writing Today" in *From My Guy to Sci-Fi: Genre and Women's Writing in the Postmodern World* (Helen Carr, ed., 1989), and "To Be Free Is Very Sweet" in *Slavery and Abolition*. Before coming to Maryland, Collins taught in both London and Grenada and served in Grenada's Ministry of Foreign Affairs. She has also been a commentator for the British Broadcasting Corporation.

Mervyn Dymally (1926–). Trinidad-born American congressman (retired). Dymally earned a Ph.D. in human behavior (1978, U.S. International

University). He helped chair the Clinton–Gore '96 campaign and is a founding member of the Congressional Black Caucus. He also has chaired the U.S. House of Representatives' Education Committee and served as lieutenant governor of California.

Patrick Ewing (1962–). Jamaican-born professional basketball player, who became a center for the New York Knicks in 1985 and was a member of the U.S. men's basketball team that won a gold medal at the 1992 Summer Olympics. In the 1985 NBA draft of college players, Ewing was the first player chosen. He signed a contract with the New York Knicks for $1.7 million, at the time the highest salary ever paid to an NBA rookie. Despite injuries Ewing was named Rookie of the Year in 1986 and led all first-year players in scoring and rebounding. Ewing considers graduating from Georgetown with a fine arts degree his finest moment and the fulfillment of his late mother Dorothy's dream. He conducted youth clinics in South Africa in the summer of 1994. Ewing has made cameo appearances in the movies *The Exorcist 1990* and *Funny about Love* and the TV shows *Mad about You* and *Herman's Head.*

Louis Farrakhan (1933–). One of the most influential contemporary black religious leaders in the United States. Born in New York City as Louis Eugene Wolcott of Kittitian and Jamaican parents, Farrakhan is currently the head of the Nation of Islam. He grew up in Boston, Massachusetts, attended Winston-Salem Teacher's College in North Carolina, and worked as a nightclub singer in the early 1950s. When he joined the Nation of Islam in the mid-1950s, he assumed the name Farrakhan. His speaking and singing abilities helped him rise to prominence within the Nation of Islam, and he led the group's mosque in Boston. After the death of Malcolm X, Farrakhan became the head of a large mosque in Harlem. In the late 1970s Farrakhan led a dissident faction within the organization to oppose changes in the major beliefs and programs that had been instituted by its former leader Elijah Muhammad. Several years later, he left the organization and formed a new organization that assumed the original name, the Nation of Islam, and reasserted the principles of black separatism. In the 1990s Farrakhan continued his call for poor African Americans to make stronger commitments to education and their families, to end black-on-black crime, and to be less dependent on public welfare. In October 1995 he led the highly publicized Million Man March in Washington, D.C. At this march, about a million black men vowed to renew their commitments to family, community, and personal responsibility.

Grandmaster Flash (1958–   ). Hip-hop artist. Born in Barbados as Joseph Saddler, Flash is one of hip-hop's greatest innovators, transcending the genre's party-music origins to explore the full scope of its lyrical and sonic horizons. He began spinning records as a teen growing up in the Bronx, performing at area dances and block parties. Over time, he has developed a series of new techniques including "cutting" (moving between tracks exactly on the beat), "back-spinning" (manually turning records to repeat brief snippets of sound), and "phasing" (manipulating turntable speeds)—in short, creating the basic vocabulary that DJs continue to follow today.

Marcus Mosiah Garvey (1887–1940). Jamaican-born black nationalist leader. Garvey established the Universal Negro Improvement Association (UNIA) on August 1, 1914. At its peak, the UNIA boasted a membership of over 4 million. The Black Star Line, one of the UNIA's ventures, was an enterprise belonging to blacks, operated by and for them, that gave even the poorest black a chance to become a stockholder in this big business enterprise. With such a large following and such ambitious ventures, Garvey was soon perceived as a threat to the system, and he was convicted on a questionable charge of mail fraud. After serving a brief time in prison, he was deported back to Jamaica in early December 1927 and spent his last years traveling in the Caribbean and Europe, always preaching about black pride.

Earl G. Graves (1935–   ). Entrepreneur. Born in Brooklyn, Graves is of Barbadian ancestry. He is president and CEO of Earl G. Graves, Ltd., publisher of *Black Enterprise Magazine*, a business publication geared toward black professionals, executives, entrepreneurs, and policymakers in the private and public sectors. Graves was an administrative assistant to the late Senior Robert F. Kennedy from 1965 to 1968. In 1972 he was named one of the ten most outstanding minority businessmen in the country by the president of the United States and received the National Award for Excellence in recognition of his achievements in minority business enterprise.

Grace Jones (1952–   ). Pop singer, born in Jamaica. Jones grew up in New York City and then became a successful model in Paris. After some attempts at establishing a film career, she produced some unremarkable disco records that sold on the strength of her style, image, and live performances. On the record *Warm Leatherette*, she developed the new wave and half-spoken lyrics that since then have become her trademark. In 1984 she diversified into films and appeared with Arnold Schwarzenegger in *Conan, the Destroyer*. A year later she played alongside Roger Moore in *A View to A Kill*.

Jamaica Kincaid (1949–   ). Novelist, born Elaine Potter Richardson on the island of Antigua. She lived with her stepfather and her mother until 1965, when she was sent to Westchester, New York, to work as an au pair. In only four books—the novels *Annie John* (1985) and *Lucy* (1990), the short story collection *At the Bottom of the River* (1984), and her nonfiction book about her home country Antigua titled *A Small Place* (1988)—Kincaid has carved out a unique place in the literary landscape. Her spare, deceptively simple prose intensely and often harrowingly describes the growing up of strong-minded girls who, very much like herself, were born into tropical poverty. Kincaid's latest novel, *The Autobiography of My Mother*, may be her most ambitious and accomplished yet.

George Lamming (1927–   ). Novelist born in Barbados, where he attended Combermere High School. He left for Trinidad in 1946 and later emigrated to England where, for a short time, he worked in a factory. In 1951 he became a broadcaster for the BBC's Colonial Service. He entered academia in 1967 as a writer-in-residence and lecturer in the Creative Arts Centre and Department of Education at the University of the West Indies. Since then, he has been a visiting professor at the University of Texas at Austin and the University of Pennsylvania and a lecturer in Denmark, Tanzania, and Australia. Lamming's first novel, *In the Castle of My Skin*, was published in 1953. His next novel, *The Emigrants*, deals with a group of West Indian expatriates who, like Lamming, resided in England. His more recent works depart from this semiautobiographical format. *Of Age and Innocence* and *Season of Adventure* take place on Lamming's fictional Caribbean island of San Cristobal. *Water with Berries* describes various flaws of West Indian society through the plot of Shakespeare's *The Tempest*. *Natives of My Person* is an account of a slave-trading ship on its voyage from Europe to Africa to the North American colonies. Lamming teaches at the City University of New York.

Claude McKay (1890–1948). Jamaican-born poet and novelist whose *Home to Harlem* (1928) was the most popular novel written by a person of African descent at that time. Before moving to the United States in 1912, McKay wrote two volumes of dialect verse, *Songs of Jamaica* and *Constab Badlands*. After attending the Tuskegee Institute in Alabama and the Kansas State Teachers College, he went to New York in 1914, where he contributed to *The Liberator*, a leading journal of avant-garde politics and art. With the publication of two volumes of poetry, *Spring in New Hampshire* (1920) and *Harlem Shadows* (1922), McKay emerged as the first and most radical voice of the literary movement known as the Harlem Renaissance. After 1922

McKay lived abroad, successively in the Soviet Union, France, Spain, and Morocco. In both *Home to Harlem* and *Banjo* (1929), he attempted to capture the vitality of the black vagabonds of urban America and Europe. Later he published a collection of short stories, *Gingertown* (1932), and another novel, *Banana Bottom* (1933). In these works McKay searched for a distinctive black identity among the common folk. After returning to the United States in 1934, McKay wrote for a number of magazines and newspapers, including the *New Leader* and the *New York Amsterdam News*. He also wrote an autobiography, *A Long Way from Home* (1937), and the study *Harlem: Negro Metropolis* (1940). His *Selected Poems* (1953) was published posthumously.

Hugh Mulzac (1886–1971). Naval officer born in the West Indies. In 1942, Captain Hugh Mulzac became the first African American merchant marine naval officer to command an integrated crew during World War II. He had earned his captain's rating in the merchant marine in 1918, but racial prejudice prevented him from commanding a ship. Later Mulzac was offered the command of a ship with an all-black crew. He refused, declaring that "under no circumstances will I command a Jim Crow vessel." During World War II, however, Mulzac's demand for an integrated crew was finally met and he was put in command of the SS *Booker T. Washington.*

Orlando Patterson (1940–   ). Sociologist and novelist, born in Jamaica. Patterson came to the United States in 1970 and taught at several universities. Apart from his academic writings, he published several acclaimed novels, such as *The Children of Sisyphus* (1964), *An Absence of Ruins* (1967), and *Die the Long Day* (1972). Patterson is a widely recognized authority on race issues in the Americas and currently teaches as the John Cowles Professor of Sociology at Harvard University.

Sidney Poitier (1927–   ). Actor. Poitier was raised on a tomato farm in the Bahamas and became the first African American actor to achieve major Hollywood stardom in successful mainstream films that depicted an African American man in a positive manner. He was nominated for an Academy Award in 1958 and became the first African American male to win the best actor Oscar for his role as Homer Smith in *Lilies of the Field*. His films never shied away from addressing sensitive issues of "race." In 2000 he received the Screen Actor Lifetime Achievement award. In recent years, Poitier became the ambassador to Japan for the Bahamas.

Colin Powell (1937–   ). Born in New York City of Jamaican parents, he rose in the military to become deputy assistant to the president for national security affairs (1987), assistant to the president for national security affairs (1987–1989), and chairman of the Joint Chiefs of Staff (1989–1993). Powell wrote about his experience in his book *My American Journey* (1995). After he retired from the army in 1994, he was widely considered as a suitable candidate for the presidency but decided not to run for that office at that time.

Hazel Scott (1920–1981). A popular pianist and organist from the 1930s until the late 1960s. One of America's foremost pianists, born in Trinidad. She received training in classical music at the Juilliard School of Music in New York City and her jazz technique, she says, she owes to Art Tatum and Teddy Wilson. In October 1940, she starred at the opening of Barney Josephson's Cafe Society Uptown, just off Park Avenue, and her pianistic pyrotechnics were acclaimed, throughout the United States and Europe as well. She appeared in the production *Priorities of 1942* and has played twice at the famed Carnegie Hall in New York City. Her motion picture career included: *Something to shout about, I dood it, Broadway Melody, The Heat's On,* and *Rhapsody in Blue.* The combination of two approaches to piano in classical and jazz make Hazel Scott an outstanding contribution to any music lover's library. Her most famous hit was "Tico Tico" and her style is a Stride/Boogie Woogie popular in the 1940s. Scott married the noted congressman, preacher, and editor Rev. A. Clayton Powell, Jr.

Cicely Tyson (1933–). Eminent actress. Tyson's family hails from St. Kitts and Nevis. She became well known as a member of the television series *East Side, West Side.* Among the films she made are *The Heart Is a Lonely Hunter* (1968), *Fried Green Tomatoes* (1991), and *Sounder* (1972), for which she received an Oscar nomination. However, her best-known roles are perhaps the one in the television miniseries *Roots* (1977) and her Emmy Award–winning roles in the television movies *The Autobiography of Miss Jane Pittman* (1974) and *Oldest Living Confederate Widow Tells All* (1994).

Derek Walcott (1930–). St. Lucian poet, playwright, and Nobel laureate. Walcott is known for his lucid descriptions of Caribbean culture and his creative use of language. He was educated at St. Mary's College in Saint Lucia and at the University College of the West Indies in Jamaica. Between 1959 and 1976, he directed the Trinidad Theater Workshop. In 1981 he moved to the United States and settled in Boston, Massachusetts, where he teaches creative writing at Boston University. Walcott has written more than fifteen books of poetry and about thirty plays and won the Nobel Prize for Literature in 1992.

Bert Williams (1874–1922). Born in Nassau, British West Indies, Williams was a formidable comedian and entertainer. In his time he was considered one of the world's finest comedians. His musical recordings were among the best-selling hits of the era. Williams lived and worked in a time of racism. He began his career with minstrel shows (which were big-time show business before radio, movies, and television), where the theatrical convention was to wear blackface and to portray the "shiftless darky." Through the eyes of the era, this was not recognized as the arrogantly racist action that it is but was simply seen as another ethnic comic type, like the drunken Irishman, the cheap Scotsman, the conniving Jew, and a number of other stock characters that comics performed in saloons, music halls, burlesque and vaudeville houses all over America. Williams worked in blackface the rest of his career, because his producers and fans never permitted him to abandon the stereotypical black he portrayed so hilariously.

Malcolm X (1925–1965). Black leader born as Malcolm Little, his mother was a creole born in Grenada. His father was a Baptist minister and organizer for Marcus Garvey. Settling in Harlem, New York, Malcolm became more and more involved in criminal activities. He robbed, worked as a pimp, and sold drugs. In 1946 he was arrested for robbery and sentenced to prison for seven years. In prison, Malcolm became a follower of Elijah Muhammad, the leader of a small black religious movement, the Nation of Islam. During this time he discarded his "slave name," Little, and took the new name "X." Malcolm improved his poor knowledge by reading, and he strictly followed the Nation of Islam's dietary laws and moral codes. After his parole in 1952, Malcolm X undertook organizational work for the Nation of Islam. At the height of his influence, Malcolm X was one of black America's most powerful voices and was particularly influential among African American youth and in progressive intellectual circles. In 1964, he went on his pilgrimage to Mecca, obligatory for orthodox Muslims. There he began to reconsider his views toward integration. In Mecca, he learned that it was possible for black and white people to live in brotherhood—an experience that fundamentally influenced him in the last phase of his life. When Malcolm X was giving a speech in the Audubon Ballroom in Harlem on February 21, 1965, he was gunned down by Black Muslims.

Glossary

Asante   Ethnic group from the Gold Coast, West Africa.

Bajan, Bajun   Short form for Barbadian (i.e., inhabitant of Barbados).

Caribs   Aboriginal Americans resident in the Lesser Antilles; ethnically pure descendants were later called Yellow Caribs, while those mixed with African blood were called Black Caribs or Garifuna.

Creole   Someone born and bred in the New World—applied to both whites and blacks; in a wider sense also refers to the process of ethnic and "racial" amalgamization.

Creolization   The demographic process in the Caribbean (as well as other New World locations) by which the creole whites and blacks became the majority; the cultural process leading to a distinctive Caribbean culture based on African, East Indian, Chinese, Amerindian, and European influences.

Levantine   Region on the eastern shore of the Mediterranean Sea, including Syria and Lebanon; people from this region are sometimes referred to as *Levantines*.

Maroon   A slave who permanently ran away from the plantation; *cimarrón* in Spanish, *marron* in French.

Middle Passage   The journey of captured Africans across the Atlantic Ocean in the slave trade.

Mulatto   Strictly a person of half African, half Caucasian descent, but more loosely any person of mixed African and Caucasian descent. The word emerged from a racist context and has a distinctly demeaning undertone.

Murthi   In the Hindu belief, the visible form that a deity assumes.

Patty   Turnover with minced beef, chicken, or vegetable filling.

Plantocracy   The system of self-government by the class of white planters and their allies; this term often also refers to the white planter class alone.

Puja   The act of showing reverence to a god, spirit, or another aspect of the divine through invocations, prayers, songs, and rituals. An essential part of puja for the Hindu devotee is making a spiritual connection with the divine. Most often that contact is facilitated through an object: an element of nature, a sculpture, a vessel, a painting, or a print.

Susu   Rotating credit association.

Selected Bibliography

Bryce-Laporte, Roy S., and Delores Mortimer, eds. 1983. *Caribbean Immigration to the United States*. Washington, D.C.: Research Institute on Immigration and Ethnic Studies, Smithsonian Institution.

Castillo, Jessie. 1994. *Garifuna Folktales*. Brooklyn, NY: Caribbean Research Center.

Chevannes, Barry, ed. 1998. *Rastafari and Other African-Caribbean Worldviews*. New Brunswick, NJ: Rutgers University Press.

Clarke, Velta J., and Emmanuel Riviere. 1989. *Establishing New Lives: Selected Readings on Caribbean Immigrants in New York City*. Brooklyn, NY: Caribbean Research Center.

Depoo, Tilokie (with Prem Misir and Basdeo Mangru). 1993. *The East Indian Diaspora. 150 Years of Survival, Contributions and Achievements*. Cypress Hills: East Indian Diaspora Press, Asian/American Center at Queens College.

Foner, Nancy, ed. 1987. *New Immigrants in New York*. New York: Columbia University Press.

Forde, Yolande. 1995. *Caribbean People Under the control of the Criminal Justice System in New York State*. Brooklyn, NY: Caribbean Research Center.

Gosine, Mahin. 1990. *Caribbean East Indians in America: Assimilation, Adaptation and Group Experience*. New York: Windsor Press.

Gosine, Mahin, and Dhanpaul, eds. 1999. *Sojourners to Settlers: Indian Migrants in the Caribbean and the Americas*. New York: Windsor Press.

Irish, J. A. George, ed. 1994. *Caribbean Heritage Resource Guide: A Handbook for Teachers Working with Caribbean Students*. Brooklyn, NY: Caribbean Diaspora Press.

———, ed. 1995. *Caribbean Students in New York*. Brooklyn, NY: Caribbean Diaspora Press.

Irish, J. A. George, and Coleen Clay. 1995. *Assessment of Caribbean Students: A Guide for Assessing Children from CARICOM Nation States and Dependent Territories.* Brooklyn, NY: Caribbean Diaspora Press.

Irish, J. A. George, and E. W. (Bill) Riviere, eds. 1990. *Political Behavior and Social Interaction among Caribbean and African American Residents in New York.* Brooklyn, NY: Caribbean Research Center.

James, Winston. 1998. *Holding Aloft the Banner of Ethiopia: Caribbean Radicalism in Early Twentieth-Century America.* London: Verso.

Kasinitz, Philip. 1995. *Caribbean New York: Black Immigrants and the Politics of Race.* Ithaca, NY: Cornell University Press.

Knight, Franklin. 1978. *The Caribbean: The Genesis of a Fragmented Nationalism.* New York: Oxford University Press.

Lewis, Gordon K. 1968. *The Growth of the Modern West Indies.* New York: Monthly Review Press.

McKay, Claude. 1940. *Harlem: Negro Metropolis.* New York: Dutton.

Mintz, Sidney W., and Sally Price, eds. 1985. *Caribbean Contours.* Baltimore: Johns Hopkins University Press.

Mortimer, Delores M., and Roy Bryce-Laporte, eds. 1981. *Female Immigrants to the United States: Caribbean, Latin American, and African Experiences.* Washington, D.C.: Research Institute on Immigration and Ethnic Studies, Smithsonian Institution.

Nettleford, Rex. 1979. *Caribbean Cultural Identity: The Case of Jamaica.* Los Angeles: Center for Afro-American Studies and UCLA Latin American Center Publications, University of California.

———. 1995. *Inward Stretch. Outward Reach. A Voice from the Caribbean.* Brooklyn, NY: Caribbean Diaspora Press.

Palmer, Ransford. 1995. *Pilgrims from the Sun: West Indian Migration to America.* New York: Twayne.

———, ed. 1990. *In Search of a Better Life: Perspectives on Migration from the Caribbean.* New York: Praeger.

Pastor, Robert, ed. 1985. *Migration and Development in the Caribbean: The Unexplored Connection.* Boulder, CO: Westview Press.

Pessar, Patricia R., ed. 1997. *Caribbean Circuits: New Directions in the Study of Caribbean Migration.* New York: Center for Migration Studies.

Portes, Alejandro. 1993. *City on the Edge: The Transformation of Miami.* Berkeley: University of California Press.

Reid, Ira De A. 1939. *The Negro Immigrant: His Background, Characteristics and Social Adjustment, 1899–1937.* New York: AMS Press.

Rodney, Walter. 1981. *A History of the Guyanese Working People, 1881–1905.* Baltimore: Johns Hopkins University Press.

Sherlock, Philip, and Hazel Bennett. 1998. *The Story of the Jamaican People.* Kingston and Princeton: Ian Randle and Marcus Wiener.

Stone, Carl. 1973. *Class, Race and Political Behaviour in Urban Jamaica.* Mona: Institute of Social and Economic Research, University of the West Indies.

Sunshine, Catherine A., and Keith Q. Warner, eds. 1998. *Caribbean Connections: Moving North*. Washington, D.C.: Network of Educators on the Americas.

Sutton, Constance R., and Elsa M. Chaney, eds. 1992. *Caribbean Life in New York City: Sociocultural Dimensions*. New York: Center for Migration Studies of New York.

Vickerman, Milton. 1999. *Crosscurrents: West Indian Immigrants and Race*. New York: Oxford University Press.

Waters, Mary. 2000. *Black Identities: West Indian Immigrant Dreams and American Realities*. Cambridge: Harvard University Press, with the Russell Sage Foundation.

Watkins-Owens, Irma. 1996. *Blood Relations: Caribbean Immigrants and the Harlem Community, 1900–1930*. Bloomington: University of Indiana Press.

Index

About the Author

HOLGER HENKE is a Research Fellow at the Caribbean Research Center at Medgar Evers College (CUNY). He is also the Assistant Editor of *Wadabagei: A Journal of the Caribbean and Its Diaspora.*